SID VICIOUS

Also by Alan Parker:

Satellite: Sex Pistols with Paul Burgess

Rat Patrol from Fort Bragg: The Clash

Hardcore Superstar: Traci Lords USA only

The Great Train Robbery Files with Bruce & Nick Reynolds

The Who by Numbers with Steve Grantley

Song by Song: Stiff Little Fingers with Jake Burns

And Now For Something Completely Digital with Mick O'Shea

Cum On Feel the Noize: The Slade Story with Steve Grantley

SID VICIOUS

no one is innocent

ALAN PARKER

First published in hardback in Great Britain in 2007 by Orion Books
an imprint of the Orion Publishing Group Ltd
Orion House, 5 Upper St Martin's Lane,
London WC2H 9EA
An Hachette Livre UK Company

10 9 8 7 6 5 4 3 2 1

A CIP catalogue record for this book is available from the British Library.

ISBN: 978 0 7528 7546 0

Printed in Great Britain by Clays Ltd, St Ives plc

The Orion Publishing Group's policy is to use papers that are natural, renewable and recyclable and made from wood grown in sustainable forests. The logging and manufacturing processes are expected to conform to the environmental regulations of the country of origin.

www.orionbooks.co.uk

Contents

For giving me the sheer inspiration to actually

sit down and write a third book about Sid Vicious,

I'd like to dedicate this book to Jane Dalton . . .

FOREWORD

BY MALCOLM McLAREN

John Simon Ritchie aka John Beverly aka Sid Vicious aka Sex Pistol aka Agent Provocateur. The most formidable and controversial icon of his generation. A questionable James Dean of Punk fashion. A surrogate Elvis Presley of Punk Rock. Sid was everything everyone else was not. Both good and bad. He impressed us all and embarrassed us all. His life was an effortless performance of style. He never saw a red light, only green. He should have been buried next to Karl Marx in London's Highgate Cemetery. That was my wish, but Anne Beverley, his mother, decided to have him cremated instead.

To look back, as I have been asked by Alan Parker, the author, at these episodes in my life and times spent with Sid, I have to wonder why so many people simply look at me in disbelief and ask, 'How did it all happen?' 'Who was Sid?' 'Was he vicious?' And the more adventurous ask, 'Are you really evil?' Well, I say, 'My son thinks so . . . Vivienne Westwood thinks so . . . other girlfriends think so, Johnny Rotten certainly thinks so and most conservative people the world over think so. The Pope probably thinks so too.' They are all right and they are all wrong. If I take a different view on all of this – one that is pragmatic rather than romantic, a view from the balcony, so to speak, what will I see? Electric guitars and cheap multi-track recorders giving license to a generation of kids with no musical training, obvious talent or permission from anyone to start bands and record music. Everyone is saying, 'I can do this' and 'I want to play that!' For a while, of course, the assumption was that to be like Sid Vicious, the right way of learning was to imitate him. How? By learning his songs!!!!? Reading the sheet music, Hah! Get a music teacher? And then go play the tunes! Because no one wants to hear your rubbish. Do what the industry expects. What they teach you to believe is good. Sid changed all that and more. Sid meant, OK, you have your bass but you don't have to play it well, or even at all. You can play it badly – and I endorsed that attitude. For if you can't write your own songs, it doesn't matter, simply steal other people's and change them the way you want. What matters is this: you are going to change the rules and in doing so, change the culture and, by that, change life. Through Punk Rock, a whole new fresh approach occurred and Sid reflected this in his sound and stance. To watch him was to watch a raw open-wounded creature being loved for doing something different. It fast became a way of life. Sid lowered the bar of entry and allowed everyone into the creative process. The line between the audience and band was blurred. Sid was a fan who invented the Pogo. It made for chaos, it threw the fan at the feet of the band and suddenly the fan was all the attention and, for that moment, the star. Sid created a new business model, as fans are also creators. Today on the worldwide web we talk about the old audience. One-time fans, passive buyers of music in stores turned into pro-active makers of the music itself. Sid was the doyenne of all our youth. He pushed the mainstream right out of the picture, inspiring us to blow off the door of the recording industry, releasing every song from the jail and letting everyone know about it across the planet. Instantly doing the work that was once the work of critics, DJs and marketing companies. And Simon Fuller, the creator of Pop Idol, where would *he* be with him?

Sid Vicious began the age of participation in which everyone could be the artist.

Alan Parker, the author of *Satellite*, has decided to analyse the short history of England's foremost Punk idol. Friend of all those once active in the 70s, he has completed the most intensive study of Sid's life and the world he inhabited.

Everyone I knew and cared for wanted to sleep with Sid and no one more so than my erstwhile girlfriend, Vivienne Westwood. She got close, very close. He was her chosen one, the original and best Sex Pistol. Sid was someone Vivienne tried to connect me with early on when I was desperately searching for a singer to front that emerging new band I had named the 'Sex Pistols'.

His power of seduction was obvious. He didn't just wear the clothes. He acted them. My taste was close to Vivienne's in this respect, but as fate would have it, I got connected to the wrong John instead. John Lydon. But I quickly changed the bass player when I got the chance. Sid didn't just play the bass and sing the songs. He caused mayhem! He was his own audience and star. The ultimate D.I.Y. Punk idol. He provided a readymade, do-it-yourself identity. Someone easy to assemble and therefore become. Sid was good-looking and cool enough to be emulated by all the disenfranchised of his generation.

He single-handedly reinvented the classic Havana tuxedo as an outlaw costume by styling it with a pair of black drainpipe jeans and what slowly would become the ubiquitous Punk garter that he wore so sweetly around his left thigh! His vocal performance on 'My Way' outpaced and, many say, out sang Sinatra's with its venomous tirade against Johnny Rotten.

How could such a creature exist! An asexual pimp, a heterosexual liar, and a homosexual flake, an authentic pin-up, a true star. He was no shoe-gazer. He tore into your heart when he sang. He made sex purposely corny and ordinary. Easy for those who needed to overcome any inhibitions they may have at

puberty. He was a dream idol for pre-teens too. He was provocative and dangerously sexy, stretching the limits in this way. His
vanity was sublime and wonderfully cheeky. He was so
typically young and foolish. Making love seemed a too-distant
subject. Too difficult to bother to even comprehend. 'Who cares
about love?' Sid once said to me. 'Love is for people preparing
to die.' He made everyone near me say this. His lawlessness and
disregard for normal values made him a serious threat in the
band and the music industry made no attempt to hide its
feelings. It continued throughout his short career to conspire
with those it thought would help get rid of him, including
Johnny Rotten.

On stage, he was the greatest amateur. He seemed to keep
everyone waiting for something to happen! And then, madly,
gladly, unknowingly and without inhibition or pretence he
would always surprise us. The audience began congregating at
the left side of the stage waiting for Sid. And by the end of the
Sex Pistols' US tour, John Rotten was left alone.

During the preparations for Sid's trial, my conversations with
various promoters had me contemplating Sid performing in Las
Vegas. I was positive about his acquittal. But Sid's trial was
going to cost a fortune and with the Sex Pistols' account drained,
I thought this was an excellent new adventure and money-
maker. Sid could sing for his supper at the Sands in Las Vegas
and pay the bills. He would have taken Las Vegas by storm. He
was the only Punk candidate to fill Elvis Presley's shoes.

Sid's mother Anne was kind enough and helped him
wherever she could. She was a small-time drug dealer. She
smuggled heroin in her cunt and entered Rikers Island, a
detention centre in New York where Sid was awaiting trial for
the murder of Nancy. She was the dutiful mother. She aided
him in his last breath, killing him and killing herself years later.

Sid saw the halo of the Sex Pistols burn out before anyone.
Almost the moment after he climbed on stage to join them.
'Disappointed Sid' set about destroying them and reinventing

them at the same time. At a soundcheck on the Dutch tour, John as usual refused to work with the rest of the band. Sid gladly replaced Rotten on vocals. He sang every song word-perfect and in tune. I'll never forget John's face drowning in his beer, Steve Jones's bemused expression, and Sid so natural. He had out-Punked them before John could even blow his nose. History would show how the group would soon descend without Sid into a middle-aged Pantomimic Rock group. Everything I had fought against from the very beginning. Sid always managed to create an environment that you could truthfully run wild in. Sid had to put the boot in somewhere, sometime in San Francisco. He was the Sex Pistols' problem but alas the rest of the band could never agree that he might also be their saviour.

Earlier that year, outside Buckingham Palace, we signed to A&M Records. Sid was the surprise newcomer to the band. He made the scene unforgettable with his swagger and nonchalant style. His ability to always look like he had just climbed out of bed was stunning. His performance at the press conference afterwards became legendary in the media when he challenged a stuffy female journalist to have sex to stop the bullshit, taunting her contradictory attitudes and causing her to cry. Today she's running a graduate course in Punk Rock at New York University. This anti-musical genre of Punk Rock should be described as a carefully managed attack on the corporate world. It is an act of irresponsible violence, of making ugliness beautiful. But it is presented today as no more than a post-karaoke nightmare.

My personal image of Sid is that of a fearless, but anxious, vulnerable youth. An irresponsible and utterly brilliant failure. He was never a benign success and Vivienne was right. Sid did sell more records back in 1978 than Johnny Rotten.

Sid is as fashionable today as he was yesterday. He is constantly studied, reinterpreted and reappraised. His iconic status remains secure. He can be seen everywhere from the sneer of Billy Idol to the drug habits and attitude of Pete

Doherty. From the pornography of Paris Hilton to the cabaret performance of Lily Allen. From the styles of Heidi Slimane to the poses and posturing in *Dazed & Confused* and *Fantastic Man*. His face has peered out of more T-shirts, posters and documentaries than any other rock star of his era. His uncanny ability to imitate art and yet at the same time make it seem so natural that he claims it as his own is a Warholian dream. Andy would often drift into my *Sex* store on the Kings Road in Chelsea and look desperately for a T-shirt with Sid's name printed on it. I'd say, 'Andy! I don't do that!' 'Malcolm', he replied, 'Just do it for me, just one!' Later he would paint Sid's portrait for the cover of an art magazine.

Sid was the precursor to the Young British Artists of the 90s, better known as the YBAs. Damien Hirst told me he would have joined a Punk band had he not managed to sell his art early on in his career. The artist Gavin Turk became Sid Vicious forever by resurrecting him as Gavin Turk, copying the classic pose and outfit Sid wore in *The Great Rock 'n' Roll Swindle*. Sid/Gavin both shooting at us from the inside of a glass tomb.

I must finally credit Jamie Reid, Sophie Richmond, Boogie, Roadent, all my team and above all Vivienne for helping inspire the bastard.

Malcolm McLaren

Hard Luck, the Only Kind of Luck

'So this is how to kill friends and influence people, fix yourself first then give them the needle, Punk Rock and lies, tattoos and alibis, don't you know Sid Vicious never really played the bass at all, oh, what a con!'

(From *Tattoos and Alibis* by Ricky Warwick)

Friday, 2 February 1979.

Sergeant Richard Houseman – a seasoned NYPD veteran who, after twelve years on the force, thought that he was beyond surprises – braced himself against the biting wind blowing in from the Hudson River. He clambered out of his patrol car and made his way up towards the first-floor apartment at 63 Bank Street, located within the heart of New York's bohemian East Village. He had been less than two hours into what he'd been hoping would be just another routine shift at Manhattan's 6th Precinct when the report of a suspected drug-related fatality had been called in. Houseman shook his head, remembering how the city's mayor Edward I. Koch had promised to get tough on drugs, but the fact remained that New York was awash with them – especially heroin, which had resulted in a steady increase in accidental overdoses. Only twelve months earlier hard drugs looked as though they were finally being swept out of Manhattan for good, but now heroin, coke, smack, crack were all freely available.

This, however, would be no ordinary case, for the deceased was ex-Sex Pistol Sid Vicious. And although Houseman had never so much as heard a Sex Pistols song and had dismissed Punk as just another musical fad, he was all too familiar with the name Sid Vicious – the English rock star was front-page news, having been recently arrested for the murder of his American girlfriend 'Nauseating' Nancy Spungen. The case had been a major talking point at the 6th Precinct, where almost all of the detectives working on it were divided as never before. Was the young man guilty, or an innocent abroad, who just happened to be in the wrong place at the wrong time?

Houseman entered the apartment's compact living room to find two women sat on the sofa, facing him. The younger of the two was Michelle Robison, the apartment's resident and Sid's new girlfriend. Crying aloud, she looked positively hysterical. The other woman was Sid's mother, Anne Beverley, who had arrived from England several weeks earlier – supposedly to take care of her wayward offspring. Anne seemed awfully calm for a woman who had just lost her only son. Both women appeared to be in a state of shock, but Robison, who was still dressed in her nightie and pop socks, managed to pull herself together long enough to escort Houseman along the narrow hallway to the tiny, cluttered bedroom where Sid's lifeless form lay sprawled upon the bed. Punk T-shirts were scattered across the floor, and the sergeant noticed that one was red with a large black swastika on it. Although it was clear that Vicious was dead, Houseman conducted the perfunctory tests before radioing the station to call the coroner's office.

While he awaited the coroner's arrival Houseman returned to the living room and began questioning both women in order to try and ascertain what had happened in the hours leading up to Sid's death. Robison was clearly distraught and could therefore offer only the most vague responses to his questions. Like a mantra, she said only 'No, no, no!' when asked anything, while Sid's mother appeared to be quite lucid. Houseman heard how the two of them had organised a 'jail-springing' party for Vicious in order to celebrate his release on bail less than twenty-four hours earlier. Anne, Robison and several members of New York's junkie set had collected Vicious from the court before returning to the apartment where Sid had availed himself of a celebratory wrap of heroin provided by his mother, while she busied herself with preparing a spaghetti Bolognese. Indeed, upon entering the apartment, Houseman had caught the faint, but unmistakable aroma of stale garlic, and several half-filled plates of pasta were still stacked up beside the sink.

Anne Beverley went on to explain that Simon (Sid's real Christian name), having soon used up the proffered heroin, had subsequently begun demanding more and had arranged for one of his friends to go out and score. When Houseman asked her why she hadn't tried to stop this friend from obtaining more of the drug, Anne responded by claiming that her son was so well-known among the city's drug fraternity that he would have simply gone out to score it himself; and that, had he done so, he would have probably been arrested for breaking curfew. The friend, Dave, accompanied by a UK photographer whose Punk street name was 'Kodick', had returned within the hour. Although none of those present knew it, the latest batch of heroin to have hit the streets was unusually strong at nearly 98% proof.

As the earlier dose had failed to satisfy him, Vicious had taken a second and far stronger hit of heroin. This had resulted in Sid overdosing, but Robison and the others had managed to resuscitate him by walking him around the apartment. At some point during the night, however, Vicious – according to his mother – must have sneaked into the living room, located the stash she was supposedly safeguarding, and proceeded to take a third and fatal dose.

Houseman had just finished questioning Mrs Beverley when the coroner, Dr Michael Baden, arrived. Satisfied that the death had indeed been an unfortunate accident, the sergeant escorted Baden into the bedroom, expecting the coroner's preliminary examination of the deceased to more or less concur with what was written down on his notepad. Within minutes, Houseman's initial assumption had been blown to pieces and the apartment had become a prospective crime scene after it became apparent that the deceased might have been helped with his final, lethal hit. Upon returning to the living room, however, Houseman discovered that Mrs Beverley, whose eyes had suddenly taken on a steely determined glint, was apparently no longer willing to talk to him. She now seemed more interested in her late son's T-shirts and other belongings: 'Take your hands off those,' she screamed at a newly arrived beat cop. 'They belong to the Sid Vicious estate!' Houseman now understood why the British press had labelled Anne 'Ma Vicious'. He turned angrily towards Robison, who appeared more agitated than ever, but although he was convinced that the girl was hiding something, she too was refusing to talk beyond her mantra of denial.

It seemed that the state of New York was happy to allow Sid's death to be the final act in what had been a very disturbing and unpleasant saga. Houseman filed his original report.

For twenty-eight years the events of that night have been shrouded in myth and mystery. But now, after several months of painstaking research, along with help from Malcolm McLaren, as well as eye-witness accounts from photographer Eileen Polk, photographer Peter Kodak and musician Howie Pyro (who were both present at 63 Bank Street that night), we can finally fit the missing pieces of the jigsaw and prove once and for all that not only was Sid innocent of killing his beloved Nancy, but that his own demise was neither suicide nor accident.

CHAPTER 1

Born to Lose

'Undermine their pompous authority, reject their moral standards.
Make anarchy and disorder your trademarks, cause as much disruption as possible. But, don't let them take you alive.'

(Slogan taken from a poster, released by the
estate of Simon Beverley)

The death certificate No. 156-79-102078, issued by the City of New York's Bureau of Vital Records, unsurprisingly bears no mention of the name Sid Vicious. It merely states that English-born musician John Simon Ritchie died of Acute Intravenous Narcotism (pending chemical examination) at an unknown hour on Friday, 2 February 1979. Had anyone bothered to correlate this document with the deceased's birth certificate, which had been issued some twenty-two years earlier on Friday, 10 May 1957 in the decidedly less salubrious-sounding Metropolitan Borough of Lewisham, they would have discovered that 'John Simon' had in fact been born Simon John. But what is one more inaccuracy in a life filled with fallacies and falsehoods?

Simon John's mother was Anne Jeanette McDonald. By the time she gave birth to her son she had just turned twenty-five years old, had already been married and divorced (briefly being

Anne Randall), dropped out of school and joined the RAF; and all at a time when an Englishwoman's place was roundly thought to be at home as a housewife.

McDonald came from a small family, having one sister, Veronica, and had struggled at school. Poor academic results and her young marriage and divorce led to numerous rows at home. She left school and signed up for the RAF.

While serving in the RAF, McDonald met John George Ritchie who was also serving in the military with the Royal Guard. Just as it was fifty years later, Great Britain was involved in several military actions around the world during the 1950s, and National Service would stay in use until 1960. Suez, Korea, Malaya, Kenya and numerous Empire outposts required British personnel. By 1956 the couple were expecting a baby. One of Ritchie's bunk-mates was Thomas 'Tommy' Whittaker. 'He wasn't a happy soul,' recalls Tommy when asked about Ritchie's time in the army. 'We used to call him "Jolly John", you know, more or less a piss-take. He was never what you'd call the life and soul of anybody's party.' When Ritchie and McDonald met, he was immediately smitten and did most of the chasing. 'I remember Anne very well,' says Tommy. 'We thought she might bring him out of himself – he was a good-looking guy, and he was besotted with this young woman. She was in the RAF for a short time – we used to call that sort the "blinkers". You know, blink and you've missed them. They'd join up straight from school, possibly even as a result of leaving school early, do the basic training then home to mum, and she was one of them.'

McDonald didn't hang around in the RAF, as she hated the whole experience from day one. The only good thing to come out of it had been her meeting Ritchie and, despite the upcoming stigma of being an unmarried mother, she decided that she'd rather face that than a second walk down the aisle. By now Ritchie had left the Royal Guard and was working as a publisher's rep in London. 'A lot of the lads stayed in touch beyond the guards,' says Tommy Whitaker. 'You make good friends in the services, forge strong ties, but not John. Last I heard he was in the publishing game, and I was still in the forces. It wouldn't surprise me if they hadn't found him swinging from a tree somewhere. There was just something about him: his glass was permanently half empty.'

When the baby arrived in May 1957, Anne was happy to give him his father's surname despite not being married. The family home was a semi-basement flat in Lee Green, south-east London, but the nature of Ritchie's job meant that he was often away for long periods. He seemed ill-suited to life in Civvy Street and Anne was often forced to accept hand-outs from her in-laws simply in order to survive. Despite financial troubles, photographs from the time suggest that this was possibly the happiest time they ever shared as a family unit.

With the 1950s drawing to a close and a new decade offering hopes of a better future, Ritchie suggested that they should leave London and all their problems behind them and begin afresh in Ibiza. The Ritchies were certainly not the first family to abandon the capital in order to try their luck elsewhere, but the majority of Londoners would have struggled to pick out Ibiza on the map, let alone contemplate relocating to the sun-kissed Balearic isle. Today, Ibiza is seen as a pill-popping Mediterranean paradise, but in 1960 it was a tranquil fishing port offering little or no prospects for an ex-Royal Guard with questionable sales skills. This proved to be a moot point, however, because Ritchie, having sent his common-law wife and child on ahead, with a promise of monthly cash to follow, failed to join them, leaving Anne stranded in a foreign land with a two-year-old child, precious little money, and no option but to rely on her wits in order to survive. 'When the first and second lots of cash don't arrive and the letters dry up fairly quickly, it's not long before you're sure he's not coming out there either,' recalled Anne. 'It was just me, no money, a part-time job and a two-year-old in tow.'

Anne managed to survive by supplementing her meagre income as an occasional typist by selling pre-rolled joints to American tourists, using a dodgy credit card, and enjoying the charity of her fellow bohemians. 'A friend of mine told me one day that the fishermen liked a joint after work, but they couldn't roll them,' she said laughing. 'I thought, what's to learn? I'd never rolled one in my life, but I practised for a few days and realised it was easy, so I bought some grass with what money I did have left and rolled a dozen joints. Then I took them to the docks and sold them, with an instant one hundred per cent mark-up. It was easy.' Although money, or the lack of it, would be a constant worry for Anne, her 'Shirley Valentine'-type existence was not without its good points. The perennial warm climate was infinitely more preferable to the dour British weather. It might be unrealistic to expect that she spent eighteen months on the island without indulging in the odd romantic interlude with a fellow ex-pat or one of the locals, and there was a short liaison with a fisherman referred to in pictures only as 'Marty'. Indeed, the endless hours of bike-riding would have done wonders for Anne's trim figure and the sight of a young single Englishwoman dancing away the long balmy evenings dressed in skin-tight jeans or a short skirt would have sent many a Latin libido over the boil. Simon, or 'Sime' as the child was eternally known to his mother, would always be sat close-by, nursing a cup of orange Curacao and amusing his mother's fellow revellers with his ever-expanding list of Spanish swear words. 'He was a super little boy at that age and quite a character,' recalled Anne with a smile. 'All my friends predicted he'd be either nothing, a total drop-out, or prime minister of England.'

For roughly eight months of their stay, Simon had a dog. They found it wandering stray on the seafront one night. Two weeks later, and despite posters in many bars, there were no takers, so the dog 'C.P.' and the boy at least had each other for company.

Coping with a hand-to-mouth existence a thousand miles from home, however, was no way for a young mother to live – especially when her son was fast approaching school age. With this in mind, Anne finally called time on the extended holiday. A friend had informed her that the British High Commission in Ibiza would help out with the return fare if she was jobless and thus a burden on their country, so Anne returned to London, where at least she had a family to call her own – her mother, and her sister Veronica.

       ❧   ❧   ❧

The return to more familiar surroundings brought neither an upturn in Anne's fortunes, nor an end to her nomadic wanderings. A short stay with her mother while she found a place of her own led to her inhabiting a nondescript one-bedroom flat in Balham, south London.

The London that Anne had returned to in early 1961, although still several years away from earning its 'swinging' reputation, was still light years ahead of Ibiza in terms of sartorial elegance, and her beatnik clothing and razor-short gamine hairstyle often elicited comments both lewd and crude. Fashion-wise, Anne had arrived back from Ibiza years ahead of her time, and her new-found look – combined with her suntan and clothing – made her stand out from the crowd. Everything about her screamed 'different'.

London in the early 1960s was still handing out smog masks due to unbreathable fogs caused by millions of coal fires spewing smoke into the atmosphere. A new Thames flood-barrier was announced and two pence was added to the price of a packet of cigarettes. The government also announced a curb on the sale of 'pep-pills' and links to more serious drugs were being investigated.

At her Balham digs Anne found that she had inadvertently acquired a permanent babysitter as the live-in landlady was house-bound and willing to look after three-year-old Simon whenever necessary. This freedom allowed Anne to get out and earn some money when she secured herself a job working nights at Ronnie Scott's jazz club in Soho. 'Looking back, that was one of the best jobs I ever had,' said Anne. 'I didn't earn fortunes, but then we didn't need fortunes at that point.'

Young Simon was starting to look just like his absent father and seemed happy enough listening to his mother's modern jazz records, but just as it seemed that a brighter, self-sufficient future might be opening up for mother and son, Anne made a significant error of judgement.

Anne was told that registered drug users could get accommodation in London almost instantly, and – never one to miss an opportunity – went to a local clinic and registered herself as drug-dependent. 'I stayed up the night before smoking grass, and they told me the secret was to prick my arms a lot with a needle, to make it look like track marks. They also went swollen and red,' said Anne. 'I looked fucking terrible when I arrived and they pretty much signed me up on the spot.' There was such a number of people finding housing in London at the time via this route that Anne wasn't even drug-tested – today, that would be the first task performed by doctors. With her new-found 'drug dependency' clearly marked out on paper, Anne went to the local housing office. They took no time in re-housing her in an old Victorian dwelling above a shop on Drury Lane. Even seedier than the former residence in Balham, the new place was clearly 'low-rent'. It lacked every modern convenience with only an outside toilet. There was no hot water. The flat also came without a warm-hearted landlady, which meant that Anne had to give up her job at the club in order to look after her son. Along with this came a bigger problem – it wasn't just the council that knew what low-rent looked like. Every drug dealer in the West End was aware that the flat above 178 Drury Lane was one of a number of properties in the centre that had been set aside for drug-dependent families – or at least so goes the popular myth.

The flat on Drury Lane was easy to find given that Anne's sister Veronica and her own son David already lived there with her mother. It might not have offered the best conditions in the world, and they were all cramped in a fairly small space, but at least the family was together again.

The idyllic, sun-filled days of just two years previously must have seemed like a lifetime ago to the once-vivacious Anne, who now preferred to remain indoors and numb her pain with a cornucopia of soft drugs. But as her life became inexorably harder, so did the drugs.

At first the kind of guys hanging around the Drury Lane flat were content to take a smoke in exchange for a smoke, but sooner or later Anne began popping pills. Like many people who find themselves on this road, Anne learned that the buses only run one way. 'I knew what I was doing was foolish, especially with a child in tow,' said Anne. 'But there comes a point when it's just you. No one else matters. In prison some inmates call heroin the "escape plan", because it takes you somewhere else. It brings down the walls.' By Easter of 1962 Anne McDonald was well on the way to heroin addiction.

❀   ❀   ❀

It is somewhat ironic that Simon's first school was the Soho Parish School situated on Great Windmill Street. Little could the five-year-old have known as he scurried to school that one of the nondescript edifices to his left would – some seventeen years later – be transformed into the cinema used in *The Great Rock 'n' Roll Swindle* where Tenpole Tudor would inform Irene Handle that Sid Vicious had been arrested for murder.

Simon's first day in school was on 3 September 1962. The school keeps a record, which dates back to around 1950. In its logbooks are the names of all the children who have ever passed through the school's doors since that time. Inspection of these books reveals that just once in fifty-seven years of record-keeping does a pupil not have three ticks by their name for the child's first day at school. That pupil was Simon Ritchie and the missing tick indicates that no one brought him to school. So at just five years of age he had walked alone from Drury Lane, which meant that he had to cross over both Charing Cross Road and Shaftesbury Avenue. The school records also show that an officer was sent out to speak with the boy's mother, but that the mother was found curled up asleep on the sofa. The remnants of a bottle of scotch were not far away, and a hypodermic needle was found on a coffee table in a saucer near the sofa.

Although Simon was predominantly a happy child, whose dark 'Chinese' eyes were permanently bright with laughter, Anne would later confess to Simon Kinnersley that his being an only child meant he was also very wrapped up in himself. Becoming used to not having to share his toys with anyone else resulted in his being either unwilling, or unable, to mix with the other children, which landed him in trouble on more than one occasion. Of the pupils in his class at the Soho Parish School it was possible, via the current headmistress, to track down one who remembered young Simon. 'I can't really say he sticks out in my mind vividly. Who does at that age?' begins Yvonne Slater. 'But one thing is as clear as if it happened yesterday. A boy who sat across from him brought in some cheese sand-wiches and crisps, and Simon just sat staring at him while he was eating them. So the boy offered Simon half the sandwich and half the crisps, and he wolfed them down so fast, it was like he hadn't eaten for quite a while.' Anne's credo, which she would later pass on to her impressionable son, was that a person should be able to do whatever they wanted just so long as they didn't hurt anyone else in the process. Simon's lack of inter-personal skills left him open to ridicule at school and after falling foul of the school bully, and the school doing little to deal with the problem, Anne decided that the easier route was for Simon to move schools before his first full year was completed.

Simon's next school, St George's, was in Farm Street, situated close to the American Embassy in Grosvenor Square. He left the Soho Parish School on 5 April 1963 and started at St George's the next day. Not only had he already lived at half a dozen different addresses in his short life but now he started a regular run of changing schools as well. Clearly, the lack of a father figure and an increasingly 'absent' mother could not be good for anyone's development.

In the present day, St George's is just one of many central London-based junior schools, but up until 1970 it was a school to which head-teachers and truant officers alike sent children who were not fitting in where they had previously been placed. Simon's report card states that he was a bright student with a particular fascination for music, but that he lacked concentration in the classroom. A final tale from the Soho Parish School backs up this assessment: 'In class he was sullen, withdrawn,' says Yvonne. 'Not really a part of it. He fell asleep once in a class – out like a light he was.'

By this time, Anne's attention was also elsewhere. After never seeing John Ritchie again, she had found love once more – this time in the arms of a middle-class intellectual from Tunbridge Wells called Christopher Beverley. The couple had met sometime during late 1964. A whirlwind romance found them married the following February. The few surviving wedding photographs show a plainly dressed yet beaming Anne, very much the cat that got the cream, standing next to the bespectacled Beverley, with the seven-year-old impish Simon standing in front of the newlyweds with his shoulders hunched and his hands stuffed deep into his trouser pockets. His front door key is hanging about his neck on a piece of twine. A 'latch-key' kid despite his mother's new-found position, his face looks a little too worldly wise to fit perfectly with his age. Anne would later describe her meeting Chris Beverley as something akin to 'winning the pools', but unfortunately fate once again pulled the rug from under Anne's feet when her new husband was diagnosed with cancer within a matter of weeks after the wedding. Beverley succumbed to the disease the following August, and although his death came before he was able to complete the paperwork necessary to legally adopt Simon, Anne ensured that her son took on her dead husband's surname, along with his home and his old nanny for as long as possible. Also at this time, according to the website Vicious Files, which is operated by Sid's Cousin David Ross, Anne held down a job as a bar manager.

Although Anne's previous misfortunes had seen her develop a thick skin to help protect her from the pain and misery that life had dealt her, Beverley's untimely death hurt her far more than she ever let on, and such was her grief that she would often make late-night forays to her husband's grave so that she could be with him, talk to him and, in doing so, prove that the entire episode had been real. 'It destroyed me,' Anne confided during the summer of 1989. 'The whole thing took me years to finally get over. I thought I'd actually found a way out, but as with all things it simply wasn't to be.'

Having been accepted into the Beverley family, Anne and Simon moved to Tunbridge Wells and set up home in a rented flat at 43 Lime Hill Road, situated behind the town's high street. The move brought another change of school, but rather than the posh private school that Chris Beverley had talked about for his soon-to-be stepson, Simon was enrolled at the decidedly less academically challenging Sandrock Road Secondary Modern – a fee-paying school. Of course, this was a step up from St George's, and with his new nanny around there was no shortage of people to take him to and from school.

'When he first arrived, he was very well behaved and didn't stand out,' recalls Jeremy Colebrooke of his former classmate in the Mark Paytress book *The Art of Dying Young*. Although Colebrooke, who shared classes with Simon from 1968–71, readily admits that they were not close friends, he does, however, remember that Simon was not only bright, and deserving of his A-stream status, but was also good at football.

As was the case during his brief tenures at previous schools, however, Simon still found it difficult to mix with the other children, which made him seem all the more aloof and secretive. That said, however, perhaps young Simon was purposely keeping himself at a distance so that he would never have to invite anyone to his home – the reason being that by this time Anne was intravenously injecting heroin again, having cleaned up briefly during her relationship with Chris Beverley. There would be little point in taking anyone home for milk and cookies when the cupboards were bare and Mum was lying on the sofa with a syringe sticking out of her arm. By now it was more than just the odd drug dealer who had found his way from London's West End to Tunbridge Wells.

In 1976, Sid would take great delight in telling *Sounds'* Jonh Ingham that he'd missed the so-called summer of love of nine years earlier as he'd been too busy playing with his Action Man, but it is more likely that he was playing with his pet ferret. Just when the ferret entered Simon's life, or where the domesticated polecat came from, is anybody's guess, but with a mother slowly and inexorably sinking ever deeper into her private heroin hell, one can easily imagine just how much the furry creature came to mean to the lonely and isolated schoolboy. Colebrooke remembers how Simon brought the ferret to school one day, stowed away inside his duffle bag. During a subsequent geography lesson, the ferret 'accidentally' escaped, much to the delight of fellow pupils and the consternation of the teacher.

It is thanks to Colebrooke's reminiscences that we get a rare insight to Simon's home life. He remembers how the boy always smelt of garlic, which, although widely used today, was less common in the UK in 1968. This obviously stemmed from Anne's time in Ibiza and reveals that she must have prepared her son many an exotic meal – or exotic for Tunbridge Wells circa 1968, at any rate. She was also known for her quiches and when later asked what her abiding memory of her son was, Anne replied that he'd loved her mashed potatoes and gravy.

The other children, having been cruelly denied the delights of Mediterranean cooking, had taken to calling Simon 'Garlic Breath', but never to his face, apparently for fear of incurring his wrath. The supposedly aloof Simon had managed to earn himself something of a reputation for thinking with his fists, and Colebrooke remembers one unforgettable incident when Simon's wrath was fully unleashed.

The episode, which had started out as a petty row over the ownership of a Manchester United football scarf, quickly spilled over into violence. 'He [Simon] absolutely pummelled the guy,' says Colebrooke. 'He cut him up pretty badly. And we're talking about a guy that could really handle himself!' It appears that Simon had been enveloped by a red mist for, not content with winning the fight, he continued to kick and punch the unfortunate unnamed individual with such ferocity that a passing motorist felt it necessary to intervene.

Future Sex Pistols roadie and Banshees manager Nils Stevenson, however, never saw this side of Sid in all the time he knew him: 'Forget the "Vicious" bit,' Nils said in 1999. 'That was all hype. He was about as vicious as yesterday's chicken. Just a name they gave him, although there are those who still see fit to think it's worth a mention. I'm sure they think they are simply adding to the legend.'

When not using his fists, Simon would actually use his brain and was something of a voracious reader, taking in everything from the *Eagle* comic to Edgar Allan Poe. When NASA was ready to put the first man on the moon in the summer of 1969, Simon – like boys the world over – was extremely excited by the prospect of watching the event live on TV. Due to the time difference, however, and a few NASA delays, the event did not happen until almost 4 a.m. UK time. News items of the previous week had kept the country spellbound by the very idea of the landing, while the newspapers of the day held the usual daily countdown stories. Everyone on the streets, at work and in schools was talking about it. With all this in mind, Anne

Beverley could not understand the letter that the school sent out to the parents of all pupils at Sandrock Road. It strictly informed parents that they should not keep their children up for the television broadcast of the moon landing. It would only make them tired at school the next day, and besides, all news programmes would be screening the event time and time again over the next few days. 'I was livid,' recalled Anne Beverley. 'I thought: who the fuck are you to tell me that my boy can't watch the first ever moon landing live along with the rest of the nation? It's not like they would be sending rockets to the moon weekly, and even if they did intend to this was the first time!'

Anne decided to ignore the letter and carefully planned the event. Simon would go to bed extra early on the Sunday evening, she would then wake him with coffee at around 3 a.m., beyond which time they would sit together and watch Neil Armstrong make history. The next morning her son was so tired that he completely missed school, and a week later the local truant officers paid Anne a visit to see where her son had been on Monday, 21 July. 'I just confronted them,' remembered Anne. 'I said, "You do know it was the moon landing on TV early that morning, don't you?" I mean, it was in all the papers, on the news, and I wanted my son to see it while it was happening, not some recording of it.' To Anne's surprise the officers agreed with her, told her they were just checking in, and that person-ally they had thought the letter to be a bit stupid.

❦   ❦   ❦

When Simon left Sandrock Road at the end of the third year in July 1971 and returned to London with Anne, neither Jeremy Colebrooke nor anyone else at the school had any reason to suspect that they'd hear of him again. Colebrooke admitted that even six years later, when the Sex Pistols were at the zenith of their infamy and Sid's name and face were plastered across every tabloid in the country, he had failed to recognise that the sneering spiky-topped loon and his one-time ferret-loving classmate were one and the same. In fact it wasn't until after Sid's death, when the *Daily Mirror* ran a photo spread that included several schoolboy photographs that the penny finally dropped.

Upon returning to London after six relatively settled years in Kent, mother and son also returned to the transient lifestyle of old, with Simon changing schools as often as his mother changed addresses. In order to help her son get to these various schools, Anne bought him a bike on hire purchase. It also came in useful at weekends when the two could go riding together. This took Anne back to the relatively care-free days in Ibiza and provided her with some solace.

Although Simon was no academic and struggled to get on at school, he showed a real talent for history. He'd often use his historical interests to amaze Anne during their weekend bike rides. As Anne later recalled, 'He soaked up every word they told him like a sponge and would often be able to explain what the history of any part of London was long before you arrived there.'

Simon's final school was Clissold Park in Stoke Newington. In 1972, aged fifteen, and against his mother's wishes, Simon bid a not-so-fond farewell to the education system. It was a carbon copy of Anne's life in the early 1950s, and she knew exactly what that meant. If academic life went against the Beverley grain, then working for a living was equally unpalatable. 'Looking back on it now, which I know is easy,' remembered Anne Beverley, 'his life took almost the same path as mine for an awful long time, yet I never saw the dangerous bits coming!' His one and only stint at gainful employment was as a trainee cutter at Simpson's – a local factory notable for producing Daks trousers. As in school, Simon appeared incapable of adapting himself to anything he considered to be mundane, and was – some thought purposely – forever miscalculating the sizes of the pockets. Despite repeated warnings, the end result was always the same, and so after one miscalculation too many, he was shown the door.

Having found himself at a crossroads, with neither interest nor inclination as to where his life was heading, Simon decided upon two courses of action: the first was to amend his name to John, as the arty-farty-sounding Simon belonged to the sedate leafy streets of Tunbridge Wells and had no place in the rough and tumble of London, although his mother and her sister Veronica would always refer to him as Simon. 'John' for them was truly a bridge too far – it opened up too many long-closed boxes. The second was to go to college to study art and photography. Anne, although somewhat less than enamoured with her son's decision to adopt his biological father's Christian name, was herself an art lover and therefore more than pleased with his decision to enter further education. He chose the local Hackney Technical College, which his cousin David, some three years his senior, already attended. This made sense in that it was conveniently situated close to home in Ayresome Road, Stoke Newington. But what Anne couldn't have known at the time was just how pivotal and life-changing her son's choice of college would prove to be. It was at Hackney Tech that the newly re-named John Beverley met a seventeen-year-old London–Irish youth with bad teeth by the name of John Joseph Lydon.

CHAPTER 2

From Nowhere to Boredom

'There's a solitary man crying "Hold me". It's only because he's lonely. If the keeper of time runs slowly, he won't be alive for long. If he only had time to tell of all the things he'd planned, with a card up his sleeve, what would he achieve? It means nothing!'

(From 'Card Cheat' by The Clash)

'The first time he came around here he had a beautiful head of hair down to his arse. He was ridiculously shy. If I just so much as looked at him, he would go beetroot red; couldn't say a word. I'd never met someone that shy before.' These were Anne Beverley's first impressions of John Lydon, the future king of British Punk, at their first meeting. Anne's view of Lydon would change over the years, culminating in a thinly disguised bitterness towards him. In her later years she thought him a coward. Every time she saw his face on TV she would say, 'There he is, doing a "Rotten", giving the punters just what they want to see. If his love for all those around him is supposedly so deep, then where was he for his so-called best mate?' To some this view might seem harsh. After all, Lydon was also just a kid when the Sex Pistols were at their peak and Anne Beverley's son needed help the most.

Right up until the day she died Anne Beverley never quite understood John Lydon. Indeed, if he was such a good friend to her son, then why did he go to great length to lambast and lampoon Sid in equal measure at the Sex Pistols' 100 Club reunion press conference in 1996?

Things had been very different back in 1973, when a shared passion for music and mischief had served to bring the two Johns into each other's orbits. In his biography, *The Art of Dying Young* (*Omnibus*), Mark Paytress suggests that the connection between the two became so intense that they were soon adopting each other's characteristics. Lydon, in his autobiography *Rotten: No Irish, No Blacks, No Dogs* (*Plexus*) admitted that John Beverley's inability to take anything seriously taught him to lighten up. Further confirmation is provided by John 'Jah Wobble' Wardle, another of the so-called 'Johns', who was already mates with Lydon at the time he was befriending the future Sex Pistols' bassist Beverley. 'He certainly brought humour into John's life,' recalled Wobble. 'He was a quiet fellow, very introverted, while Sid [Beverley] was an extrovert, a real character.' Although Wobble made the effort to get on with Beverley, he now admits he did so mainly as a concession to Lydon and that he never felt entirely comfortable hanging out with him. 'You couldn't have the conversations that you could with John [Lydon]. Sid was just one of these nutty geezers you knew,' he says by way of explanation. Nils Stevenson, who managed Siouxsie and the Banshees and was the Pistols' tour manager, had similar memories of the young pre-fame John Beverley: 'He was up for anything for a while. People would suggest things, and I'd be thinking forget that, we can find something better to do than that, but Sid already had his jacket on.'

Lydon was the oldest of three brothers born to Irish parents and was a little over a year older than John Beverley. Growing up in Finsbury Park, Lydon grew sick and tired of the education establishment and thought it best to form his own ideas and philosophies. He was the perfect match for Beverley's equally pissed-off worldview. 'There's a few things about John and Sid at the beginning that aren't really discussed now, you know, Punk Rock legend has written a different story,' said Nils Stevenson. 'At the start Sid was the fashionable one, the one who took chances, the good-looking kid, the kid who stood out. John [Lydon] was a shy kid, very intelligent, but shy.'

John Lydon's view of Britain had been ingrained in his psyche from an early age. The whole education system had said to him that anyone, including himself, from the wrong side of the tracks had no prospects going forwards into the 1970s. The rising unemployment, social and political unrest and the militant strikes that would plunge the country into darkness were the perfect breeding grounds for the movement that Lydon would lead later on in the decade.

❀   ❀   ❀

By the time John Beverley entered the red-brick edifice of Hackney College of Further Education in September 1973, he was obsessed with David Bowie, the one-time elfin folksinger who had recently reinvented himself as the androgynous space-age superstar Ziggy Stardust. Not content with having posters and news clippings of his metamorphic hero covering every inch of wall space in his bedroom in the high-rise council tower block on Evering Road, Stoke Newington, John Beverley had begun copying Bowie's style and image. Gone was the 'Marc Bolan' curly perm, which Lydon reckoned made his mate look like 'an old woman', to be replaced with a Bowie-esque feather-cut which was dyed bright red at the front. At this stage he had yet to discover the benefits of using hairspray to spike his hair, and would plaster it in Vaseline before then placing his head in the oven to achieve the desired effect. 'Have you ever heard anything like it in your life?' laughed Anne Beverley. 'I walk in the kitchen and he's got his head in the oven, I said, "What the fuck do you think you're doing?" and he told me, "No mum, it works, honest." Oh yes, and like everything else at that time it was stylish, so it had to be done.' He'd also taken to wearing colourful and flamboyant clothes. He was unafraid of experimenting with his image, while also seeking to develop his own individual sense of style. Lydon would later berate his mate for being a hapless fashion victim, interested only in whatever the latest magazines were telling him to wear. They had much in common, and Lydon hadn't failed to notice this: 'We got on alright, because he stood out from the crowd, you know, and couldn't fit in, just couldn't fit in like the rest of us. Like all my friends, really. It's tough being an individual in a society that seems to frown upon such activity.' Lydon never thought it OK to be frowned upon by anyone and his time at Hackney was not a happy one, though he did make some links that would stay with him for years to come.

'I got on there really well with John [Lydon], and I got on there really well with the black kids,' recalled Beverley. 'They were fucking great, the spades in that college. They were really cool, know what I mean? They used to have reggae discos with massive sound systems – they were really loose. But everything else was shit, I hated the lot [and] never did anything at all. I never did a single thing and I used to be always making excuses.'

❋ ❋ ❋

Towards the end of Beverley's first academic year at Hackney, he managed to make the pages of the local newspaper after a brush with the law. In the early hours of Sunday, 27 May 1974, hours after a female fan was killed and over 600 were injured at a David Cassidy concert at White City, the police were called out to quell a disturbance at a party in Coronation Avenue, Stoke Newington. They made one arrest – of an individual, later identified as John Beverley, who was 'shouting at the top of his voice', and who appeared to be 'berserk'. The arresting officer, PC Leslie Pollard's report describes how the accused had struck both himself as well as his colleague PC Glenn Mooney, and later put his shoulder through a glass panel of a door at the station, sustaining a laceration to his shoulder that required stitches. In his defence, John claimed that his behaviour that night was completely out of character and due to someone having laced his drink with methylated spirit. This claim was supported by Pollard who later informed the court that he had indeed smelt methylated spirit on the accused's breath at the time of his arrest. Although some sources also claim LSD was used that night, there is not a shred of evidence to back it up. Anne Beverley appeared as a character witness and testified that her son seldom drank, which at the time, by all accounts, does look to have been perfectly true. She must have been fearing the worst regarding the striking of two police officers, not to mention damaging police property. This usually meant a custodial sentence. John later added that he was 'extremely sorry for any trouble he had caused'. The magistrate, however, having taken into account that John Beverley was of previous good character, and assuming that no right-minded seventeen-year-old O level student would knowingly drink methylated spirit, decided to be merciful and granted him an absolute discharge on all three charges. He was ordered to pay £10 costs and £5 compensation for the broken window. 'That was a very tough time,' said Anne Beverley. 'We were starting to have the usual mother and son teenage arguments, and yet I also had to stand by him when he genuinely needed me.'

Although the charges had been dropped, the kudos from having assaulted not one, but two police officers propelled John Beverley's standing among his college peers into the stratosphere. 'I remember him telling me years later,' says Nils Stevenson 'that certain people who used to give him a hard time at college suddenly backed off in the wake of that incident.'

The event, along with the subsequent court hearing, was deemed newsworthy enough to make the local gazette, whose main headline read 'Was Hackney Student Drugged At Party?' Bizarrely, Anne Beverley actually took a cutting of it from the newspaper and kept it, like some parents might keep a press cutting if their offspring had done well at a swimming competition.

❀   ❀   ❀

In the summer of 1974 John Lydon was happy to bid farewell to Hackney Technical College, but rather than go out into the world and seek employment, he instead elected to enrol for another year of further education. Kingsway College, which is located at the King's Cross end of Gray's Inn Road, appeared to cover the entire student spectrum as it catered not only for A level students and day-release apprentices, but also for wayward disruptives such as Jah Wobble who'd been expelled from Nautical School, and were belatedly sitting their O levels. General collective opinion seems to be that anybody who wanted to attend Kingsway College simply had to ask and they were in.

John Beverley, meanwhile, was starting his second year at Hackney and displaying an increasing aptitude for art. Some of his student work from this time – line drawings, sketches and watercolours – still exists today, and can command higher prices than the majority of his recording work. Some of his pictures are credited to 'The Highway Man', a pseudonym he often used at college, and these come complete with a small doodle – often in pencil – of a devil holding a pitchfork. In 2004, a 24" x 18" Dali-esque illustration, bearing the signature of John Beverley circa 1974, executed in coloured pencils with what appears to be a watercolour wash over it, sold at auction for the respectable sum of £1,912. Needless to say, this interest was probably a result of Sid's celebrity status as a rock 'n' roll martyr rather than the quality of the work itself. The bulk of this collection is now the property of his cousin David, who has some of it on display on his Vicious Files website.

Anne Beverley always believed that had her son's life taken a different turn he could have developed into a promising artist, but ex-Hornsey Art College student Henry Sabini, who was the beneficiary of the aforementioned auctioned artwork (having been given the piece by the aspiring artist himself), thought the piece to be 'very adolescent' and 'pretty poor art'. He has always assumed that the illustration, which features decapitated limbs mounted upon sticks, and a statue with a bloated, elongated arm that 'comes to life', was Beverley's attempt to manifest his feelings over their rivalry for the affections of a mutual friend called Mandy. 'We talked a bit about art,' recalls Sabini. 'John would always complain that his tutors were prats. He didn't see why it was necessary to learn life drawing. I tried to explain that once you knew how to draw properly, then you really can start playing around, but he didn't want to take that step.' As in his later career with the Sex Pistols, it seems that John Beverley was incapable of doing the groundwork and simply lived for the end result. One of the paintings, however, shows a mosque by a river in a red misty sunset. Drawn from memory, this was hung over the fireplace at Anne's home in Swadlincote and did indeed show some artistic flair. Other works included layered photography and photographs treated with charcoal, plus cartoons and a picture of a saxophone – an instrument that Sid would later briefly play.

Despite his growing enjoyment of art, John quit Hackney after the second term and, although Anne would later attribute her son's decision to his teachers having supposedly kept badgering him to take subjects that weren't to his liking, the absence of his best friend John Lydon must have been a key factor. Though he was unable to enrol at Kingsway, this did not stop him from latching onto the college's social scene and he became something of a semi-permanent fixture in the common room. By this time he had undergone another image makeover, which earned him the nickname 'Spiky John'. Gone was the Ziggy feather-cut, to be replaced with a shorter proto-Punk hairstyle that was swept back from his forehead. His clothes were now predominantly black. 'He looked like Johnny Depp in *Cry Baby*,' recalls Simone Stenfors, who herself would later become a Punk scenester. 'I first met him at a Hallowe'en party in October '74,' she says. 'He looked completely different to everyone else. It was a fancy dress party and I'd gone dressed as Morticia Adams and my husband, Chris Carter [later in the band Throbbing Gristle], went as a Swedish au pair, but Sid simply went as himself. I fancied him immediately.'

It's not hard to see why 'Spiky John' stood out from the crowd. While the other attendees, at least those that weren't in Hallowe'en garb, were dressed in typical mid-1970s attire of leather bomber jackets and flared and patched denim, Beverley was dressed in straight-leg jeans, black cap-sleeve T-shirt, and a leather-studded wristband. Simone now admits that, 'I was so taken by him that I sent my new husband [of just two days] away to get drinks, while I sat chatting Sid up!'

To complete his outfit for the night, Beverley wore a small padlock hanging from a chain about his neck, although this is not the 'Rabbit' padlock with which he would later become synonymous.

From photographs taken that night it is also noticeable that Beverley had an air of arrogance about him. While the other students in the pictures were striking suitably mock-macabre poses or looning at the camera, Beverley appeared poised and calculating as he stared directly into the lens. This could simply be as a result of the knowledge he'd gained from his photography course, or perhaps because he believed that he might one day be famous and that he should therefore avoid potentially embarrassing photos that might come back to haunt him in the future.

'Spiky John' Beverley was starting to gain a reputation in student circles for being on the cutting edge of fashion. Mike Baess was attending Kingsway to study art and languages at the time and first encountered Beverley during a student sit-in in mid-November 1974. A group of students barricaded themselves inside the Sidmouth Street campus to protest over subsistence-level grants. 'He was dressed head-to-toe in black, and he had black spiky hair at a time when the rest of us wore it shoulder-length,' recalls Baess. 'His heroes must have been the leather-era Elvis and James Dean. He was the one that everyone looked at when he walked into a room. I think he knew that he had that power and cultivated it. He looked like a cross between a Warhol superstar and a Teddy Boy – interesting, but slightly dangerous, too. He was a genuinely unique person, and kinda looked like a rock star.'

This image hadn't gone unnoticed at home either. 'Almost immediately after the Bowie phase, came the all-in-black look,' remembered Anne Beverley. 'I used to say, "Sime you look like an unemployed gunslinger." We'd both laugh at that, but everything had to be black.'

John Beverley had come upon the demonstrators by chance while looking for his friend Lydon, but readily accepted Baess's offer to join them. While ploughing his own furrow he was also keen to be accepted and join in with friends when he could. His participation at the sit-in was ironic given that he himself had yet to formally enrol at the college. Even when he did become a student, he was one of the worst culprits for collecting his grants while absconding from lessons. Baess and the other militants were clearly in it for the long haul, having set up a mobile disco for entertainment, as well as bringing in sandwiches and, more importantly, a stash of weed. Perhaps not surprisingly, given that there was a mobile disco blaring away in the background, the conversation soon turned to music. 'I was really into Hawkwind and the Pink Fairies, so we talked about them for a while,' Baess later told Mark Paytress. 'John liked Roxy Music and David Bowie, although I was impressed when he started talking about Syd Barrett [the original front-man of Pink Floyd], as he didn't strike me as the kind of guy who would.'

Just how in-depth John Beverley's knowledge of Syd Barrett was, Baess doesn't say, but little could either of them have known at the time that, within a matter of months, 'Spiky John' would had been consigned to the identity dustbin to be replaced by 'Sid' in supposed homage to the psychedelic '60s eccentric. Lydon, who was responsible for providing John Beverley with his soon-to-be-iconoclastic *nom de guerre*, has always maintained that 'Sid' was named after the Lydon family's pet albino hamster. Either way, Beverley had half of the name that would make him famous.

Anne Beverley's son, although still in his teenage years, had undergone many changes through his life and the search for an identity that he was happy with was understandable. Changes in family, abode and school were just the backdrop to his changes in name and personality. Simon Ritchie had become John Beverley, and Spiky John had now become Sid.

Today, whenever someone says the name Sid it is likely that you think of Sid Vicious, but back in 1975, with Syd Barrett having disappeared off the radar, the only famous 'Sid' that would have readily sprung to mind would have been Sid James from the *Carry On* films. Sharing one's name, albeit a nickname, with a balding middle-aged actor, regardless of the latter's successful film and TV career, was not going to earn him any Brownie points in the coolest nicknames stakes. The fact that the Sid nickname stuck came down to Beverley's mistake of telling John Lydon that he hated the 'poxy' name Sid. As Nils Stevenson explained, 'If you didn't want John [Lydon] to keep on about something, the worst thing you could say was that you hated it – [it was] red rag to a bull stuff.'

❀   ❀   ❀

Having discovered that they shared a mutual passion for underground music, Sid, as he was now known to all his friends, and Mike Baess started hanging out together at weekends. On

Saturdays the pair would meet up with friends before heading down to Portobello Road market to buy bootleg records and tapes, while Sunday afternoons, which where always seen as a quieter affair, were reserved for visits to the Roundhouse in Chalk Farm. Baess offers an interesting insight into Sid's musical predilections during this period as it appears that he had a soft spot for jazz-rock, no doubt derived from his mother's record collection, and enjoyed getting stoned listening to Weather Report and Stanley Clarke albums. 'People honestly believe that the jazz thing is all manufactured, that he never actually listened to it,' recalled Anne Beverley. 'It's nothing huge for people to understand. I had jazz records and he didn't have an awful lot of money, so you do the maths.'

Baess also described Sid as being charming, witty and possessing an intelligence that was often purposely suppressed in order to play out his adopted role of class buffoon. Although Baess readily admits that his friend was indeed anti-social and possibly out of control, he is quick to stress that the rebellion was more 'cheeky chancer' than Che Guevara. 'He never paid for anything,' offers Baess, by way of explanation, 'be it fags, beer, records, you name it. He just seemed to blag his way through life. He didn't give a fuck about anything, which from a teenage point of view seemed fantastic.' This theory is supported by Nils Stevenson: 'I remember being in Covent Garden with him once, and he said, "Are you hungry?" I was, as it happened, so he walked over to this fruit stall, struck up a conversation with the barrow boy and, while he was doing so, picked up two apples, started eating one and threw me one, about five minutes later we wandered off. The guy on the stall was all smiles and waves, and I never saw a penny change hands, and this was way before any fame came his way.'

Another of Sid's associates during the latter months of 1975 was 'Mandy Pete', so-called due to his ability to provide his friends with a seemingly inexhaustible supply of Mandrax tablets. Mandrax, or 'Mandies' to use the barbiturate's street name, is a sedative; in drug terms, it is the 'yin' to accompany the amphetamine 'yang'. By this time, Sid – having spent his formative years watching his mother sink ever deeper into drug dependency – had been desensitised by drugs and had even begun injecting speed, making full use of an old metal syringe that could be boil washed, and which belonged to his mum.

'John [Lydon] and I were round at Sid's place in Queensbridge Road, Hackney, one afternoon,' remembers Jah Wobble. 'Sid's sat there with his mum on the sofa and they're both jacking up! I was only sixteen at the time, not even old enough to buy a drink in a pub, and I'm sat watching my mate and his mum sticking needles in their arm. Sid may have only been banging-up with speed, but it was still freaky watching him slump down the wall leaving a greasy vaseline smear on the wallpaper.

'You get a certain vibe around drugs,' he adds. 'It's different to booze, which is more manic, like anything can happen. But with drugs, especially smack, all you can sense is darkness. I don't just mean literally, though it certainly wasn't a bright flat. It was metaphorically dark.'

The Queensbridge Road flat's inherent darkness only served to heighten Anne Beverley's sense of hopelessness. She yearned to feel the Ibizan sun on her skin once more, and to drift off to sleep to the sound of cicadas. But that seemed a lifetime ago.

'Hindsight is easy isn't it?' said Anne. 'Looking back now, I guess the real problems began at Queensbridge Road, because I was in no real state to look after myself, and [Sid] started injecting speed, which was the beginning of his downward spiral.'

John Gray, another friend of Lydon's who would complete 'The Johns', also recalled feeling uncomfortable watching on as Sid nonchalantly sterilised his mother's old-fashioned metal syringe in a saucepan of boiling water before proceeding to inject himself with amphetamines. One friend who positively enjoyed visiting his friend's high-rise abode however, was future Clash and PiL guitarist Keith Levene. Although himself something of a burgeoning drugs aficionado, he had another reason for his Wednesday night visits. He had come to realise that Wednesday was Anne Beverley's chosen bath night, and not only was she a creature of habit, she was also averse to towelling herself off afterwards, preferring instead to dry off naturally as she walked naked around the flat. 'I've always dried naturally, love, you know?' said Anne with a sly grin. '[It's] just one of those things. It's my house and that's how I am!'

❀   ❀   ❀

Although Sid would sporadically return to his mother over the next two years, it was during the autumn of 1975 that he left home for good. He had previously tried to flee the nest shortly after his mother's return to London four years earlier, but after two weeks of sleeping rough he'd scurried home with his tail between his legs. The legend of squat life might well have sounded incredible when re-told from distant memory by some Glam Rock star in the *NME*, but the reality was grim. On more than one occasion for the future Sex Pistol, the chance to move back home won hands down. Anne, although still deeply devoted to her beloved Simon, was relieved to see him go as the tiny council flat was not big enough for two free-spirited people. 'I said, it's either you or me, and it's not going to be me, so you can just fuck off. I don't care if you have to sleep on a fucking park bench.' In addition to this, of course, the track marks which Anne Beverley had faked only a few short years earlier, to help her get financial aid in returning to London, were by now only too real. Anne need not have worried about her son having to wrestle with tramps for bench space in Hyde Park, for within days of leaving home he had found a relatively safe haven in the form of another squat in Hampstead.

New Court is one of two intimidating five-storey tenement blocks that were due to be given a new lease of life through a refurbishment programme by the Churches Housing Association. The tenements are believed to be London's earliest examples of social housing and were originally built in the 1880s to house the servants of well-to-do families living in the nearby elegant Georgian townhouses in Flask Walk and Lutton Terrace. By the mid-1970s, with the servants long-since liberated, the blocks had been transformed into flats, but as the renovations did not stretch to the buildings' foreboding exteriors they still resembled nineteenth-century prisons. 'Fucking A1 squalor – the sort of place rats are happy to vacate given the option,' remembered Dave Jones, an old Glam scene guitar roadie and ex-resident of many a London squat.

'New Court was a bizarre place,' adds Baess, who was a frequent visitor to the building throughout 1975 and 1976. 'It had these huge fifty-foot chimney stacks and looked like workhouses. Yet up the alley and round the corner was Heath Street where all the posh boutiques are.' The fact that John Lydon, having incurred his father's wrath, was also a temporary resident during 1975 has seen New Court become enshrined in Sex Pistols folklore. Lydon's expulsion from the family home in Finsbury Park was on account of his having undergone a metamorphism from long-term Hawkwind fan and resident longhair at the local college, to *Clockwork Orange* proto-Punk. His father had apparently insisted that his eldest son get his hair cut, but rather than seek professional assistance, Lydon took a pair of scissors to his hair before then dyeing it blue. Unfortunately, the dye was designed for clothes rather than hair, which resulted in his hacked-off locks turning a vile cabbage-green colour. In his autobiography, Lydon likens New Court to a Victorian slum dwelling which lacked the basic amenities of electricity and hot water, and which had become so dilapidated that the local council had declared it illegal for people to live in. But New Court was not quite the 'squatters' shithole' that Lydon would have us believe. It would seem that a lot of the squat life of mid-1970 pre-Punk London has been given an extra twist to portray something approaching Charles Dickens' standards somewhere along the line.

'It wasn't even a squat,' says Mandy Pete, who spent several months sharing floor space at New Court with Sid. 'It was a ground-floor flat in the block on the left-hand side as you come out of Flask Walk, and was leased by the Housing Association to a woman called Barbara. The flat was always very tidy. The carpets were clean and Barbara would always do the washing up.' The Barbara in question was in her early thirties and had a young daughter called Zoe. She obviously saw herself as something of a cross between surrogate mother and Samaritan to the waifs and strays that were sharing her spare room, as she even neglected to charge them rent. 'She was very much the motherly type, and had a very calming influence on Sid,' adds Pete. 'Maybe that was his attraction to her. He seemed like the kind of guy who needed a mother about.'

Pete readily admits that he and Sid made strange bedfellows. 'Sid was a peacock and always fretting about his appearance while I was more of a free-festival sort of guy. He probably would have spat at me if we'd have met twelve months later,' he told Mark Paytress. Polar opposites in the sartorial stakes they may have been but, as with Baess, Pete found that he and Sid shared a mutual passion for music and drugs. 'We did a lot of speed together. We had parties where we'd stay up for days on end listening to music, smoking spliffs, snorting sulphate and popping Mandies,' he admits today. 'Sure we were careless, because we didn't give a shit. But it wasn't so much that we were seeking oblivion as simply having a good time. As far as I'm aware Sid didn't shoot up in those days but he did do a bit of dealing. Everyone did, but it wasn't regarded as dealing. It was more of a community thing, helping out your mates while making a little bit on top.'

Drugs and wide-awake parties weren't the only things that Sid is remembered for during his time at New Court, however. There are darker tales of deeds such as strangling cats and mugging elderly residents. 'There was a story of Sid mugging an old lady,' confirms Wobble. 'It was only a rumour, but I couldn't say that he wasn't capable of it.'

'Some of the stories wouldn't surprise me, but some of it is pure comic book stuff,' said Nils Stevenson in 1999. 'I mean, Sid sings, "I killed the cat" in 'My Way', thus he must have killed a cat. I doubt it strongly – it's media machine stuff. I know how Malcolm works, and that sort of thing looks good on a press release.'

Although a change in name doesn't necessarily bring about a change in personality, especially when the said name is bestowed rather than chosen, the sullen and introverted Simon John Beverley that Jeremy Colebrooke remembers from Tunbridge Wells had well and truly disappeared into the ether by 1975; even Spiky John had been forced into the shadows now that Sid was in town. But even allowing for teenage bravado, or drug-dependency, it is still hard to conjure up the image of Sid lurking within the dingy alley behind New Court passing the time throttling cats while waiting to relieve unsuspecting old dears of their pensions. That said, however, Baess, during one of his nightly sojourns to New Court, encountered his friend in the alleyway. 'I could tell that he was speeding his tits off. He told me that he'd just mugged an old lady and produced a flick-knife and a small leather purse full of money as if to prove it.'

Mandy Pete also confirmed the mugging stories to Mark Paytress, and even went so far as to claim that Barbara was aware of her spiky-haired lodger's Turpin-esque antics and would joke that, 'He's been up to no good again.' But either Pete was attempting to beguile Paytress by over-egging the pudding or he'd simply been raiding the medicine cabinet again – Barbara's turning a blind eye to Sid robbing her neighbours at knife-point is clearly at odds with her supposedly philanthropic nature. Of course it could also be possible that, given the amount of drugs being taken by everyone in and around Barbara's place at the time, these memories might not be the most reliable.

As well as the possible muggings, Sid topped up his dole money by spending a few weeks working as a rent boy under the pseudonym 'Hymie'. He printed out photos of himself posing in black jeans, sunglasses and T-shirt with the hand-written message, 'I'm Hymie, Try Me'.

When asked some years later by *Uncut* magazine whether he thought Sid was gay, Malcolm McLaren replied, 'I have no actual evidence that Sid was gay, but he had all the trappings. He had a fascination with treating himself as an object of desire for both sexes. He never thought of himself as a complete heterosexual. It was mostly gay people who fell in love with him. I certainly never slept with Sid. My partner, Vivienne Westwood, was absolutely infatuated with him and was desperate to sleep with him. She did attempt to do so on several occasions. As a jealous partner, I prevented her from doing so.'

By the autumn of 1975 Sid was not just pushing the bound-aries on his sexuality but was also pushing ways of making money and, despite his mother's advice of doing anything so long as it didn't hurt anyone else if it meant a few pounds, he'd go for it. Mike Baess personally witnessed an incident during October that serves to illustrate the emergence of Sid's darker side. 'A mate of mine called Chris was having a twenty-first birthday party at his house in Oxford,' he says. 'Me, Sid and a few other mates went up there by coach and God only knows how Sid paid for his ticket. He'd brought along some white powder that he tried to pass off as speed, but was in fact the domestic cleaning agent Vim. He actually sold some to one guy who took it and had to be rushed into hospital to have his stomach pumped. That wasn't funny. The guy could have died.'

❀   ❀   ❀

John Lydon had been laying concrete with his dad for £70 a week. Upon being thrown out, the job went with it. After a short stint in a shoe factory, dismissed by Lydon as nothing more than farce, he started working at Cranks health food restaurant situated at the top of Heals Department Store in Tottenham Court Road. He and Sid worked together cleaning the kitchens.

The money wasn't perfect but there was always plenty of food left over every day, so at night, once the bosses had gone home, they would stuff their faces with freebies. With the building deserted until the next day, it became their playground, and the pair would run havoc until the morning. They would leave around dawn, already coming down from the speed that had kept them up all night.

At around this time Lydon met some people who would change his life, and the face of rock music, forever. Sid had told Lydon of a shop he'd seen at 430 Kings Road called SEX. At the time of Lydon's first venture to SEX, Malcolm McLaren was looking to find a singer for a band he was putting together.

'Johnny Rotten wandered into the shop one evening to buy a pair of brothel creepers in black suede,' remembers Malcolm McLaren who owned the shop with Vivienne Westwood. 'He had green hair and very bad teeth. He was wearing an old second-hand tuxedo, as if it were the original teddy-boy drape. He was immediately press-ganged into auditioning, singing Alice Cooper's 'Eighteen' with the jukebox. He gave an impression of being in pain, and of needing to hide that pain. He was angry and the anger was clearly masking a shyness that made him appear vulnerable and, in some way, cool. It was very seductive. The sound he brought to the group wasn't melodic; his style didn't borrow from the blues or from soul or from any of the conventional roots of rock and roll. He created anthems of despair — loud, relentless, unforgiving.'

Saturday lad, and prospective member of the new band, Glen Matlock remembers the general vibe in the shop very well: 'Bryan Ferry was swanning past and Malcolm thought they were all a bunch of tossers, so we did, too. They were all multi-millionaires. Or we thought they were, and we didn't have a pot to piss in but we laughed at them cause y'know, it was if we seen them in the pub, and it just gave us a good attitude right from the get go, and then Steve [Jones] and Paul [Cook] started coming in, Steve mainly to nick things, I think.'

Lydon's impromptu audition led to him being asked to front the band and the original Sex Pistols line-up was complete. Sid took the news badly. 'I remember Simon coming round to see me, and he was really down,' recalled Anne Beverley. '"It's a bit much," he said. "Especially as it was me that took him [Lydon] down there in the first place. He would never have even gone in there if I hadn't forced him to go down the Kings Road."'

Anne was referring to the day that her son informed her that John Lydon, the same John Lydon who, twelve months previously, had seemed extremely shy, had been sequestered by Malcolm McLaren to sing with the fledgling Sex Pistols. 'It should have been Simon. He was really put out at that,' said Anne years later. 'I remember him coming home one day with this lettuce-green dye, and wanted me to dye his hair for him. In a way he was a Punk before Malcolm McLaren even came on the scene. He was a Punk right from 1975 when he first dyed his hair. He carried it all the way through. Then the group took off and they got their songs together and he thought they were the dog's bleedin' dinner. "Aw, Mum," he said. "I've been to see them and they're fuckin' brilliant!" He was big enough for that. He wasn't a mean-spirited person at all.'

It was quite possible that Sid himself could have been put into the place of singer if he hadn't been working on a market stall on Portabello Road when Lydon called into SEX. Vivienne Westwood, having been suitably impressed by Sid's style and charisma, had put his name forward as a possible candidate for Steve Jones' group – a hotchpotch of ex-thieves and fledgling musicians named The Swankers. 'Steve and Paul had a band going and I think Paul's brother-in-law was in the band as the bass player, but he weren't turning up or taking it seriously. I don't think there was anything to take seriously at that stage,' says Glen Matlock today. 'I overheard them talking 'cos they were trying to get Malcolm involved somehow, and I said, "Well, I'm playing bass, you know. I'll come down and have a play with you." So that was it, we formed the band.'

Unfortunately for Sid, Vivienne had yet to know him by his new nickname and was still calling him John, which supposedly led to Malcolm confusing Sid with John Lydon, whom he was also aware of thanks to his associate, and future Clash manager, Bernie Rhodes. Rhodes had spotted Lydon sporting a cabbage-cut and an 'I Hate Pink Floyd' T-shirt, while making a nuisance of himself on the Kings Road. Had Sid happened to wander into SEX that fateful Saturday in late August 1975 then perhaps it might have been he and not Lydon who was invited to join the group, and rock 'n' roll history would surely have taken an altogether different path.

CHAPTER 3

Sex Pistols Will Play!

'When we started we thought we were great
Though nobody else agreed,
Just you and I wasting our time
Playing and singing out of key,
And they said we played too loud
Cos we didn't play for their crowd
But we just told them "Wait and see"'
(From 'Wait and See' by Stiff Little Fingers)

By 1975, Malcolm McLaren and Vivienne Westwood had been running their clothing emporium for four years and, like its bastard offspring, Simon John Beverley had also undergone three name changes during this period. 'That was some place, that shop,' remembers original Pistols biographer Fred Vermorel. 'For two years they never paid any tax on it. You know, when they were finally asked, they didn't think they needed to, because the lease wasn't originally in their names!'

The shop had first opened its doors as Let It Rock, selling both authentic and reproduction 1950s clothing to cater for the then-current Teddy Boy revival and was even commissioned to provide costumes for Ray Connelly's 1972 film *That'll Be The*

Day (starring David Essex and Ringo Starr). Future employee Alan Jones says, 'I remember Vivienne coming along, then SEX happened and of course this was when the whole of the Punk ethos was born.'

'After a few weeks of renting a corner at the back of the shop, to sell everything myself and Vivienne had' says Malcolm today, while breaking into a laugh, 'the owner, this black Teddy Boy, threw me the keys one night and said, "Take a small commission on the stuff of mine that you sell, I'll be back in a while." But he never came back, and slowly we transformed the shop in our own image.'

In order to accommodate the switch from drapes and crepes to studs and leather, the pair decided to rename the shop Too Fast To Live, Too Young To Die, which had become something of a maxim among American biker gangs in homage of the iconic actor James Dean. 'I would now sell such things as dog collars, whips, chains, tit-clamps, rubber T-shirts, rubber skirts,' recalls Malcolm. 'Bang on the Kings Road, opposite Woolworth's.' Although Malcolm and Vivienne were intent on distancing themselves from the Teds (in earlier Let It Rock days Malcolm had worked in the shop in full Teddy Boy drapes), they were still happy to take their money, and not only continued to keep the Let It Rock range on sale during this period but also retained the name as the brand label for future in-house designs. 'They went in for shock designs. It was done around the group, but a lot of the T-shirts didn't even name-check the group anywhere,' says Fred Vermorel.

       ⟦   ⟦   ⟦

By the time Sid and The Johns began hanging out at SEX, Malcolm and Vivienne had begun selling a range of rubber and fetish wear, which had previously been the sole exclusive of the back pages of seedy porn magazines. 'I used to be a speed freak at one time before I joined the band,' Sid would later confess on

BBC Radio 1. 'I used to deal speed and I was shooting speed all the time. I had track-marks down my arm, and I used to sell it in Malcolm's shop.' What attracted Sid and John Lydon, as well as their future co-conspirators Steve Jones and Paul Cook, to the shop, however, was not the skin-tight rubber outfits, but rather the range of titillating T-shirts such as the legendary 'Two Cowboys' design. There was also the added bonus that the near-destitute youths could hang about in the shop all day without being pestered to buy something, which was something of a rarity on the mid-1970s Kings Road. 'That shop was incredible, if you think about a normal clothes shop – all "Good morning sir, can I help you?" Yet in there, different rules applied,' remembers Nils Stevenson. 'You could walk in around noon, put some money in the jukebox, pop open a can of coke, and still be there chatting at 4 p.m. It really was more like a drop-in centre of sorts.' And that wasn't all. 'They had an interesting wage policy,' remembers Fred Vermorel. 'For the kids who worked at the shop, Vivienne would say, "Just take what you think you've earned today." So these kids had plenty of money, and clothes just went missing on a daily basis.'

Around this time, Sid found out where Bryan Ferry lived. In the words of John Wardel: 'He wanted to go round there with a bottle of Martini and demand to be let in. John would have had too much pride to want to be seen trying to get in, even though he desperately wanted to. Sid wouldn't worry about that, he'd just steam in.'

Standing in the shop today (still owned by Vivienne and called Vivienne Westwood: World's End – one of three stores selling her latest designs in the capital alone), it is hard to imagine how the tiny corner edifice, which is no bigger than an average-sized living room, could have possibly been the epicentre of London's last true counter-culture movement. Indeed, SEX's interior floor space must have been akin to that of Dr Who's Tardis in order to house Malcolm and Vivienne's designs, the designers themselves, Jordan and the rest of the staff, the Sex Pistols and their entourage – and that's without the surgical bed and jukebox. It must also be the only Kings Road shop that doesn't have a staff toilet.

*   *   *

The coming together of Malcolm McLaren, a middle-class effete haberdasher, and Steve Jones, the ragamuffin, near-illiterate street urchin, must have seemed an unlikely friendship. But Malcolm, who would later present himself as a Fagin-esque embezzler, had been totally captivated with Jones' light-fingered antics, which had resulted in the group amassing an impressive array of musical instruments, including an entire PA belonging to David Bowie that had been purloined from the Hammersmith Odeon during Bowie's Ziggy Stardust farewell tour in July 1973.

McLaren's idea of pop Svengali was more in the tradition of late 1950s and early 1960s pop impresarios such as Larry Parnes or the Beatles' Brian Epstein, a by-gone era of guys who just fancied a dabble with this 'pop music thing', rather than becoming a full-on rock manager such as Led Zeppelin's Peter Grant or The Who's Kit Lambert and Chris Stamp. McLaren had already dipped his toe into the murky waters of rock 'n' roll management by attempting to revive the fortunes of American trash-glam rockers, the New York Dolls, during his stateside visit in the early 1970s. His idea had been to dress up the group in red patent-leather outfits (designed by Vivienne, naturally) and have them perform in front of a giant hammer and sickle backdrop. 1970s America, although reeling from the triple whammy of the Watergate scandal, Nixon's resignation and the on-going stalemate in Vietnam, still wasn't ready to embrace 'Commie Rock' and the group had disintegrated during a mini-tour of Florida. By his own admission Malcolm wasn't your average manager. As he said, 'I adored it when they were angry, fed-up and constantly on the search for the impossible.'

Before returning to London, McLaren had spent several weeks licking his wounds in New York where he had witnessed the emergence of a new and exciting musical scene at CBGBs, where groups such as Television and the Ramones were playing a stripped down version of rock 'n' roll. This had reminded him of the early rock 'n' roll pioneers from his youth. His initial intention had been to lure Television's charismatic bassist Richard Hell into accompanying him to London in order to front Steve Jones' fledgling group. Hell considered the proposal but then, suffering from a combination of cold feet and cold turkey, had pulled out at the eleventh hour. McLaren may not have got his man, but Hell's radical image – hacked-off hair and torn clothes festooned with safety-pins – was easily trans-portable. All that was needed now was to find someone capable of carrying it off. This ultimately led to John Lydon being asked to step into the breach.

Sid and Lydon had not been the only two considerations for McLaren's new front-man. The original person to be offered the job was a then-unknown charismatic Scottish kid named Jim 'Midge' Ure. McLaren had come upon the interesting-looking Glaswegian during a business trip to Scotland with Bernie Rhodes, but Ure had politely declined the offer on account of his already being in a group which had just cut a recording deal with Bell Records. Bell was home of fellow Scots the Bay City Rollers and the reigning king of Glam Rock, Gary Glitter, so the deal was both sound and solid. The group in question was Slik, a Glam-orientated outfit that would hit the top of the UK chart in February 1976 with their debut single 'Forever And Ever'. McLaren's initial intention had been to mould Jones' new group into London's equivalent of the Bay City Rollers, and although Ure would have fit the bill perfectly, fate had other things in store for the diminutive Scot.

❀   ❀   ❀

After playing their first gigs at college venues towards the end of 1975, the Sex Pistols, under McLaren's loose tutelage, were writing songs and preparing for their first demo sessions with producer Chris Spedding, who was a regular at SEX. The earliest gigs were directly aimed at the art-school crowd. St Martin's School of Art, the Central School of Art and the Chelsea School of Art hosted some of these fledgling shows. McLaren's managerial interest stretched no further than his agreeing to pay for them to use a succession of rehearsal spaces. He regarded the group as little more than portable mannequins with which to model the shop's new clothes. This would not be the case for long. Within eight months, the group changed its name from Swankers to the decidedly more interesting Sex Pistols, and Lydon was re-christened Johnny Rotten by Steve Jones, on account of the poor state of his teeth. McLaren was astute enough to realise that the group was not only attracting media interest but also a steadily increasing number of social and musical misfits who were all disillusioned with the current state of the self-indulgent music industry.

By April 1976 the Sex Pistols had branched out from the ubiquitous college gig circuit, had gained their first column inches in the *NME*, and had also acquired a Tuesday night residency at the 100 Club on Oxford Street. But it was their gig supporting The 101'ers at the Nashville Rooms in West Kensington on the 23rd of that month that would formally tattoo the Sex Pistols onto the musical map – a photograph showing the group involved in a scrap with several members of the audience was deemed newsworthy by all three of the leading music weeklies. *Melody Maker* went so far as to feature a photograph showing the group in mid-brawl on its front cover. For McLaren, this was the sort of publicity that money couldn't buy.

The 'fight', which according to those in attendance was little more than handbags at five paces, had started out as an innocuous argument between Vivienne and a girl over rightful possession of a chair. This escalated into a scuffle between

McLaren and the other girl's long-haired boyfriend. The sight of McLaren with his arms wind-milling as he waded in to defend his woman's honour should have been enough to reduce the group and its audience into fits of hysterics and may well have done so had it not been for Sid. 'My impressions of Sid were immediate before being introduced,' remembers future film director Julien Temple. 'I saw the Pistols' second gig at the Central School of Art, and the thing that jumped out as much as the band was the few fans they had in the audience, with Sid being the main one of them. They looked to me even then like a bunch of cartoon superheroes, something otherworldly about that whole embryonic scene that was just edgy and dangerous, and Sid was at the centre of the group of kids that would go wherever the Pistols played in those early days.'

Missing out on the opportunity to be the Sex Pistols' singer may well have left Sid feeling deflated, but if he couldn't be in the group itself then he would content himself with being their number one fan. Sid certainly made a sartorial effort when attending the Pistols' gigs. On the night of the brawl he was looking resplendent in a gold lamé jacket and spiked coif, sold to him by none other than Don Letts, under the pretext that Elvis had owned it. 'I still laugh at that today,' says Letts. 'He wanted the jacket, then he wasn't sure and it fit him perfectly, so I mentioned that it had been owned by Elvis, purely on a wind up, and he bought it, in more ways than one.'

It was also around this time that the Bromley Contingent, a bunch of Sex Pistols fans from South London, were invited onto Janet Street Porter's Sunday morning *London Weekend Show* to talk music and fashion. They were picked simply because they looked so different, being spotted at various gigs by the show's research team. Sid who not only wasn't a member of the 'contingent', but most certainly didn't live in Bromley, was invited onto the show and lumped in with them. Bertie 'Berlin' Marshall takes up the story: 'Sid was sitting at the end of my box, picking his nose and spitting and fiddling with something that dangled from his lapel – a used tampon. Sid was mumbling over Janet's autocue rehearsal, then spitting and talking.' The conversation that followed between Sid and the show's presenter went like this:

'What a load of bollocks.'

'Oi, you shut up!'

'Up yours!' spat Sid.

'I said fucking shut up,' Janet hissed.

'Fuck off, cunt!' Sid yelled.

'What ya call me?'

'A cunt,' said Sid and flung his tampon in Janet's direction. She ducked.

'Fucking wanker!' she screamed as the bloody tampon sailed past her ear.

For this account we have Bertie's excellent biography *Berlin Bromley* to thank. Remember, all this was played out during the show's rehearsal. Had it taken place on screen, then notoriety could have been made that very day. As it was, Sid would make his own headlines soon enough.

The Sex Pistols played regularly during April and May 1976, including a regular spot at the 100 Club. It was at this venue that Sid would cement his 'Vicious' pseudonym, whether warranted or not, at the Pistols gig of 29 June. But before the night in question there would already be conflicting stories about the name. 'Sid couldn't fight his way out of a paper bag,' John Lydon told a Japanese reporter in 2002. '[He was] a very physically weak person, but hilarious, one of my best friends ever. Sidney was his nickname, not Vicious. Vicious was a joke.'

Lydon also claims in his autobiography that his albino hamster was responsible for providing Sid with the second, and more damning, part of his enduring epithet as a result of the rodent supposedly having savaged his father's finger. However, there is no record of anyone calling him Sid Vicious until the following summer.

NME writer Nick Kent first ran into Sid in late May outside Earl's Court, where the Punk was trying to get a ticket for that night's Rolling Stones concert. Sid was pointed out to Kent by members of a new band called The Damned, who Kent was with and who had offered Sid an audition earlier that year. Sid, like many a teenager, had spent his formative years dreaming of emulating his pin-up heroes David Bowie, Marc Bolan and Bryan Ferry. Having watched his best friend go from unknown non-entity to front-page news, however, was evidence that the dream could be made reality. Sid began taking steps to form his own group from among the nucleus of fans that were now turning up at every Sex Pistols show. Having neither interest nor inclination to learn a musical instrument meant that there was but one role available to him – that of lead singer. Sid's initial idea to set himself up with an all-girl backing group came a good ten years before Robert Palmer's video for 'Addicted to Love'. He had, in fact, been invited to an audition by the young Chris Miller (aka Rat Scabies), to be front-man in a new group being formed by himself and Brian James, from the ashes of the London SS and James' other group Bastard. Rat had picked out Sid on image alone, as he certainly looked the part, but the fledgling group also had their eyes on another equally eye-catching young fellow named David Letts (aka Dave Zero aka David White). Letts had a passion for vampire films and had taken to dressing like Christopher Lee circa 1972 and answering to the much more 'street' Punk name of Dave Vanian. On the day of the audition, Sid failed to wake up on time, and thus David Letts, the only person to actually turn up for the try out, became the singer in The Damned.

At the 100 Club, Nick Kent was in attendance with a couple of music industry representatives, Island Records' Michael Beale and Howard Thompson, who'd just so happened to have recently signed the Sex Pistols' adversaries Eddie & The Hot Rods to their label. More tension was in the air because Kent was seen as an outsider to the McLaren camp, although the pair had been close a year earlier. Numerous versions of what happened have surfaced over the years but what seems certain is that a couple of songs into the Pistols' set, Sid attacked Kent for no apparent reason and left the writer bleeding profusely.

Although Sid would later cite 'not having liked Kent's trousers' as the reason for his attack, a second, and far more sinister version of events is that he attacked the journalist (who had at one time jammed with the soon-to-be Sex Pistols before Lydon's introduction to the group) at either Lydon's or Malcolm's behest over some now long-forgotten slight. 'That was madness taken to the extreme,' says Nils Stevenson. 'So this guy from the *NME* gets beaten with a bike chain and he's bleeding, but what for? Ah, nobody can remember, but oh yeah, maybe he had it coming.'

Jah Wobble, who was party to the assault, claims that the attack on Kent wasn't premeditated in any way and was merely the end result of a bit of pushing and shoving. If Wobble's version of events is true, then why was Kent the sole recipient of a bike chain lashing, and not the guys from Island? Kent still believes that Sid's assault was at Malcolm's behest. 'It was Malcolm's way of saying "You're out",' he told Mark Paytress. 'They [SEX] had done this T-shirt: "You're Gonna Wake Up One Morning And Know What Side Of The Bed You've Been Lying On". My name's there on the 'Loves' side with all Malcolm's favourite people. So I'd gone from being cool to uncool for doing nothing, man.'

Kent claims to have later confronted Sid about the attack and asked why he'd done it, to which Sid had supposedly said he couldn't remember. Kent accepted that answer, knowing that Sid was off his head on speed and didn't really know what he was doing. Whatever the reason, Sid was now universally known as Sid Vicious.

❀   ❀   ❀

The summer of 1976 had been the UK's hottest on record in the twentieth century and the Sex Pistols' momentum seemed to be rising in tandem with the temperature. Two shows at Manchester's Lesser Free Trade Hall had helped kick-start a Punk scene of sorts within the city, and the group had also made its TV debut by performing the soon-to-be debut single 'Anarchy In The UK' on Granada's late-night music show *So It Goes* – a programme hosted by Granada News anchorman and future Factory Records boss Anthony H. Wilson. Sid's desire to be in a band of his own grew even stronger.

Also in attendance at the 100 Club show had been 'Palmolive' (real name Paloma). '[Sid] looked really mean and was determined to get noticed by being obnoxious,' she told journalist Pat Gilbert for a February 2005 *Mojo* story. 'He wanted to be in a band, we all did. His voice wasn't very good, but his strength was his Punk image. He could be funny, but he was also unfriendly and moody.' Steve Jones confirms this view of Sid. 'Well, it didn't matter too much that he couldn't play too well,' he says. 'He was the face of the movement, he looked the part, did Sid, and ultimately that's what mattered.'

Sid was joined in the venture with a tight-knit group of fans that started jamming together under the band name The Flowers of Romance. This title had been borrowed from the short-lived Sex Pistols song of the same name (Lydon would later reclaim the name for the title of Public Image Limited's third album). The group's initial line-up consisted of future Slits guitarist Viv Albertine and drummer Palmolive, along with Paul Cook's then girlfriend Sarah Hall on bass and Sid's old college mate Steve England. The line-ups were fluid, so at one time or another, future Clash/Public Image Ltd guitarist Keith Levene and Steve Walsh also jammed along.

Rehearsals, if indeed the ad hoc jamming sessions could be described as such, were conducted in the cramped basement at 42 Orsett Terrace in Westbourne Grove, the squat where Spanish émigré Palmolive lived with her own boyfriend of the time – Clash front-man Joe Strummer. Viv Albertine later told Jon Savage in *England's Dreaming* that, 'It was a bedroom band. We played Ramones songs and couldn't keep time. Sid went from being a singer to playing sax. It was a bunch of interesting looking people, so we'd get interviewed and we'd never done anything and could hardly play.'

The eclectic group of wannabe musicians rehearsed several times, but there is no known recording of any of these sessions. It *is* known that they played around with covers of the afore-mentioned Ramones and even Frank Sinatra. Most interestingly they fooled around with several of Sid's self-penned ditties such as 'Brains on Vacation', 'Kamikaze Pilot' and 'Belsen Was a Gas'. The latter was later adopted by the Sex Pistols in the latter half of 1977 with a Johnny Rotten re-write in an attempt to add variety to what was fast becoming a stale repertoire.

The main problem facing the other members of the Flowers was that Sid, being imbued with a very low boredom threshold, could never be bothered to apply himself to any given task. Having a front-man that preferred to drown out the drudgery of his day-to-day existence with speed or any other drugs close to hand, did not bode well for future success. There was little point in trying to confront or reason with him as he had an irri-tating ability to alter his viewpoint on a given subject halfway through the conversation.

There was also the question of Sid's political naivety. He, along with several members of the London Punk scene's inner circle, was fascinated by Hitler's Third Reich and Nazi imagery, which wasn't going to make for inner-group harmony. This was especially true with Palmolive, who'd been forced to flee her native Spain to escape General Franco's oppressive right-wing state. 'We got into a conversation about politics,' Palmolive told Pat Gilbert. 'He made a statement about liking Nazis and being a racist. But when I told him that I didn't agree with his point of view he kicked me out of the group. My perception was that he was a kid who was childish and rebelling against everything.

I think the whole thing with the hate and anger of Punk took him further than he actually wanted to go. There was a dark force that seemed to be pushing him on. We were all playing with it. We liked to show off and look mean, but you have to be careful you're not taken in by it.'

At this point in his life Sid was obsessed with what people thought of him, although unlike Rotten he hadn't simply fallen into what became a successful band. Having grown up without a father, Sid needed to be accepted. If he couldn't achieve this because of any musical prowess, he'd try and do it via the way he looked. He would often change his image. Unlike Wobble, he wasn't a genuine street-smart tough guy ('Stab him in the back was his idea,' says Steve Walsh) and unlike Jones he wasn't simply into the scene based on which 'bird' he could 'shag'. The path for Sid was already very different.

'Let me tell you about the Flowers of Romance,' said Anne Beverley. 'They certainly all seemed keen. Although from what Simon told me, even after their first day together it looked very obvious that they would never stay together. He looked upon it as something to do until something better came along. He was very excited. Everything was going to happen there and then. He was very much the group's leader, and would talk the others through what they would need to wear. It was mostly black leather but some pink stuff as well for the girls. I remember something about how he'd told the girls that their being in his group meant that they would be able to get a discount from Vivienne, but the truth of the matter was that he was the only one who would be getting the discount. It was only after they had picked out the clothes and placed them on the counter that they realised they were still going to be charged full price.

'He had never been part of a gang, always something of a loner right through school. People did come around but I was never aware of any names, they all just came and went. But the Punk scene was different. It was a bond for him, a reality. Suddenly his world was full and I knew everybody by name.

The impression that I got right from day one was that he felt very much like he belonged.'

In the midst of this, Malcolm McLaren came up with the idea of a two-day Punk festival at the 100 Club in late September. The chosen dates were Monday 20th and Tuesday 21st and McLaren set about booking Punk bands, which weren't exactly common at the time.

The Sex Pistols were already scheduled to play Cardiff's Top Rank on 21 September so they would headline Monday night's bill, which also included The Clash, as well as another Bernie Rhodes group, Subway Sect. Tuesday night's bill was filled with The Damned as headliners, The Vibrators, Manchester's Buzzcocks and French Punksters the Stinky Toys. But with only three groups confirmed for Monday night's bill, McLaren was scraping the barrel to complete the line-up. He heard about a brand new group that had been put together by 'Candy Sue' Ballion, who would shortly reinvent herself as Siouxsie Sioux. She'd already taken to drawing a swastika 'beauty spot' on herself and her later name change to the initials 'SS' reflected this. McLaren added her group to the bill for the opening night, but there was just one problem. The band – then called Suzy & The Banshees – did not exist anywhere outside of Sue's fertile imagination.

Having tricked McLaren into adding her name to the bill, Sue cajoled Steve 'Spunker' Bailey, a fellow member of the Bromley Contingent, to be the bass player, and the pair then set about trying to find like-minded individuals who'd be crazy enough to join them on stage.

When Sid first heard about the festival he was upset that he hadn't used his contacts with either the Pistols or McLaren to shoe-horn The Flowers of Romance onto the roster. So when he found the chance to get on stage with Siouxsie he didn't need to be asked twice, regardless of the fact that she herself had already claimed the microphone. 'It was just the fun of maybe irritating people that were there to see "groups", you know, young little combos that had rehearsed and everything,' said Siouxsie. 'It was almost a bit of fun really to see if we could annoy people with finding out what a bass guitar is on stage, and making a very touching improvisation of the Lord's Prayer.'

The movers and shakers within London's nascent Punk scene may have been openly lauding Punk as music without actual musicianship, but Siouxsie was astute enough to realise that she would at least need one bonafide musician possessing a modicum of musical know-how. Thanks to a mutual friend in the form of Sue Catwoman, she was able to call upon the services of future London and later Adam & The Ants guitarist, Marco Pirroni. The position had initially been filled by future Generation X front-man Billy 'Idol' Broad, but Punk's male pin-up had since had a change of heart – he was in it for the long haul and hadn't abandoned his studies at Sussex University in order to make a fool of himself. This left but one role available to Sid – that of drummer – regardless of the fact that he had never so much as sat on a drum stool, let alone tried to maintain a beat. It shows how badly he wanted to be involved that Punk's self-styled peacock agreed to be hidden away out of sight at the back of the stage. He was desperate to emulate his friend Lydon by playing in front of an audience.

❀   ❀   ❀

It had been agreed that the Banshees could borrow The Clash's equipment for what was supposedly intended as a one-off performance, but the offer was subsequently withdrawn due to both Siouxsie and Sid incurring the wrath of Bernie Rhodes over their decision to take to the stage wearing swastikas. The situation may well have been diffused had it not been for Sid calling Bernie a 'mean old Jew'. With only a matter of hours remaining before the festival was due to commence, it seemed as though Sid would have to settle for standing in front of the stage rather than on it, but fortunately for him and the rest of the group – if not the audience – Malcolm McLaren came to the rescue by offering the Banshees the use of the Pistols' gear. Having booked the festival himself, Malcolm was in no position to be losing bands at less than half a day's notice.

Earlier that day, Sid, Siouxsie, Steve and Marco had convened at the Clash's Chalk Farm rehearsal space in order to rehearse, but as the gig was intended to be a one-off, and with Marco being the only one with any knowledge of an instrument, there seemed little point in actually doing anything other than running through how to plug in the equipment without electro-cuting themselves in the process. En-route to Oxford Street, the gang decided to call in at The Ship public house on nearby Wardour Street for a little Dutch courage. The four had barely set foot through the door before being ordered back out again by the landlord – although the nondescript pub would soon become synonymous with the London Punk scene, there wasn't, and never would be, any tolerance there for the swastika. The only member of the group not wearing a swastika that day was Steve Bailey.

❀   ❀   ❀

With no songs to call their own, the Banshees performed a twenty-minute-long meandering, cacophonic dirge, later referred to as a 'medley', containing snippets of Deep Purple's 'Smoke On The Water', The Beatles' 'Twist & Shout', and Bob Dylan's 'Knockin' On Heaven's Door'. Over the rising cacophony, Siouxsie narrated the Lord's Prayer.

'We did a Velvet Underground thing for what seemed like hours and hours,' remembers Marco today. 'It was horrible. Sid was doing Moe Tucker and I was doing "Sister Ray". I remember me and Sid looking at each other, we were both fed up so we just stopped.'

By actually playing at the festival Sid had, as the Eddie Cochran song goes, taken the second step to heaven. The first step had been his being hailed as the creator/inventor of the pogo 'dance'. This simply involved jumping up and down on the spot à la the pogo stick, the outdoor toy for children that was patented in 1919 by the American George Hansburg and was still popular during the early-to-mid-1970s. Although the pogo was a dance of sorts, it had actually been born out of Sid's desire to see his heroes on stage when he'd been following them around in late 1975 and early 1976. The third step, and by far the most significant, however, would be played out the following night.

'The myth is that Simon left The Flowers Of Romance to join the Banshees,' Anne Beverley explained years later. 'But that wasn't the case at all. He simply did something to help his friends. That was him all over.'

The soon-to-be-ex road manager of the Sex Pistols, Nils Stevenson, was moved enough by the Banshees' performance to immediately offer his services as manager. Twenty minutes in the spotlight had been enough to convince Siouxsie Sioux and Steve Spunker/Severin to take up Nils on his offer. 'The first night [of the 100 Club Punk Festival] was all about Sid making a name for himself on stage,' remembers Stevenson. 'The second night was the one that set the name "Sid Vicious" in stone far more than anything that happened between him and Nick Kent. The second night was the stuff of legend.'

Early in the night, club promoter Ron Watts had accosted Sid backstage as he was threatening members of the Stinky Toys with a knife. 'Sid came at me with a chain once,' he told the website www.punk77.co.uk. 'I confiscated it and wish I still had all these weapons as I could put them up for sale at Christies, couldn't I? And I saw Sid with a knife, threatening Elle, the singer out the Stinky Toys, with it. I took that off him and gave it to Malcolm McLaren. Wish I'd kept it.'

The Damned closed the festival on the second night, but Sid, who was watching from the floor alongside Steve Severin and Siouxsie Sioux, was not impressed with the show. 'I remember saying something to Sioux about The Damned being rubbish,' says Severin today. 'And the next thing I know, Sid gulps down the rest of his pint and hurls the glass at the stage.' Vicious' throwing accuracy seems to have been about as good as his musicianship as the glass missed the stage but instead struck one of the basement club's supporting pillars and showered the audience with shards of glass, with one girl taking a piece in the eye.

Like many of the great Punk stories, there are several conflicting versions of this one. Journalist Caroline Coon has claimed that Sid couldn't have thrown the glass in question because she saw it sail past his head. The 100 Club is far smaller in size than in stature and although the club was packed to the rafters, Severin's assertion that Sid did indeed throw the glass is given added weight by the fact that no one, with the exception of Coon, appeared to be willing to defend him.

Coon had been championing the Sex Pistols, as well as the whole Punk scene, for the past six months and was at the 100 Club to cover the event for the *Melody Maker*. When the police arrived, Coon's attempts to wrestle Sid away from them were not solely to claim a scoop for her editor, but rather because of her involvement with RELEASE, the organisation she had founded in 1967 to provide support for those arrested on drug charges. Her efforts to free Sid, however, would prove to be in vain, for the police, who had followed the sound of the ambulance siren to the venue, were fully convinced that they had their man. All Coon achieved was to get herself arrested – she paid a late-night visit to West End Central on nearby Tottenham Court Road. 'Sid was very disturbed,' Coon later told Jon Savage. 'But I don't think that he threw the glass. I think it was the first-time Punks who had come to the festival, and thought that this was what they had to do.'

The incident may have helped propel Sid into Punk folklore but it did little to help his future bandmates, or any other Punk group for that matter. Ron Watts, the club's promoter and the man responsible for giving the Sex Pistols their Tuesday night residency, revoked his invitation and banned Punk Rock from the 100 Club. Despite being handed the baton for starting the glass-throwing craze at the 100 Club by the UK music press, the Sex Pistols were miles away – at The Top Rank in Cardiff – when it all kicked off.

Sid paid a price for the incident – seven days at the Ashford Remand Centre. Anne Beverley always maintained that her son's spell in Ashford triggered the final act in his metamorphism from fun-loving fool to Punk pariah. Although seven days ensconced in a remand centre doesn't sound like much of a punishment for having possibly blinded someone in one eye, it was one week too long for a soft-centred soul such as Sid. In fact, the girl in question was never photographed, nor was she ever called upon to provide testimony. She has never been interviewed by anyone and seemed to vanish from existence that very night.

Ashford Remand Centre is a holding cell for those either awaiting trial or allocation to another prison, many of whom would have been serial offenders familiar with the dog-eat-dog existence within such institutions. These individuals would have easily sussed out the not-so-Vicious Sid, as confirmed by Sid's vehement refusal to allow Anne to visit him. 'He told me not to visit him because the other lads would think he was a mummy's boy,' she said. 'He said that the violence dished out in there was very real and nothing like the cartoon violence that the others spoke about, though just who these "others" were I never did find out. I used to cry myself to sleep with some of those letters. Looking back on it now, it marked the death of Simon and the birth of Sid, but at the time I buried that away inside my head. I didn't want to think about it.'

One motherly figure that was allowed to visit Sid in Ashford was Vivienne Westwood. Rather than try to point out the error of Sid's ways, she simply fuelled his desire to set himself up as a Punk martyr by presenting him with a copy of Vincent

Bugliosi's *Helter Skelter*, the account of Charles Manson's trial and the harrowing Tate-LaBianca murders of August 1969. Anne Beverley, on the other hand, sent him copies of *Spiderman* comics and *MAD* magazine.

Upon his release from Ashford, and finding himself out of favour with landlady Barbara over the glass-throwing incident, Sid sought refuge in The Clash's Chalk Farm rehearsal space. Bernie Rhodes, who owned the building, must have undergone a radical change of heart during Sid's brief incarceration. Although the isolation and loneliness of Ashford had been the stuff of nightmares, Sid thought his dreams had come true upon discovering that he had been elevated to superstar status among his peers.

Hoping to cash in on his new-found Punk kudos, Sid immediately renewed his involvement with The Flowers Of Romance, but when the time came to rehearse, all he seemed to want to do was sit around and take drugs. This reduced the sessions to little more than social get-togethers. Sid wasn't alone in this, either, as other members of the group had already seen friends elevated to some kind of 'stardom' in other groups, while they hadn't seemed to move a step forward. Steve Walsh, an aspiring guitarist and occasional writer for Mark P's seminal Punk fanzine *Sniffin' Glue*, spent several weeks of non-rehearsing with the non-group and vaguely remembers engaging in a few half-hearted attempts to put a melody to Sid's scribbled lyrics. These were very much written in the Ramones' '1-2-3-4 Hey Ho/Let's Go' style. By this time, the leather-clad four-piece from Queens had long-since replaced Stanley Clarke in Sid's musical affections. Walsh also felt that Sid's 'hard man' image was definitely staged. 'If there was a serious punch-up where it looked as though someone might get hurt, but the numbers were equally matched, then he'd stay away,' says Walsh. 'But if he could smack someone in the head and run like hell, then he'd be cool about it. At the same time though, if a mate was in trouble he'd be the first to join in, regardless of the odds.' One person who can testify to Sid's seemingly blatant disregard for self-preservation is journalist Kris Needs, who recalls the time when he had been cornered by a gang of Teds who took instant offence to his being a Punk. 'The bastards were giving me a real beating when suddenly, out of nowhere, Sid comes flying in armed with half a brick in each hand. He whacked a couple of them around the head, which made the others back off long enough for us to get away.'

Nils Stevenson believed that Sid didn't purposely act out the role of hard man, but seemed to think that he had to play the part whenever John Lydon was around. Of the 'Four Johns', Lydon's new found status as Lord Johnny of Rotten had elevated him to the status of commander-in-chief. 'John Rotten may have been the big chief, but he was a strange choice to have as a leader,' Anne Beverley said while barely hiding her contempt for him. 'He might well be the first to tell everyone to do something like jump off Tower Bridge, but if there was any jumping to be done you can bet he was the last one in the queue. He just hid behind Steve English or Rambo [the Sex Pistols' security men], who were both genuine hard men. I used to call them the "Martini Men", because those two boys were always up for a scrap, anytime, anyplace, anywhere.' As the band would soon find out, the fight was just about to start.

CHAPTER 4

Aloha From Denmark Street

In British cultural history there are two major events running through 1977 – the Queen's Silver Jubilee and the Punk movement. Punk was an accident just waiting to happen.

From the Sex Pistols' earliest days on the college circuit, they had been slowly building to some kind of crescendo. Not even Malcolm McLaren could be sure what this would entail but he knew it would be momentous in some way. The fact that Elizabeth II had been on the throne for twenty-five years was just good luck on the band's part – it was like throwing petrol on a bonfire.

The last months of 1976 had seen Punk begin to infiltrate the consciousness of the general public. Punk fashions were starting to gain a foothold with teenagers up and down the country with ripped jeans, leather studs and coloured haircuts becoming more commonplace. The majority of the British population thought – and hoped – that these badly dressed, obnoxious, spitting, swearing, talentless 'musicians' would disappear just as quickly as they had arrived. While Sid was basking in his 'glory' of a week in Ashford, the Sex Pistols had been busy on the road. Their stop-off for the first night of the 100 Club Punk festival had been just one of more than two-dozen shows played between September and November, including their first sojourn overseas when they played a couple of shows in Paris. Members of the Bromley Contingent accompanied the band. Siouxsie strode around wearing stockings and a 'titless' bra, and with a swastika armband in full view. Locals were equally bemused and hostile and the band was escorted from the club into a waiting van.

EMI finally released the Sex Pistols' debut single 'Anarchy in the UK' on 26 November 1976, and it was then that the backlash began. 'Anarchy' was a perfect slice of Rotten's provocatively enunciated lyrics, churning guitars and a sprinkling of humour. Having a laugh was not at the top of many agendas at this time. Not long before, 40,000 people had gone on strike in anger at public-sector cuts and the Tories were making gains in a series of by-elections.

If some people were uncomfortable with the lyrics of such a raucous 'noise', they were downright horrified after the group – at the behest of EMI press officer Eric 'Monster, Monster' Hall – stepped in to fill a gap left by the band Queen on Thames Television's *Today* programme presented by Bill Grundy. The show's host had downed a drink or two before the live filming began, and the proceedings famously sank to gutter level very quickly when the band and assembled entourage began trading insults and profanities with Grundy. The tabloid press was all over the story in a flash and the public outcry erupted.

Although Sid had not been present at the time, he later told a radio DJ on San Francisco's K-SAN: 'That Bill Grundy thing, that wasn't put on at all. He asked for it and he got it, you know what I mean, and they did it in a really clever way. They were just themselves, they made mincemeat of him. Because he's a total fool and he's a grown-up and they were kids and how could he compete?'

The Grundy incident happened on 1 December, just two days before Malcolm McLaren had the 'Anarchy in the UK' tour slated to begin in Norwich. Predictably, each venue was picketed by local-interest groups and local councils put pressure on many venues leading to sixteen of the shows being cancelled and only eight actually being played. The band was now a household name around the UK, but the tour chaos netted a loss of around £10,000.

Slim Whitman, Abba and Glen Campbell had been topping the charts during the lead-up to Christmas 1976 and the Sex Pistols were clearly the antithesis of these acts. The media took notice, but public pressure and the bright glare of Fleet Street's spotlight did nothing to help the already growing tensions within the band. Things were moving a little too fast, too soon. The principal frictions erupted between Glen Matlock and Johnny Rotten. 'It started with Glen and John falling out really,' remembers Paul Cook. 'Over what, I don't really know. Just a clash of personalities.'

This clash of personalities was sometimes aired very publicly. One night at the 100 Club matters came to a head when a more than pissed off Matlock had taken to singing, 'You're a cunt' instead of the usual backing vocals to 'Pretty Vacant'. Rotten walked off stage in anger and was later found at a bus stop on Oxford Street by McLaren. He was waiting for a bus to Finsbury Park.

Matlock was a key piece of the Sex Pistols puzzle. As well as being the most accomplished musician, he also co-wrote most of the material. He had provided a lot of input to the overall sound of the band, drawing on his early influences of Little Richard, Jerry Lee Lewis, the Kinks and the Small Faces – who the Pistols often covered in their early shows.

During the first few days of 1977 the band played four shows in Holland. The gig at Amsterdam's Paradiso Club on 7 January was Matlock's last with the group. A meeting at the Food For Thought vegetarian café in Covent Garden was the venue for the final meeting in which McLaren tried to patch things up between the bass player and vocalist, but to no avail. Nils Stevenson was also dropped as road manager. His kiss-off totalled just £300 for a year's work, and he was replaced by John Tiberi, an Anglo-Italian answering to the nickname of 'Boogie'.

At the shop in Kings Road, the writing was on the wall. 'At the time I just thought that Glen had had enough,' remembers Alan Jones who worked at SEX. 'To be honest, the impression he gave to me was, "I've had enough, I'm bored of it, I want to do something else." OK, Malcolm might have wanted to have edged Glen out at some point, but I think it was a mutual thing. There was this guy waiting in the background, Glen wanted to go, I think it was just as simple as that.'

Glen Matlock's explained that much of the political manoeuvring came from Malcolm McLaren. 'If there was an argument in the band,' said Matlock, 'instead of it being resolved, [McLaren] would prolong it, set people against each other so there was always friction when friction wasn't necessarily the best thing to have at that time.' But the final straw was the clash with Lydon. 'There was obviously a big problem between me and John. I felt that once John got his face in the papers he became a different person, which I didn't particularly like. When we went to Holland, my last gig with them was at the Paradiso, I felt like everyone was on my case.'

Surprisingly there was almost nothing publicly planned for the band over the next six months, save for a couple of shows. There had been talk of stealing Paul Simonon from The Clash, or simply swapping him for Glen Matlock, depending on whose version you choose to believe, but the realistic replacement for Matlock was always going to be from a short list of one – Sid Vicious.

The Sex Pistols' decision to replace their only recognisable tunesmith with a self-confessed non-musician may have come as something of a shock in the music industry, but it was something of an 'open secret' for those within the Sex Pistols' inner circle. Many had been aware of the ever-widening gulf between Glen and John and had therefore known about the intended decision for several weeks prior to the official announcement.

'He was really good at the start of the Pistols, it was really good things,' John Lydon would later tell BBC Radio 1. 'We were really swinging when we got Sidney in, and the fact that he couldn't play was absolutely irrelevant. It was part of the fun of it all.'

On Friday, 18 February 1977, after having passed his audition earlier that week while being on a short list of one, Sid Vicious was officially unveiled as Glen Matlock's replacement. Matlock was given a pay off of £2,966.68 – not exactly rock 'n' roll retirement status money, but enough to buy his first car. 'Well, for a start the line-up is much more handsome now,' quipped Sid. 'And this is a fact. And we play the songs much faster now, and also I write differently from the way Glen used to. I haven't written very much lately, I mean since I've been in the group, but I'm starting to [write] now more. And just the fact that I'm there instead of Glen means that the others do everything differently, I think, 'cos they have to adapt it to fit in with me. Whenever there's a change in something, a change is a change, so if something changes it is different. It has to be, obviously – it can't be the same otherwise.'

Before the axe had fallen, Matlock himself was aware of what was transpiring. Having long since grown tired of Lydon's self-aggrandising and constant sniping, Glen was already contemplating a future away from the Sex Pistols and was even offering to teach Sid the basics. 'Me and Steve [were close] I suppose and John thought that by bringing Sid in, he'd have someone there,' Paul Cook says today. '[Sid was] like a partner, someone a bit closer to him.' The fact that Sid couldn't really play bass was beside the point.

'The Sex Pistols were leaders of the movement and Sime was their biggest fan,' said Anne Beverley. 'If they had kept Glen and decided that they needed a violinist, he still would have joined. But if I had a pound for every music business executive that I've spoken to since Sime's death who's said that he should have been a singer then let's just say I'd be a lady with a house full of money.'

Sid's 'thick as thieves' bond with Lydon meant that he was privy to the singer's simmering dislike of 'Mummy's Boy' Matlock, which placed him in an ideal position to put himself forward for the soon-to-be-vacant role of bass player. 'It was John who insisted that Sid was in the group,' Julien Temple later told Jon Savage. 'It was John who got rid of Glen. Sid was John's protégé in the group really. The other two just thought he was crazy.'

While Matlock was going through his final days in the band, Sid had already started trying to get his act together. With no experience of playing bass, he started to try and teach himself by jamming along to The Ramones' seminal eponymous debut album while speeding on 'black beauties' (Biphetamine). The New York band were Sid's current favourite and his love affair with The Ramones even stretched to his mentioning them whenever possible in interviews. When asked by Judy Vermorel about songwriting he answered, succinctly, 'What I want to do is put something out that I like, and whoever else likes it they'll find it, you know what I mean? And if nobody else in the whole world fucking likes it I couldn't give two shits, if it doesn't sell one copy, who gives a fuck? The point is that it's what you want to do. You have fun making it and you have fun listening to it. I listen to our records a lot, 'cos I like them, I think they're good records, otherwise I wouldn't have had any part in them. I like our music to listen to as much as I like The Ramones to listen to. The Ramones are my favourite group, by the way. Do you know what I mean?'

Vicious later managed to meet his hero Dee Dee Ramone and as Ramones manager Danny Fields recalled in *Punk: The Whole Story*, the friendship might have been more than just talking about music. 'I think Sid Vicious had a crush on Dee Dee,' he revealed. 'I don't know for a fact, but I've got a pretty good idea of what went on. After Nancy Spungen, wouldn't you rather have Dee Dee Ramone in your bed?'

One month's rehearsal time was never going to be enough time for Sid to master an instrument with any degree of compe-

tence. For the past three decades Sid's lack of musical profi-
ciency had been the metaphorical rod with which his detractors
had incessantly beaten him. Sid, though, was more than happy
to step into the role of band buffoon for a press that had by now
latched onto the Pistols and was following the band around like
a 'pretty pot of glue'. Sid was anything but stupid – he was
astute enough to realise there was little point in his hiding away
in Denmark Street learning the Sex Pistols' back catalogue when
he could be out having fun, since no one, perhaps with the
exception of Lydon, Jones and Cook, was really interested in the
music. Fleet Street's finest did not care whether this or that
song's verse and chorus structure happened to be in the same
key as its bridge. They were interested only in the acerbic
rhetoric of Chairman John. 'The band wasn't a band,'
remembers Sophie Richmond, Malcolm McLaren's secretary at
the time. 'It was a name for four people operating. They didn't
rehearse, they couldn't bear to be in the same room together half
the time. John moaned about Steve and Paul a lot. It was a real
effort in spring 1977 to get them to go to Denmark Street to write
new tunes. Glen could write tunes and they couldn't. They
could produce words and chords, but not tunes, and they were
finished as a creative unit once he'd gone.'

Matlock went on to form the Rich Kids with Midge Ure and
guitarist Steve New who, some eighteen months earlier at the age
of just fifteen, had auditioned for the abandoned role of second
guitarist in the Sex Pistols. During February 1978 the Rich Kids'
eponymous debut single, which was written by Matlock,
reached No. 24 in the UK charts. Lacking one of their key song-
writers, the Pistols were now due to enter the Wessex recording
studio with producer Chris Thomas at the beginning of March to
work on their intended second single, 'God Save the Queen'.

❀ ❀ ❀

Steve Jones was not overjoyed at Matlock's departure. 'I kind of
regretted [Glen] leaving,' he said, 'because Sid couldn't play a

fuckin' note.' Vicious was as aware of his musical shortcomings as anyone and had secretly taken steps to try and improve. In fact, Sid had – without telling the others – asked Motörhead leader and all-round hell-raiser Lemmy to teach him to play bass, but after an hour or so of trying, he'd decided that Sid was a non-starter on the instrument. '[Sid] used to sleep on the couch,' Lemmy recalled. 'We had a squat in Holland Park, nice house. I tried to teach him to play bass. Couldn't do it though. No aptitude for it whatsoever. I said, "That's it, Sid, you can't play bass, I'm sorry." He said, "Yeah, I know." He was all upset.'

'Two months later I bumped into him at the Speakeasy,' Lemmy told *Jack* magazine. 'He said, "Hey Lem, guess what? I'm in the Pistols." I said, "But you can't play bass." He just grinned and said, "Yeah, I know, but I'm IN THE PISTOLS!" He was a nice enough geezer, I got quite friendly with him, but he used to get in too many fights.'

Sid's first official duty as a Sex Pistol came on Sunday, 13 February when he participated in a live transatlantic telephone radio interview with renowned Los Angeles DJ Rodney Bingenheimer. A month later he was involved in a more public event at, of all places, Buckingham Palace.

In the midst of the personnel changes, the Sex Pistols had one other major piece of news early in the new year. EMI had already grown tired of the developing circus around the band and had terminated the band's contract on 8 January 1977. So a band that had yet to record its debut album had already sacked its road manager, changed its bass player, been on national TV, caused a public outcry and been banned from most of its first major UK tour. Now it didn't even have a record deal. What it did have, however, was a £30,000 golden goodbye from EMI – part of the original advance, plus some cash from publishing rights, which the label washed their hands of. This money allowed McLaren to bide his time over looking for a new label.

By the beginning of March there were but two serious contenders vying for the Sex Pistols: Maurice Oberstein's CBS, and Jerry Moss' and Herb Alpert's A&M. Whether McLaren's decision to choose A&M over CBS had anything to do with the latter label having already signed The Clash back in January has never been truly established, but in choosing A&M he single-handedly killed off any hopes Oberstein might have been nurturing of sending the two groups on the road together as a Punk package.

With the benefit of hindsight, CBS would perhaps have been the more prudent choice since the company was a major player in the world market and Oberstein, although far from a Punk aficionado, was at least *au fait* with the English Punk scene. A&M, on the other hand, was a sedate 'family-like' label with a small stable of artists including Supertramp, Rick Wakeman, Peter Frampton and a globally huge brother-and-sister act, The Carpenters. The label therefore had little or no understanding of the new music craze that was currently sweeping the UK. As both Jerry Moss and Herb Alpert were based in the USA, they were forced to rely on the judgement of Derek Green – the head of A&R (Artist and Repertoire) at A&M UK. As a label they had never seen a headline that was not singing the praises of one of their artists or simply marvelling at the huge amount of albums they had shifted on both sides of the Atlantic. Once McLaren had made up his mind that A&M was indeed the right home for his boys, he flew to Los Angeles on 13 February with his lawyer Steven Fisher in order to meet with Moss.

Green, although normally astute and wily in his business dealings for A&M, had made one small – yet cataclysmic – blunder during his negotiations with Malcolm: he neglected to meet the group in person before sealing the deal. This was usually a personal prerequisite of Green's when poised to sign a prospective new group or solo artist, but having already been made aware of the Sex Pistols and what they supposedly repre-sented – due to media overkill in the wake of the Bill Grundy fiasco – a tête-à-tête meeting had been rendered obsolete. Green would later admit that his decision not to meet the group in person was for fear of being put off. He had spent several weeks listening to Dave Goodman's demos, which had been recorded at Gooseberry Studios back in January with Glen Matlock still in the band, as well as familiarising himself with the group's biography. As far as he was concerned, he liked what he heard and he'd covered every word – or so he thought.

EMI may have been scared off by a few untimely expletives, but Green was willing to put the Pistols' bad-boy behaviour down to youthful exuberance and believed that he would be able to keep the band on a tighter leash. After all, wasn't it McLaren himself who had told Green, at almost all their meetings, 'Boys will be boys Derek'?

There was, however, one slight oversight in that the demos and photos supplied by McLaren all included Glen Matlock in the line-up and the biography had purposely omitted any mention of Glen's departure or the name of his replacement. 'My own staff in the UK who were aware of the Pistols, the younger staff, were really quite against the idea for whatever reasons,' recalled Green in 2004. 'We went into what was an extremely difficult and protracted negotiation for finding the right terms. I can't be sure of the reasons but I did something I'd never done before and I decided I wouldn't meet the Pistols before signing them. I guess I didn't want to be put off. It was at that moment that Malcolm then told me to change the name on the contract from Glen Matlock to Sid Vicious, and I'd never heard of Sid Vicious and I mean, "What, Malcolm, what? Who is he?" and Malcolm said, "Well, he's the new member of the band," and I said, "Well, how does he play? Is he a good musician?" And he said, "He can't. He'll learn." I was just lost for words.'

'I was an extreme svengali in those days,' admitted Malcolm McLaren. 'People, for me, were like puppets. You colour them up and you put them all together and you make them all in that format and you give them a title, and that's it and the way it goes.' With this approach in mind he'd lined up the potentially controversial 'God Save the Queen' as the band's second single.

The contract was signed by the band on 9 March at the offices of Rondor Music, the American label's subsidiary publishing company. It was a deal worth a hefty £150,000 over two years. For McLaren this was vindication – not only had he walked away from EMI with a tidy little sum, but he'd already signed a larger deal already and had other offers too. He'd been inundated with calls from Richard Branson, who wanted to sign the Pistols to Virgin. In fact, Branson had been courting Malcolm even before the group had signed to EMI, and although today Virgin is a multi-faceted conglomerate, back in 1977 it was still a small up-and-coming record company, which was riding the coat-tails of Mike Oldfield's *Tubular Bells*. McLaren neither liked nor trusted Branson and viewed the turtle-neck-sweatered Virgin supremo's label as being little more than 'hippy central'. This left A&M as the only real alternative.

Alan McGee was working as a 'plugger' for A&M at the time and was astounded by Green's signing of the Pistols. 'We were just amazed that we'd signed this band, but Derek had realised that we needed something like this to bring us up to date.'

The 'official' contract signing at Rondor was a very low-key affair with only the group, their management and A&M's lawyers in attendance, but the following day's promotional contract signing, which took place on the traffic island opposite Buckingham Palace, would prove to be anything but low-key. Imagine Green's consternation as he stood upon the traffic island opposite Buck House a little after 9 a.m. on a chilly Thursday morning watching on as the group tumbled, very much the worse for wear after nearly twelve hours straight drinking the day before. The setting was perfect. 'God Save the Queen' was about to be unleashed and it was Jubilee year, but contrary to John Lydon's wilful boast in *The Filth & The Fury*, Sid's dad, the ex-Grenadier Guard, wasn't on duty that day, having long ago left the service.

The group themselves were in no mood to hang around answering inane questions. Judging from Julian Temple's footage of the mock signing which later appeared in *The Great Rock 'n' Roll Swindle*, Sid was the liveliest of the four, but then again this could simply be due to his being the 'new kid in school' and therefore believing he had something to prove. It was almost as though he had won a competition to spend a day with the Sex Pistols and intended to fully merit his *Jim'll Fix It* badge. It might also have been because he'd already downed half a bottle of Bacardi on the way to the palace.

NME photographer Chalkie Davies was on hand for the event, and after ten minutes the band was being hustled away. 'About then a big blue police van rolled up with more coppers in it,' Davies told *Q* magazine in 1995. '[They] seemed to understand what kind of stunt was being pulled, so we were outnumbered and we just legged it away as fast as we could.'

With the contract signed, the group posed for a few photographs with the assembled media, flashed a few 'V' signs at the police car, which by this time was making its second circumnavigation of the traffic island, and then jumped back into the Daimler waiting to ferry them to the Regent Palace Hotel in Piccadilly for a Beatles-style press conference. A&M had intended this to be the re-birth of the group – forget all that drunken Grundy nonsense: this was a new deal, and a new start.

The conference was scheduled to commence in the hotel's Apex Room at 11 a.m., but such was the Daimler driver's hurry to offload his troublesome cargo that the group arrived some fifteen minutes early. This was more than enough time for them to mount an attack on the complementary drink. Sid, having staked his claim on the solitary bottle of Cossack vodka, saw little need in bothering with accoutrements such as ice and lemon, or even a glass for that matter, and instead proceeded to gulp down the vodka neat. By the time the assorted national and international press and music journalists had taken their places, he had succeeded in polishing off half the bottle and was thoroughly enjoying his new life as a pop star.

Green, acting as master of ceremonies, opened the proceedings by introducing the group to the assorted press before then fielding questions. Perhaps not surprisingly, the first question fired at him was whether A&M would fare any better than EMI had done in controlling the Sex Pistols. Green had been prepared for that particular question and intended to answer it by questioning EMI's decision to drop the Sex Pistols over their appearance on the *Today* show, when the corporation had recently signed the Rolling Stones, who were, at the time, involved in a scandal that was threatening to topple the Canadian government. But before Green had the chance to offer a response, Sid literally stole his thunder by leaning across his chair and farting loudly. He then proceeded to lay into the female journalist by asking her why she had bothered to ask such a 'dull fucking question', and before the poor girl could respond he stunned her into submission by insinuating that he'd caught her sucking on someone's cock the previous week.

Sounds' Vivienne Goldman, who was on first-name terms with Rotten on account of their mutual love of reggae music, inquired of her friend as to why the group had chosen Sid to replace Glen Matlock. Rotten, who prior to Sid's joining the Pistols had been granted carte blanche to deal with the press, found himself beaten to the punch by Sid, who informed the startled Goldman that he had been given the job on account of his having assaulted her fellow journalist Nick Kent. When it was revealed that the Sex Pistols were considering playing a benefit concert at the beginning of April, *Melody Maker's* Brian Harrigan, who unlike his colleague Caroline Coon was no lover of Punks or Punk Rock music (and would later describe the Sex Pistols as 'ugly', 'shabby' and 'exceedingly unpleasant'), jokingly inquired as to whether the benefit was for the beleaguered Rolling Stone guitarist Keith Richard. Sid retorted by informing Harrigan that he wouldn't have pissed on Richards if he'd been on fire.

Harrigan later cornered Sid, who by this time had downed all but the last couple of inches from the Cossack bottle, in the hotel foyer in the hope of gaining an exclusive quote for his paper. Sid duly obliged by informing Harrigan that he'd been docked his previous week's wages by Malcolm McLaren on account of his having been naughty. Just what he had done to justify having his wages docked, however, was not disclosed. Harrigan, however, although happy to include the quote in his article, remained unimpressed with the Pistols' new bass player, whom he later described as 'looking a little like a corpse freshly fished from the river after about ten days of floating around', and 'possessing a complexion akin to that of a slab of Polyfiller', an 'expression of congenial idiocy' and 'eyes like razor-slashes'.

Next on the day's agenda was a brief stop-off at Wessex Studios in Highbury where Chris Thomas was holed up mixing 'God Save the Queen'. Prior to leaving the Regent Palace Hotel the group had grabbed up several bottles of spirits with which to alleviate what might otherwise have been a dull afternoon. After Wessex, the group then headed off to Rondor's offices in New Kings Road, there they had but one simple task – to choose a B-side for the forthcoming single. Green had already pretty much set his mind on using 'No Feeling' – a song that would later be re-titled 'No Feelings'. En route, Sid and Paul resumed an earlier argument as to who was the toughest Sex Pistol. The argument, fuelled by the free booze, quickly escalated into a back-seat brawl with Paul coming off worst by suffering a black eye. Why Sid chose to pick a fight with the otherwise mild-mannered Paul can be easily explained – he was Sid Vicious and therefore desperate to prove the validity of his acquired nickname, but therein lay the problem. There was no way that Sid would have challenged Rotten to a fight, because the singer was not only his best friend but he had also been responsible for getting him into the group, and Steve would have probably chinned him. This only left Paul. In retaliation for the assault on

Paul, Steve relieved Sid of his shoes and threw them out of the Daimler's window, which resulted in Sid suffering a cut foot on a piece of broken glass. During the mêlée, Rotten's watch – a brand new black-faced digital with bright red numbers, which had been a Christmas present from his mother – was damaged. He was not best pleased.

The principal aim of the Sex Pistols' visit to Rondor's offices was in order for everyone to listen to Thomas' efforts on the A-side mix, to choose the B-side and to meet the staff who would be working on promoting the single. By this stage of the proceedings, however, none of the group was in a position to even pass wind, let alone give an informative judgement on their new single. This was especially true of Sid, who being both shoeless and off his head, ensconced himself in the nearest executive chair and duly passed out.

Rotten, seizing an opportunity to gain revenge over his broken watch, grabbed up a daffodil from a nearby vase and placed it in Sid's lap before attempting to revive his friend by hurling a glass of wine into his face. Sid, having been rudely awakened from his slumber and having no idea where he was, limped out of the office towards the secretarial pool where he thrust his bleeding foot in one unfortunate girl's face and ordered the 'bitch' to find him a 'fucking plaster'. He then disap-peared inside the gents', where he somehow managed to smash the toilet's cistern and send a torrent of water flooding out into the corridor.

'It wasn't management of any kind other than mismanage-ment,' Anne later claimed. 'No one with an ounce of sense of what was right would put four teenage kids in the middle of a bucket-load of hard drink, and then wonder why the day turned into chaos. I know the Sex Pistols weren't angels, but surely there was a better way to handle the situation. McLaren just seemed to always find the wrong way to handle things.'

By now Green had clearly reached his wits' end and all he wanted to do was to get the group out of there as quickly as possible, but getting anyone to agree to anything was proving a forlorn task. He therefore took it upon himself to make an executive decision. Having selected 'No Feeling' as the B-side, he hurried everyone back upstairs only to discover that the Daimler's disgruntled driver was refusing to take the group back to Denmark Street and would be sending A&M a bill for damages to the car. Steve, who had been missing for most of the afternoon, finally reappeared while the others were awaiting the arrival of a hastily booked mini-cab. It later transpired that he had wandered off upstairs in search of a toilet, and, having worked his charms on an unsuspecting secretary, accompanied her into the ladies toilets for a few moments together.

Upon arriving back at Denmark Street, an NBC TV film crew was already set up and waiting for the group, although just what the Americans were expecting to glean from four woefully inebriated Sex Pistols is anyone's guess. Sid threw himself onto Steve's bed and – before going out for the count – informed NBC's Tony Potter that he'd just had the greatest time of his life, and that as far as he was concerned it was fucking great being in the Sex Pistols.

The following day – the same day that the selected mix for 'God Save the Queen' went to press – Rotten made an appearance at Marlborough Street Magistrates Court, where he was duly fined £40 for possession of amphetamine sulphate. Later that evening – after yet another day's serious drinking – he and Sid, with faithful sidekick Wobble once again in tow, headed for the Speakeasy in Piccadilly (a favourite drinking haunt for rock bands since the Glam era) to meet up with Steve and Paul. 'We'd go down to the Speakeasy and there'd be all these rock biz types who'd had their noses put out of joint by Punk,' Wobble later told Jon Savage for *England's Dreaming*. 'It was a bit like when we were put out by the Blitz [the London nightclub which gave rise to the New Romantics] scene in 1978. They'd get a bit paranoid and comments would be passed, then glasses would be passed, if you see what I mean.'

When asked by Judy Vermorel about the incident at the Speakeasy (which resulted in Jack Lewis of the *Daily Mirror* interviewing Sid), Sid set off on a ramble that illustrated what a mess he was becoming. 'Because just previous to that there had been some incident at the Speakeasy where somebody had got injured, and of course John Rotten and I were suspected. Of course, we had nothing to do with it whatsoever, and he picked me out to interview because my name was Vicious, and it was obvious he was trying to find out from the questions he asked, he asked me if I was violent and things like that, all very subtle, designed to put a person of low intelligence, obviously such as myself . . . I would be totally fooled by this and he would get it all out of me and I would say, "Yes, I'm big, tough and vicious and I beat up all these people and split people's heads open,' and this was what he came along to do and he was so sure he was going to get that. So I told him exactly the opposite of what he wanted to hear. I said what a nice, intellectual boy I was and I wouldn't dream of doing anything like that, and I had pet hamsters and things like that, you know what I mean, and made myself seem like butter wouldn't melt in my mouth and this fucking jerk-off fell for it. They're just so thick, those arseholes, they wouldn't know a string quartet from a string vest. They make me sick, they make me physically ill because they're not in touch with what's going on at all, they've got no idea of what is happening. As far as I'm concerned, anyone with any suss looks at the picture of me standing there and looks at what I've said – the two don't go together. Of course, he lacked the intelligence, like most grown-ups, to do anything of the sort. When flared trousers, for instance, were in and long hair, grown-ups said they were *awful* and *shocking* and you should have short hair and wear straight trousers. And now the grown-ups have long hair and think long hair is fine and wear flared trousers.' He ended his rant on a less than positive note: 'I can die when I'm around about twenty-four . . . I expect . . . if not sooner.'

Steve and Paul, who by this time were regular habitués of the music industry's most salubrious watering hole, were already inside when the others arrived. Rather than find a secluded corner, the four Sex Pistols and Wobble chose to remain by the bar – centre stage, so to speak – where they could laud their recent signing to A&M over their wannabe contemporaries and jaded pop stars of yesteryear. Fuelled by drink and drugs, the highly volatile Wobble took it upon himself to question 'Whispering' Bob Harris – the ex-policeman turned DJ and compère of the BBC's late-night music show *Old Grey Whistle Test* – as to why the Sex Pistols had not been invited onto the programme. Harris, a self-confessed aficionado of Progressive Rock, who had famously branded the New York Dolls as 'mock rock' when the American outfit had performed in the studio twelve months earlier, would have sooner had his testicles skewered upon a knitting needle than have the Pistols on his show and more or less conveyed this sentiment to Wobble.

Harris, believing that the discussion was at an end, went to rejoin his companions, the *Whistle Test*'s studio engineer George Nicholson and a Prog Rock outfit called Bandit. Wobble, however, was far from finished, and with the ever-eager Sid in tow, the pair went in search of an argument which culminated in Harris fearing for his life and Nicholson being struck on the head with a beer glass, then requiring fourteen stitches. Harris and Nicholson luckily managed to beat a hasty retreat and spent the early hours at a Hammersmith hospital. This was yet another example of Sid's willingness to cause trouble where none existed. Another who had been party to other such incidents was Don Letts, as he explained to author John Robb in his book *Punk Rock: An Oral History*. 'He would stare into people's faces walking down the street, or if you were on a train he would gob on the window right next to a passenger,' said Letts. 'We were always frightened because we knew we'd have to get involved.'

Sid and Wobble probably went to sleep after the Harris incident believing they had struck a blow for Punk and that the incident would have been forgotten by Monday morning. Little could either of them have known at the time of their tête-à-tête with Harris that their actions would have far-reaching repercussions.

Harris, who was a personal friend of Derek Green, had wasted little time in instructing his solicitor/manager Philip Roberge to issue a stern letter to Glitterbest, McLaren's management company, threatening legal action against the Sex Pistols. Although the matter was serious, Malcolm would have been confident that his own solicitor, and Glitterbest partner, Stephen Fisher, would be able to come to some sort of arrangement with Roberge. Unfortunately for Malcolm, Roberge's partner was Dee Anthony, who happened to be the manager of Peter Frampton, whose latest album *Frampton Comes Alive* had just gone platinum on both sides of the Atlantic. Legend has it that few homes in the USA were without a copy by the end of 1976, making him A&M's most successful artist to date.

Green may have been prepared to turn a blind eye to the Sex Pistols' boisterous behaviour, but their having physically attacked one of his closest friends was a step way, way too far. On the morning of Tuesday the 15th, Green abandoned his post for the day and instead drove down to Brighton where he spent the afternoon sitting on the beach, casting pebbles into the surf as he pondered his options. The decision to sign the Sex Pistols against the wishes of the majority of his staff had been his to make, and his alone. Now his reputation within the industry would suffer if he were to offload the group, but deep down he knew there was but one course of action open to him. It was he who had signed the band and so he would do the honourable thing and resign. As soon as time zones permitted, Green called Jerry Moss in New York and explained that although he was no longer willing to work with the Sex Pistols, he believed that A&M should persevere with the group as they would be successful. Moss, however, was not willing to trade a bunch of limey Punk Rockers for his most-trusted lieutenant. Herb Alpert was in total agreement. As far as A&M was concerned, Derek Green was a money-making machine and the Sex Pistols could rot in hell. 'There's been lots of versions of this and I never commented, but it was a very personal choice,' remembers Green. 'I became very uncomfortable working with them personally, and I also felt a bit of a hypocrite. I wasn't an angry rebel and I wasn't about to pretend I was one. I probably lost my nerve because it's not an environment I enjoy, it was just distasteful. So I said, "I'm afraid we have to just cancel the contract." The price of our get-out was £75,000.'

Green immediately drew up a terse four-line statement for the press and also gave orders for the production of the 'God Save the Queen' single to be halted. The 25,000 or so finished copies of the single were ordered to be destroyed, including the metal masters, but one quick-witted employee at the pressing plant had the foresight to realise that the Sex Pistols were destined for greatness and spared one box from the incinerator's maw. The withdrawn single quickly became a much sought after item on the collectors' market and today a genuine copy can fetch upwards of £6,000. It is thought that fewer than fifty copies have survived.

At 2 p.m. on Wednesday, 16 March, Green summoned Malcolm McLaren and Steven Fisher to the offices of A&M's solicitors where he informed them of his decision. Needless to say, McLaren was shell-shocked. The height of the Silver Jubilee celebrations were now less than three months away and the single had been scheduled for release later that month. His attempt to assuage Green fell on deaf ears. As far as Green was concerned, A&M's statement would be going out to the press at 6 p.m. that evening. The contract was dead in the water and all that remained open for discussion was how to dress up the corpse.

McLaren walked away with a cheque for £25,000, which was the outstanding balance of the first year's advance, while Rotten, although reticent to dedicate an entire song to the A&M debacle so shortly after penning the eponymous acerbic rant against EMI, could at least use the American label's name as the song's coda. Being paid £75,000 for seven days' work (or the distinct lack of it), which, when added to the £40,000 pay-off from EMI, would see the Sex Pistols being voted 'Young Businessmen Of The Year' by the *Investors Review*, was all well and good in terms of publicity. But Malcolm had one eye on the clock.

McLaren knew he needed to get the record out in time for the Silver Jubilee or its publicity potential would be rendered obsolete. The Sex Pistols were fast becoming music industry pariahs. But all was not lost – Polydor's Chris Parry and Richard Branson over at Virgin would still return his calls. By now the UK press had taken to calling Punk 'dole queue rock', but Sid wasn't remotely happy with this description, as he told Judy Vermorel in the excellent *Sex Pistols: Inside Story* (Omnibus Press). 'Oh my God, dole queue rock!' he ranted. 'I'm not on the dole. I was never even on the dole before I joined the band. I think I went down there one week and from then on I couldn't be bothered to go down and collect 'em. I could ponce more than like £10 in a week, do you know what I mean? I had no source of income whatsoever, but I never starved. That's for sure.'

❀   ❀   ❀

Sid's live debut with the Sex Pistols came on Monday, 21 March 1977 at the Notre Dame Hall, situated just off Leicester Square, where the group had played the previous November. This particular show, footage of which can also be seen in the *Swindle* film, had been a complete sell-out, but this time around the hall was less than half full. This surprisingly low attendance had nothing to do with the Sex Pistols' fall from grace since their recent sacking from A&M, but was rather due to the venue's owners – an order of Roman Catholic priests. They had grave misgivings about being associated with the group and so restricted admittance to just fifty or so punters. Malcolm

McLaren had arranged the show as a showcase for *NBC News* as part of the American network's on-going documentary about the Sex Pistols, and – having discovered that it wasn't only record companies that were closing their doors on the group – had been forced to go cap in hand to the priests at Notre Dame. He reached a last-minute decision so that the doors would be open on strict invite only to the chosen few.

'I didn't find out until three hours before the show,' remembers Simon Barker, a one-time member of the Bromley Contingent and a former SEX employee. 'I was working in the shop when Malcolm came in and told me to spread the word. This must have been about 3 p.m. and so by 5.30 p.m. there were about five hundred people outside Notre Dame desperate to get in. Sophie [Richmond] spoke to the priests and managed to persuade them to increase the limit to one hundred and fifty, but that still left a lot of angry people outside.'

Photographer Ray Stevenson, who, up until his brother Nils' dismissal from the court of King Malcolm, had served as the group's semi-official lens man, was present on both occasions and remembers that the show was something of a let down. 'There was no atmosphere at all,' he remembers today. 'The Pistols came on, played a shorter set than usual, then went off again and everybody went home. It just didn't work.' (Some footage of the show can be found on the *Classic Albums* DVD *Never Mind the Bollocks.*)

It certainly worked for Sid. He didn't care about who was inside and who'd been left out in the cold, as the last time he'd ventured across Notre Dame's threshold he'd been one of the little people. But now he was a star. Sid's shortcomings as a bassist would have proved something of a handicap in the recording studio, but playing live was a different matter entirely and no one was going to chastise him for accidentally hitting the wrong string or playing the occasional bum note. Punk Rock was about attitude rather than aptitude – a scene in which musical deficiencies were secondary to image and on-stage charisma. Sid had both of these in abundance, and – unlike his predecessor – he was not afraid to hog the microphone. Sid looked striking that night, dressed in trainers, a pair of jeans with the knees ripped out and a 'Vive Le Rock' T-shirt with his brand-new Fender Precision bass dangling about his knees in the style of Dee Dee Ramone.

'I honestly couldn't say whether Sid ruined the Pistols as a musical unit as I never saw one of their gigs,' mused Glen Matlock recently. 'Then again, there was nothing to stop them from turning down his bass in the mix.' Although this was true towards the latter stages of the group's time together, both Paul and Steve would later cite Sid's early gigs as some of the best they ever played. Listening to recordings from this time proves that, unless another bass was overdubbed later, Sid's playing was quite adequate.

Sid Vicious' elevation from 'face about town' to 'bass-wielding clown' may have added extra impetus to the group's visual dynamic, as well as providing the soon-to-be-obsessed media with a second seemingly larger-than-life Punk personality with which to titillate their readers. But not everyone was impressed with Sid flagrantly flaunting his faux 'Vicious' persona in front of the cameras. Later that night as Sid emerged from the Notre Dame, probably expecting to be mobbed by his fans, a voice shouted out accusing him of having 'sold out'. Sid whirled round defiantly with his fists clenched, ready to challenge whoever it was to repeat the accusation, but he immediately backed off again upon discovering that his detractor was Michael – a genuine East End hard case who, along with his twin-brother John, sold hot-dogs in Piccadilly Circus. The twins were both fans of the group and acquaintances of Steve's, and the guitarist would later reveal during an interview for *Classic Albums* that it had been the twins who had inadvertently provided the Sex Pistols with the title for their album, since 'never mind the bollocks' was their stock-in-trade catchphrase.

'I went along to the Notre Dame show, principally because I wanted to be there for his "big night",' said Anne Beverley. 'It was a great show, full of atmosphere, with John and Sid playing at band leaders. Vivienne, whom I didn't much care for, was hopping about like Alice in some bizarre Wonderland of her own making; Malcolm was desperately wanting to impress the Yanks by trying to show that he was in control when it was obvious to anyone that the task was beyond him. And finally Boogie, whom I really liked, a nice guy who looked after Sid.'

Anne could not have known at the time that she and Vivienne were not the only females within the Notre Dame that had their eyes on Sid that evening. There was a diminutive bottle-blonde dressed in black jeans, black leather jacket, studded belt and a SEX 'hangman' string mohair jumper.

'One Saturday morning, an American girl appeared, a chemical blonde whose stiff, brittle hair ranged in colour from white through cadmium yellow to the black of her dark roots,' recalled Malcolm McLaren. 'She was an odd thing to look at. She wasn't plump but swollen. The eruptions across her skin were covered in a thick, chalky make-up, and her lips were painted blood red. She was wearing the ubiquitous New York "rock chick" uniform — leather jacket, short skirt and boots. She came straight up to the counter and dumped her bag between her feet. "I'm looking for Jerry. Is he around?" There weren't many people in the store; it was still early. "You know, Jerry Nolan? The drummer in the Heartbreakers? He used to be with the New York Dolls? He said he was a friend of you guys." "Yeah, so?" "Which one of you is Malcolm?" She continued with a dull confidence and instant familiarity that only Americans seem to possess. "I got in from New York this morning." Her voice was cigarette-stained. "Jerry said he'd meet me here. He said this was his hang-out." She had come directly to the shop from the airport. She looked through the racks of clothes, dropping names whenever she could. She wanted to appear important — as if she were trying to locate fellow stars in what she believed to be the new London scene. She lingered over each item of clothing for the longest time and somehow managed to keep herself busy for the entire day. Hours later, she finally did buy something – a cobwebby, black mohair sweater. At closing time, I was sure she'd disappear. She didn't. She actually followed us – me, Vivienne, the shop assistants, Paul Cook and Steve Jones – into the pub. There was nothing we could do to stop her, nothing we said, however abrasive, seemed to penetrate. And it was, after all, Saturday night. We moved on to Louise's, once a lesbian hang-out and now a Punk gathering place. Madame Louise still sat at the door every night in her mink stole, as she had for at least two decades. The place was reminiscent of its time — a pick-up clip joint, with red flock wallpaper, velvet cushions and a tiny dance floor. Its "clientele" was made up of prostitutes, waifs, gays, lesbians, bisexuals and nonsexuals. Anything and everything went, as long as it was aesthetically extreme. Prostitution had become a fashionably noble pursuit among the members of the anarchic group of Punk Rock fans. Prostitutes were models for our own clothes. The Seditionaries label, on the inside of our clothes, was dedicated to anarchists, soldiers and prostitutes. At a place like Louise's there would regularly be topless women, or women in just bras, and others, men and women, in only knickers and tights. Their attitude wasn't one of seduction, it was confrontation. They might add a swastika armband and a leather peaked cap — anything that might hit a nerve. We still hadn't shaken the American, who by now had discovered Sid. Sid stood out that night. He'd just become the group's bass player and was wearing a pair of pink, pegged slacks, and was sitting with Johnny Rotten, who wore a blue lamé Teddy-Boy jacket. The American was Nancy Spungen.'

CHAPTER 5

Ever Get as Cheated as You've Been Feeling?

Nancy Laura Spungen was born on 27 February 1958, the eldest daughter of a moderately well-to-do Jewish middle-class family. The Spungens lived in a four-bedroom colonial house in the Philadelphia suburbs of Huntingdon Valley. The actual town was called Mainline. Her doting parents, Deborah and Frank, were overjoyed at Nancy's arrival, but the dream life that they had envisioned for themselves and their first-born quickly descended into a nightmare.

Had Nancy been born in the present day she would have been recognised as a 'cyanotic birth' – the term given to babies born with the umbilical cord wrapped around their necks, causing a deficiency of oxygen in the blood – and would have been treated accordingly. Back in 1958, however, doctors were completely ignorant of the condition and therefore unaware of its side-effects.

The first warning sign that all was not well with Nancy came when she was three years old and was prescribed Phenobarbital in a bid to quell her incessant high-pitched screaming. Although the drug silenced Nancy's screams, the Spungen household, which by this time included a second daughter Suzy and a baby brother David, suffered constant turmoil as a result of Nancy's uncontrollable tantrums and oft-violent mood-swings. One month shy of Nancy's fourth birthday, her parents sought professional help and sent her for what would be the first of many psychiatric evaluations. In hindsight her mother believes that her very early childhood traumas contributed to the destructive and additive tendencies that would plague her later life.

'I talked to a few of her friends and they seem to feel that it did start between sixteen and eighteen, although she professed to being an addict much earlier,' remembered Deborah Spungen. 'They lived with her at school and she wasn't on drugs, but I think it started because she had been medicated since the time she was three months old. I complained of her crying and the doctor, as if to shut me up, gave her Phenobarbital, a sedative, and each doctor successively tried to treat her with drugs. So she started to self-medicate because it gave her a different reality which she thought was probably better.'

By the age of fifteen she had spent time in, and escaped from, a home for disturbed children; was regularly tripping on LSD; made at least one attempt at committing suicide by slashing her wrists; had carried out a DIY self-abortion with a wire-frame coat hanger and been diagnosed as schizophrenic. At sixteen, and with her academic aspirations all but ruined as a result of her being expelled from the University of Colorado for stealing, Nancy decided to take a walk on the wild side and became a 'groupie'. Although Nancy, dressed in the time-honoured groupie chic of stilettos and spandex to ingratiate herself with the in-crowd, didn't keep a log of all the musicians she bedded, it has been established over the years that various members of Queen, Bad Company, Aerosmith and the Pretty Things were all grateful recipients of a so-called 'Spungen Special', long before Sid Vicious arrived on the scene.

'I met sixteen-year-old Nancy Spungen for the first time at Max's Kansas City at a Heartbreakers gig,' recalls New York photographer Eileen Polk. 'She told me that she had run away from home, that she hated it, that she was a prostitute, and that she was carrying drugs for the band. I was not shocked by her occupation or the drugs, it was her honesty that surprised me. Most groupies would have said they were a "model" or "dancer". She was very jaded and cynical for someone so young. I didn't think she was bitchy or tough. Instead she seemed to be really gullible and trying hard to make people like her. A lot of the people on the scene tolerated her but made fun of her behind her back. She was an outcast trying to break into a scene where everyone knew each other and there were some heavy rivalries. I remember hearing some pretty catty remarks about Nancy from the Max's groupies. Having sex with guys in bands and acquiring a few notches on the garter belt was par for the course with those girls, but it was said that Nancy had slept with all the Heartbreakers, and every member of Aerosmith. Nancy didn't just screw rock stars, she fucked whole bands. None of the Max's groupies would have admitted to that, but Nancy bragged about it, which was pretty shocking. It was akin to shagging the whole football team or the whole platoon. That was considered sluttish and it just wasn't done, well not intentionally. Nancy's boasting about behaviour that others would never admit to was done to shock. I guess that's why I liked her – she was not a phoney like some of those girls who were whores and pretended they were not. Nancy was painfully honest about things like that.

'Sometimes she would pal around with Sable Starr, another young groupie who was really cute and had been Johnny Thunders' jailbait girlfriend when she was still in high school. Sable was also a bit of an outcast too, since she was from L.A. and her cuteness made the other groupies envious of her. The two of them began stripping at the same clubs together and Nancy was Sable's side-kick for a while. She learned a lot from Sable, who could get some "John" to buy her dinner and then invite all her guy friends to join their table, order drinks and stick the poor sucker with the cheque. When Nancy finally earned enough for a ticket to London she began her master plan to bag a rock star.'

During the autumn of 1975, Nancy was living in New York and working as a go-go dancer to pay her rent. It was later that she turned to prostitution in order to feed a burgeoning heroin habit. Nancy had been drawn to Punk like the proverbial moth to a flame and with her hair now bleached peroxide blonde began hanging out at the Big Apple's premier Punk hangouts, Max's Kansas City and CBGBs. Here she met many of the leading lights from the New York Punk scene, including Richard Hell, Johnny Thunders and the soon-to-be-famous Debbie Harry, who was waiting tables at Max's.

Nancy's self-professed talent for giving great blow-jobs certainly made her popular with the guys, but most of the women on the scene took a dislike to her and gave her the nickname 'Nauseating Nancy'. 'Nancy did get herself a reputation,' Eileen Polk recalled. 'She got friendly with the bands and so their girlfriends assumed that she was seducing them with drugs and then fucking them so that she could add another notch to her belt.'

One musician that took up several of the aforementioned notches was Jerry 'Niggs' Nolan. Nolan was the drummer in fellow ex-New York Doll Johnny Thunders' new outfit, The Heartbreakers, which at one time had also featured Richard Hell in the line-up. Nancy, who would later confess to having loved the Dolls because they were 'nasty and mean, played god-awful rock 'n' roll, wore make-up, had good names and equally good hair-dos', believed that her having landed a real-life ex-New York Doll was just the coolest thing ever. However, Nolan regarded Nancy as little more than a fuck-and-junk buddy. He'd already called time on the 'relationship' long before he and the rest of the Heartbreakers departed for London to participate in the Sex Pistols' ill-fated 'Anarchy' tour. 'They were a good band live,' remembers photographer Peter Kodick. 'But Johnny [Thunders] had lots of problems. He was heavily into heroin –

that was a problem, I mean the whole band were. These were guys who all had tons of money, they'd go down to the record company and get £100 out, which, at the time, was a lot of money. They had money for drugs and everything.'

When the tour came to an end the Heartbreakers elected to remain in London where they hoped to make a name for themselves in the nascent London Punk scene, and they could also score Methadone (a synthetic heroin substitute) on free prescription. 'Everyone was on speed at that time anyway, or Mandrax, the drug of choice at that time, the downer of its era,' remembers Alan Jones. When Nancy realised that the band wasn't coming back to New York she made new plans of her own.

'When the New York Dolls broke up, Arthur Kane escaped to Los Angeles to get away from his former girlfriend, a psychopathic groupie named Connie who was stalking him,' says Edith Polk. 'One night, some of us gathered at my mother's house to call Arthur and see how he was doing. The group of us, including Nancy, Anya Phillips, Sylvain Sylvain and Pete Jordon sat at my mother's kitchen table and took turns talking to Arthur. That was the night Nancy told me of her grand plan to go to London and get a real rock star boyfriend. One of her favourite bands was Bad Company and she planned to see them, as well as Jerry Nolan and Johnny Thunders of the Heartbreakers who were in London at that time. She didn't really look like a groupie then. She had frizzy brown hair and was not fashionably thin, but she had flashing eyes, a beautiful smile and long fingernails. And she had ambition. In her mind, having sex with men was a means to somehow getting into the music business as a manager or agent or something like that. I'm sure Nancy would have liked to have been in a band, but she didn't want to work for it. I don't think she had a clue as to how to do anything but satisfy her immediate needs. Her primary goal was always to hang her self esteem on someone else's fame.'

By the end of February 1977, Nancy had made her plans and set off for London where she went straight to SEX. 'Who was this Nancy?' asks Malcolm McLaren, looking back. 'I phoned friends in New York. She was, I discovered, a confirmed heroin addict. And she was trouble. In New York, my friends told me, they were so pleased when she left town that they threw a party to celebrate.'

Nancy had heard all about the Sex Pistols and their supposed bad-boy reputation, having read an unfavourable review of one of the group's shows in an American magazine. She wanted to experience this band first hand and so began pestering her mother for cash for the air fare. Although Deborah Spungen had grave misgivings about her daughter's decision, she knew that there was nothing she could possibly say or do to dissuade Nancy from going. She reluctantly cashed in $500 of the $1500 savings certificates that her late father had bequeathed to each of his three grandchildren, and purchased an open-ended round trip to London via Amsterdam. Nancy departed from New York's JFK airport brimming with hope and excitement and roughly enough money to pay for several nights in a hotel, but somehow she managed to miss her connecting flight from Amsterdam, which resulted in Deborah having to wire more cash so that Nancy could buy a ticket for the boat-train to England.

Although Deborah Spungen would later cite 11 March as the day her daughter met Sid Vicious for the first time, it is more likely that the meeting occurred several days later, as Nils Stevenson and Simone Stenfors first encountered Nancy on 15 March at the Heartbreakers' flat in Pimlico. 'I remember Johnny Thunders playing a guitar, while falling asleep and scratching his nose,' says Simone today with a grin. 'It was my birthday, and Nils told them, but that only seemed to start Nancy off with tales of her own eighteenth birthday. In fact anything anyone mentioned that night only seemed to start Nancy off with another self-obsessed tale of her own. She didn't seem to like the fact that another girl had landed in what she considered her space, but it was obvious they didn't want her there anyway. All of the Heartbreakers' girlfriends and wives were due to arrive from the USA the next day, so Nancy was a problem. It seemed obvious from her conversation that she wanted a Sex Pistol as a boyfriend. I think she first shagged Steve.'

'After a while Johnny [Thunders] decided to go to bed,' says Simone. 'He mentioned he was going to lock his door because he didn't feel safe with Nancy around. Myself and Nils made up a bed on the floor, when in walked Jerry, who simply climbed into bed at my side, and told the pair of us that he wasn't "trying anything on", but he "didn't feel safe with Nancy in the house". It made for a very uncomfortable experience trying to sleep, in between Jerry and Nils, because Jerry was wearing his very itchy SEX mohair jumper.'

Kris Needs backs up the theory that Nancy did seem to arrive on the UK Punk scene that night, in his book *Trash: The Complete New York Dolls*: 'One night we were sitting about in the front bar of the Speakeasy, me, Mark Perry, Mick Jones, Topper Headon, Joe Strummer, Sid Vicious and Paul Cook,' he states. 'There was this girl tottering about in black leather mini-skirt, fishnets, etc, trying to bum cigarettes and talk to us. She was obviously up for anything, especially if it led to drugs. She was said to have had her sights fixed on Johnny Rotten, because the Heartbreakers had been less than overjoyed to see her. Nancy turned up at the flat that Rotten and Sid shared in St James' Park, which belonged to an ex-prostitute. Rotten hated her so she made straight for big, gullible Sid.'

If Simone needed any further proof that Nancy was someone to be avoided at all cost, it came several days later when the two happened to bump into each other at the Music Machine in Camden Town. Nancy's forearms were swathed in bandages as a result of her having slashed her wrists in what was either a fit of temper or yet another suicide attempt.

In Nina Antonia's biography *Johnny Thunders: In Cold Blood*, there is a Jerry Nolan interview taken from the *Village Voice*. 'We hung out a lot with the Sex Pistols,' he said. 'I was the first guy to turn Johnny Rotten on to heroin, the first to shoot him up. I'm not proud of that, I learned a lesson. I didn't like the feeling I got from it, and I changed my mind about turning people on to drugs. I didn't do it any more after that. Nancy, who I introduced to Sid [Vicious], was the first to turn Sid on.'

Heartbreakers manager Leee Black Childers disputes this fact. 'I will go to my grave swearing that, weird as he [Sid] was, he was not a junkie at that time,' he says. 'I do believe Jerry Nolan's account that he introduced Sid to heroin.' Given that Johnny Rotten has never publicly admitted to even trying heroin and given his stance against the drug, this would seem to be something he would have gone some lengths to avoid. It looks like the Heartbreakers' drummer didn't know his Rotten from his Vicious. But what this does prove is that the long-told story that Nancy first turned Sid onto the drug that ultimately killed him, is just another case, in a long line, of apportioning too much blame onto the Romeo and Juliet of Punk. 'She showed up with Sid,' remembers Steve Jones in the film *The Filth & The Fury*. 'I'm thinking, "Who the fuck is this cunt? This is a horrible person." It was like the weirdest thing. I've never felt such a negative energy from someone, it was just a dark cloud with this bird and I fucking hated her.'

Spungen certainly made an impression wherever she went. In the words of tour manager John Tiberi, 'Nancy wasn't very nice to look at, not very attractive at all. But she did have this fascinating New York accent. Dangerous, that was my reaction. Sid wasn't a smack user until she came along.' However, Anne Beverley didn't blame her for introducing Sid to heroin. 'I'm not going to win any medals for "mother of the year" with some of the stories you've heard already,' she said. 'But I know his introduction to heroin came from somebody other than Nancy. Sure, he was injecting speed, possibly even coke, and who knows what else, so he was a perfect candidate, but I knew heroin was danger and I always said, "For Christ's sake, Simon, stay away from smack." But of course being star-struck and wanting to be one of the lads will lead an awful lot of people down the wrong roads.' Whoever it was who actually helped Sid shoot up heroin for the first time, this move certainly pushed him closer to the edge.

'Pre-Nancy, Sid was up all night on speed and absolutely fine,' explained Alan Jones. 'Post-Nancy, he would be more of a recluse, spending time together – they were inseparable.'

'The Punk thing at that time weren't clean cut. People were taking speed and drinking a lot and smoking spliffs, but there was never any heroin around in England until the Heartbreakers arrived,' says Glen Matlock. For years, the Heartbreakers have carried around the tag of being the group who brought heroin to these shores, and thus the London Punk scene, on their own. Johnny Thunders' party piece was to sit waving a needle full of heroin at any new kid on the block, before uttering the words, 'Are you a man or a mouse boy?' Most kids would give it a go purely because they were in sheer awe of this New York Doll, this low-slung Manhattan guitar hero, the man who almost re-invented rock 'n' roll decadence on his own. 'He was highly influenced by people around him,' John Lydon told the BBC. 'Nancy completely influenced him, and there was very little you could do to stop that, because you could say, "Look Sid, all this drug nonsense, this is all just New York phoniness – you don't need it, it's not what we're about." His immediate answer would be, "You're just jealous." And you can't get over a stumbling block like that, so you have to just let it run its course. Hopefully people will fast become bored with it, but he didn't, and he was too naïve to realise what was really going on.'

Having already visited SEX, where she purchased several items to expand her meagre wardrobe, Nancy returned to the Kings Road boutique with a view to getting herself a job. Although Malcolm McLaren had been happy enough to have provided Nancy's fellow American Chrissie Hynde with a job while she was flitting between Paris and London, he couldn't wait to get rid of Nancy, and later confessed that he considered having the shop fumigated in order to expunge her overbearing negativity. It was while she was making her way back down the Kings Road with no idea as to what she should do next that Nancy bumped into Linda Ashby.

Ashby was not only a SEX habitué and Punk fan but also a dominatrix whose apartment in St James' overlooked the Houses of Parliament, where most of her clientele had their day jobs. She didn't realise the repercussions that her generous offer would bring, but she invited the homeless American to stay at her place. Spungen thus not only had a roof over her head but also gave her a means of earning some easy money by taking on Ashby's overflow business. Besides, most of the girls from the shop (including Little Debs and Tracy), made some extra cash by turning tricks for Linda.

It was at the flat in St James' that the genuinely bizarre squalor of Nancy was exposed. Bertie Marshall, a fully paid-up member of the Bromley Contingent who answered to the name Berlin, was a young homosexual who often crashed at Linda's after various nights of gigs and clubs in the capital. One morning he arrived just as dawn was breaking, but the flat was full to capacity. Nils and Debbie were in the spare room, and Sharon and 'Black' Simone were taking up both sofas, so Linda offered Berlin the kitchen floor – a graffiti-covered room with piles of washing-up and a small bed pushed into one corner. Berlin noticed that the bed was covered with coats and assorted fur rugs, and that underneath these was a shock of bleached hair poking out. Nancy was completely out of it, having been given six Tuinals by Linda. Berlin inquired about the possible return of Sid, only to be informed that no one knew where he was anyway, and if he did come back the door would be locked. In his exhausted state Berlin crawled into bed and drifted off to sleep. After a few hours he awoke and got up to make a cup of tea, but he felt very itchy and began to scratch at his belly, crotch and his ass. Eventually he pulled down his trousers, and at that point he noticed a mole move! But moles don't move. He announced to

Linda that he thought something was wrong, he'd been itching a lot and one of his moles had clearly moved. But Linda informed him it wasn't a mole – he'd caught crabs, simply from occupying the same bed as Nancy. When told of this story, Simone Stenfors laughed: 'Well, that was one of my first impressions of Nancy. She did come across as rather dirty – grubby even.'

By this time, Ashby's flat had become something of a home from home for the Bromley Contingent and assorted Sex Pistols. It was always going to be the place where Sid would first meet his junkie Juliet. Vicious may have had the hots for Nancy, but she, being a groupie, was not interested in putting out for any old Sex Pistol and had set her sights on Johnny Rotten. Rotten, however, having dismissed Nancy as a piece of dirty carpet upon which many a man had wiped his feet, shunned her advances and, as a joke, 'passed her on' to Sid, believing that he would also send the brash American tart packing. Unfortunately for Rotten, the joke backfired because Sid was still in awe of his best friend and readily accepted anything that Rotten said, did or gave him, whether it be a new nickname, a gig with the Sex Pistols or an obnoxious drug-dependant girlfriend.

According to legend, and a full blown confession in *The Filth & The Fury*, Steve Jones – the guitar swinging lothario with a huge appetite for sex – shared an intimate encounter with Nancy prior to her union with Sid, although for Jones this would clearly be nothing more than another notch on his bed post. Nancy already knew there was no love lost with the management or the other group members, when she told Julien Temple: 'He [Rotten] didn't like me because I was a junkie, he tried to keep me and Sid apart for months and months and months, and we had to keep it clandestine, secret, everything. And finally he just gave up, he couldn't deal with it, he just couldn't do it. Sid just kept saying, "Look, I wanna hang around with who I want to hang around with, and I'll have stay in my place who I wanna have stay in my place, and you're not going to tell me not to. So just fuck off."'

Sid and Nancy going public caused problems for Malcolm McLaren. He'd tried to steer the band away from heroin and everyone knew that Nancy was a junkie. The relationship between Vicious and his manager was deteriorating as Sid only wanted to take orders from Lydon. In the usual manner Sid was happy to follow Lydon's lead and slag off McLaren to the press.

'The band's never been dependent on Malcolm,' Vicious told Judy Vermorel. 'That fucking toss bag. I hate that geezer. I'm not dependent on him at all. I'd smash his face in quite happily. I depend on him for exactly nothing. Do you know, all I've got out of him, I think, is £15 in all the time that I've known the fucking bastard, and a T-shirt. He gave me a free T-shirt once, years ago. And once he gave me a fiver and I stole a tenner off him a little while ago, and that's all. Loathsome creature. Hate him.'

Meanwhile, McLaren was focusing on trying to secure the group a new contract in order to release 'God Save the Queen' in time for the Jubilee. 'That was the problem with Nancy's appearance on the scene in the first place,' says Nils Stevenson. 'The timing was fuckin' terrible – it was hardly business as usual for the Pistols, and the people who should have been watching out for Sid were all busy elsewhere.'

'When this Nancy came on the scene it'd be, you know, "You're the star of the show, Sidney,"' John Lydon told BBC Radio 1. 'And he'd begin to believe this, that's when things went sadly wrong.'

'She was here in London to teach Sid all about sex and drugs and the lifestyle of a New York rock chick,' said McLaren. 'Nancy had a guy. She could dominate him, he could support her. And she had someone to control, some of the time. But her face was often bruised. Thereafter, she was rarely seen without sunglasses. She and Sid were constantly fighting. I never felt sorry for her. She turned Sid into the monster child she wanted.' The drugs, the fights and the prostitution meant there was little chance of a happy ending.

'When you realise just how many men [Nancy] had to have sex with to support her and Sid's addiction, and her lifestyle, maybe it wasn't all her fault,' says Eileen Polk. 'Maybe some of those people who were shocked and horrified by the infamous couple in the tabloids didn't even realise that they had had sex with her and had helped create this monster. I think Sid liked Nancy because she was an underdog and she fit into his style of provoking people just for the hell of it. Plus she was doggedly determined to get what she wanted. In New York that's called *chutzpah* and Sid liked that.'

❀   ❀   ❀

Malcolm McLaren's first port of call in finding the elusive new deal had been Chris Parry at Polydor, but Parry had recently signed The Jam to his label, and was therefore no longer quite so desperate to acquire the Pistols. Having tried and failed to secure any genuine interest at Decca and Pye, and unable to give any serious consideration to his one-time hero Larry Parnes' offer to set up a new label to cater for just the Sex Pistols, Malcolm went cap in hand to EMI. The distant hope of negotiating a second chance unsurprisingly fell on deaf ears. CBS was still interested in signing the Sex Pistols but rather less willing to offer the group an advance on the grounds that they had already banked over £100,000 from their dealings with EMI and A&M. Word of the group's day of debauchery at A&M's offices had obviously done the rounds, because not only was CBS unwilling to have the group anywhere near its offices (McLaren was told that all meetings would take place in Soho coffee shops), but they also wanted Malcolm to sign a legally binding document stating that he would keep his charges under full control. Needless to say, McLaren passed on the proposal. Not because of CBS's refusal to pay an advance, or indeed the label's reluctance to entertain the Sex Pistols on home soil, but rather the clause which would have made him liable for any further misdoings. It would have been easier bailing out the sinking *Titanic* with a leaky bucket than to try and keep the Sex Pistols free from trouble. 'I've always thought that was the funniest deal ever placed on the table in the history of UK Punk,' says a grinning Nils Stevenson. 'I wonder if they ever actually wanted to sign the group. Or did someone in A&R have a free afternoon and just want to have a go at winding Malcolm up.'

McLaren then hit upon the idea of staging a showcase to entice prospective A&R guys to come along and see what they would be getting for their money. The only problem was that the Sex Pistols had been banned from the majority of leading London venues and he'd made such a big deal of this in the weekly music press that even the few venues that hadn't been aware of the situation were now. So McLaren turned to his friend Roger Austin, who ran the Screen on the Green in Islington.

The free entry showcase on Sunday, 3 April 1977 finally got underway at midnight. This was Sid's first bonafide live show and was probably one of his worst, which is saying something. 'I remember bumping into Sid and he said, "We are doing a gig at Screen on the Green, but it's like private entry, so it'll be just mates." So we decided to go along,' recalls Simone Stenfors today. 'When we got there I'd never seen a longer queue. Turns out Sid told the same story to everybody he saw that week.'

The reason for his shoddy performance was subsequently put down to his having contracted Hepatitis B, but unlike Joe Strummer, who contracted the disease from inadvertently swallowing a gob of saliva while on stage, Sid's illness came as a result of having shared an infected needle while jacking up. He'd actually played the show stoned and then disappeared with Keith Levene to score some more dope – a telling indication of where his priorities now lay. It didn't help matters and the poor show meant that there weren't any labels willing to sign the band based on that performance.

There was one still option left open for the band, even if it was the one that McLaren was leaving as the very last resort –

Virgin Records. Richard Branson later admitted in his autobiography that he'd been paying close attention to McLaren and the Pistols. He claimed to know that McLaren would have a best-seller on his hands and he longed to sign the band to help eliminate the 'hippy' tag that he was eager to lose. Branson approached McLaren safe in the knowledge that the decision was his alone to make – he had no shareholders or board of control to report to.

While getting wrapped up in the contract dealings, McLaren off-loaded the growing problem of Sid's drug-dependency. Instead of giving Sid an ultimatum to choose between heroin and the Sex Pistols, or placing him on a drug rehabilitation programme, he offloaded Sid and Nancy onto Anne Beverley. Given that Anne herself was a recovering heroin addict, this was hardly an ideal solution. Anne said that her own heroin addiction had been so heavy that a piece of needle had snapped off and remained embedded in her right arm until the day she died. McLaren was counting on the old adage that 'home is the place where they have to take you in'. Although Anne was totally devoted to her only son and would have gladly done anything for him, she had by this time managed to find some stability in her life as well as a new partner. This was Charlie, a part-time drug dealer and full-time good laugh. Because of her home life she initially refused to acquiesce to Malcolm's proposal. 'I'll be honest with you,' Anne said pointedly. 'When I was first given the option of taking in Sid and Nancy, I told Malcolm to forget it. I said to him, "You're the one who let it get to this stage and then you pass them on to me!" But like everything else that happened I thought, well, who else if not me?'

❀   ❀   ❀

The Sex Pistols officially signed to Virgin Records on Friday, 13 May 1977, but as Sid was at the end of a month-long hospitalisation recovering from Hepatitis he didn't sign until the 16th. 'He immediately began to take heroin like an addict,' said John Tiberi of Sid's exit from hospital. His prolonged incarceration within St Anne's Hospital in Tottenham had not only cleaned up Sid's jaundiced liver but had also served to flush the heroin from his system. This could have been an ideal opportunity to place the detoxed Sid under a responsible wing, but Sid was left to the care of others. Unfortunately, the 'others' were a bit thin on the ground as Lydon, Cook and Jones were otherwise occupied laying down tracks at Wessex Studios, with Jones being called upon to play both lead and bass guitar on all but two songs. With the exception of Sophie Richmond, no one else within the Sex Pistols camp could be bothered to visit Sid, which left Nancy to assume the role of Florence Nightingale.

Upon his hospital release the pair briefly lived in Chelsea Cloisters, a decidedly shabby-looking block of flats just off the Kings Road. They had no idea that it was also occupied by Syd Barrett, and there is no record of whether they ever met. Lydon also lived there for a while, although he hated the place and claimed the hallways stank of 'old women's fannies'. Sid and Nancy were subsequently thrown out when Glitterbest forgot to pay the rent, by which time Lydon had left anyway. 'Everyone knows when a bird starts poking her nose into a rock 'n' roll band it's suicide,' says Steve Jones. 'That's when [Sid] really started getting fucked up and not caring about playing. I didn't want anything to do with her.'

One of the conditions that had been included in the Virgin contract was a get-out clause that stated the band could leave if Virgin failed to get the 'God Save the Queen' single into the shops in time for the Jubilee. Virgin used the CBS factory to have its records pressed, but the plant in Aylesbury was in the midst of an industrial dispute. The workers were refusing to handle the record and were considering strike action. Fortunately for all concerned, the dispute was resolved without too much of a delay and 50,000 copies of the record were pressed. The single was housed in a picture sleeve featuring

Jamie Reid's adaptation of the Cecil Beaton official Jubilee portrait of Elizabeth II. It hit the shops on its original scheduled date of Friday, 27 May 1977.

If the Sex Pistols thought they'd rattled a few cages by saying 'fuck' on live TV, then they were about to discover the true meaning of what it meant to be branded 'public enemy number one'. On 7 June, Jubilee Day, the band played at their infamous boat party on the river Thames. The Pistols performed to an invited audience and sailed down to the Houses of Parliament in a promotional stunt, which was brought to a premature conclusion by the Thames river police. Ron Watts was on the boat that night. 'I was actually on deck, and the boat was going downstream, back towards Westminster Pier,' he told the website www.punk77.co.uk. 'The Pistols were playing, and it got a bit jostley. You know, a bit of charging about in a small space 'cause [the boat] wasn't very big. So, I went out on to the deck by the railings, and a couple of other people come and joined me. There was plenty of food and drink, and I had a beer and a chicken leg or something and I'm looking and I can see these two police boats, and they were a way off. Downstream, I could see two more police boats, and they were a way off too. I carried on eating the chicken and drinking the beer, looked round, and they were all there, together, at the same time. I mean the degree of professionalism was just amazing! And then they were on that boat in force, like about twelve or fifteen coppers, in moments. The boat was quite high-sided, but they were up there. And you know what they were doing, they were up there and on that boat and we were escorted into the Westminster Pier basin.'

The early end to the show resulted in Malcolm, Vivienne, Jamie Reid, Sophie Richmond and several other members of the entourage being arrested. Amazingly, all of the band managed to slip through the chaos and escape into the night.

Anne Beverley was also on board that evening and later recounted the events. 'We had to be at the pier for 6 p.m. and they cast off not long afterwards,' she recalled. 'Quite a number of people got left behind at the quayside, but looking back on it now I suspect that it was all part of Malcolm's plan to show everyone that he was in charge. Richard Branson was very nice and polite. He offered me a drink and wanted to know all about Sid. It was the usual faces on board, except for Nancy, who assumed that the nicer she acted towards me the more chance she had of borrowing money. She kept insisting on calling me Mom, which I didn't like one bit, I can tell you. The group played later in the evening on a makeshift stage which was ever so tiny, although they didn't get too far into their set before somebody turned the power off and then the police arrived. I don't know what Malcolm thought he was going to achieve, beyond what did happen, as the whole idea had chaos written all over it.' Richard Branson was happy enough to argue with the river police that the only reason they stopped the party was because it had the Sex Pistols on it. Elsewhere some genuine punishment was being handed out by Her Majesty's finest to, among others, Jamie Reid, who would later appear in court with a walking stick.

Johnny Rotten may have escaped the clutches of the law, but there were plenty of wannabe vigilantes who'd been fuelled by the media's anti-Sex Pistols stance, which meant that he, as the Sex Pistols' public persona, was a marked man. Ten days later, on 18 June, after a day's recording in Wessex Studios, he was attacked by a gang of razor-wielding, Punk-hating thugs outside the nearby Pegasus pub, and required hospital treatment. The following day Paul Cook was attacked outside Shepherd's Bush tube station by a gang of middle-aged Teddy Boys, but Cook himself would later play down the incident by claiming that he'd been attacked solely because the Teds had taken offence at his choice of footwear (brothel creepers), rather than as a result of any pro-monarchy backlash. Either way, he was coshed over the head for the crime of trying to enter a public tube station.

* * *

'God Save the Queen' was one of only two numbers on the finished album that Sid actually played on, although after Steve Jones' overdubs you'd be hard pressed to hear him. The song was an iconic snapshot of mid-1970s England. The football-esque chants of 'no future' summed up the decade's terrace fighting and unemployment, while Lydon's sardonic vocals attempted to snap the nation's malaise and the guitars stamped out all resistance. This was the Pistols at their peak – unfortunately they'd never be able to repeat it.

There has been much speculation over whether the powers that be conspired to block 'God Save the Queen' from getting to the top of the singles charts. Woolworth's, which was a major player in the UK singles market at the time, was so intent on keeping the Sex Pistols' single out of the public domain that the shop was even refusing to acknowledge the record's existence and had a black line running through the No. 2 slot on their in-house chart billboard. 'I was arrested,' says Malcolm McLaren. 'Our portrait of the Queen [with a safety pin through her nose] was printed in the papers and "God Save the Queen" became a best-selling record, even though it was banned not only from the radio but from most conventional consumer outlets. It outsold the pop favourite at the time, Rod Stewart, by two to one. Yet no official chart allowed it to climb higher than No. 2. I sent my son, Joe, who was then eleven years old, to the nearby retailer W.H. Smith to ask for the record. "We don't sell anything like that here," the shop assistant said. "But", he'd been told to protest, "Isn't it No. 1?" "We're not allowed to mention that."' The British Market Research Bureau (BRMB) was responsible for compiling the weekly singles chart and remained adamant that there had been no underhand dealing and that the Pistols had simply been pipped to the post by Rod Stewart's single, 'I Don't Wanna Talk About It'/'The First Cut is the Deepest'.

Stewart's record had already enjoyed several weeks at the top of the chart and was therefore on the wane, while the Sex

Pistols were in pole position to replace him after having stormed into the penultimate spot after only two weeks in the charts. Virgin's in-house sales showed that 'God Save the Queen' had sold 200,000 copies during its first week of release and was outselling Rod by two-to-one, which resulted in a distraught Richard Branson contacting John Fruin, who at the time was not only responsible for the BMRB but was also head of the BPI (British Phonographic Industry), in order to question the discrepancy. Not surprisingly, Fruin denied any knowledge of a covert plot to keep the Sex Pistols off the No. 1 slot, but it is worth noting that Fruin was also the managing director of WEA Records, and would later fall from grace in 1981 after irregularities were uncovered regarding the dubious chart placings of several of his label's acts.

Branson's suspicions that the chart had been rigged were given further credence after he received a late-night telephone call during which the caller, who chose to remain anonymous, allegedly informed the Virgin boss that the BPI had issued a secret directive to the BMRB which saw all chart-return shops connected with record companies dropped from the weekly census of best-selling records during Jubilee week. This included all shops which weren't Boots, W.H. Smith or Woolworth's. It could be argued that the directive, if indeed it did exist, would have affected every artist in the top ten chart, but when one stops to consider that the leading high street stores, as well as many other record outlets, were already refusing to stock the Pistols' single, then Virgin's temporary removal from the BMRB list almost certainly guaranteed keeping it off the coveted top spot. With Boots joining W.H. Smiths and Woolworth's in the boycott, this meant that half of the single's potential chart sales were taken away before the campaign began, and yet it still clocked up sales of 200,000.

The British establishment has always gone to great lengths to show Britain as a true bastion of democracy – a 'social condition of classlessness and equality' – and it has been equally determined to propagate democracy's most fundamental right: freedom of speech. But, as Joe Strummer would later testify on The Clash's 1982 single 'Know Your Rights', people only have the 'right' to free speech. As the Sex Pistols found out to their cost, this is a different concept entirely from trying to put that right into practice.

Although the group's debut single had also been banned, the ban had only actually extended to the airwaves (although true to form, John Peel at BBC Radio 1 had ignored the ban on the grounds that he transmitted after the 9 p.m. watershed), and the record had remained freely available to buy.

Whether 'God Save the Queen' did or did not accrue enough sales to merit the No. 1 slot, the fact remains that four working-class kids from the wrong side of London's tracks had forced the establishment into a corner whereby it was forced into action. However, the Sex Pistols' victory was a pyrrhic one because the 'establishment' doesn't like being made to look foolish – from that moment on, the powers that be in Whitehall would purposely go out of their way to ensure that the group's subsequent career would be blighted by both bureaucratic interference and the by now obligatory council bans. As if all that wasn't enough, the media's on-going anti-Pistols smear campaign was showing little sign of abating. The Sex Pistols began to develop a siege mentality.

At 4 a.m. on the morning of Monday, 27 June 1977, a highly agitated Sid, with ringleader Nancy, roused McLaren from his slumber to request, nay demand, that he [Malcolm] get his arse in gear and get the Sex Pistols out of the country. McLaren's response was to organise a two-week tour of Scandinavia.

The tour commenced on 13 July at Daddy's Dance Hall in Copenhagen, Denmark, in order to promote the release of their next single 'Pretty Vacant'. Rather than accompany the group on tour, Malcolm McLaren handed the reins over to Boogie before flying out to Los Angeles to meet up with Hollywood director Russ Meyer to begin work on the proposed Sex Pistols film. By this time, the film project, tentatively titled *Who Killed Bambi?*, was at the top of McLaren's agenda.

Sid Vicious' agendas were quite different, and sometimes at odds with his perception as a drug-fuelled buffoon, and he enjoyed meeting fans, especially younger ones who he could bond with without any inherent cynicism. 'Those people need to be got off their behinds, fools, that's why we're here,' Sid exclaimed when asked about the tour. 'Most of the general public are so contrived themselves they just naturally assume we are as well and I'm afraid we're not. We don't hold ourselves back for grown-ups, why should we? If they can't take the pressure then it's their tough luck. Grown-ups are people who have become redundant. I'm going to be dead before I'm anywhere near that age. You can be grown-up at any age. There are sixteen-year-olds who are grown-ups. We're just a bunch of kids and we always will be kids and that's why we will never change. When we toured Sweden there was these two little kids, they worked in a Punk shop, and one of them was twelve. These kids were incredible. One of them had an Iron Cross tattooed on his chest. I spent the whole day with them. They were shoving me around. We had really good fun. They took me round and bought me a load of sweets. They were really brilliant. They were fantastic. I gave one kid my favourite T-shirt.' Vicious in a nutshell: hard on the outside when he needed to seem so, but soft underneath. Happy to play around with kids – the child in a hooligan's body, afraid of growing up and the responsibilities that would bring.

CHAPTER 6

A Cheap Holiday, in Other People's Misery

'The man who said I'd rather be lucky than good, saw deeply into life.'

(Woody Allen)

Sid Vicious' first trip to Europe as a Sex Pistol had been when John Tiberi took the band for a sightseeing tour of Berlin in the wake of the A&M fiasco. On the advice of Nora Foster, the future Mrs Rotten, they booked into the upmarket Kempinski Hotel and the visit to Hitler's former capital inspired Rotten to write the lyrics for 'Holidays in the Sun'. The group themselves were unable to do more than 'look over the Berlin Wall' into East Germany as Sid left his passport at the hotel that day. The band spent its time driving around in a hired VW, visiting – among other places – the Reichstag and Brandenburg Gate, while also finding time to check out Chez Romy, a transvestite disco that was a favoured haunt of David Bowie. 'It was fucking brilliant,' John Tiberi told *Mojo*'s Pat Gilbert. 'We had to go easy on room service. Nobody knew who we were, so there was no hassle, though I remember telling Sid not to wear his Vivienne T-shirt with the upside-down German eagle on it.'

The later Scandinavian dates also provided the Sex Pistols with some breathing space away from the British media microscope – not to mention an escape from the threat of attack from pro-monarchy vigilantes – even though some journalists accompanied them. It also allowed the group to relax and concentrate on doing what it did best: playing live. 'People have slagged off Malcolm for years,' says Nils Stevenson, 'but that was a shrewd move. When your group can't operate in your own back garden, get them out, get them away, and do it fast.' The twelve shows in seventeen days certainly provided Sid with the chance to improve his stage act and to perfect his catch-all Ramones riff. The high of simply being on stage had, albeit temporarily, replaced heroin as his drug of preference, and the absence of Nancy also meant for a more harmonious tour bus. Indeed, the footage shot by Boogie of the show in Trondheim on Thursday, 21 July, shows all of them laughing and smiling with the audience, with Sid on good form. The tour was well covered by the UK press, since Virgin had insisted that journalists from every leading tabloid newspaper should come along for the ride. This provided the group with seemingly endless double-page spreads. In less than a month the Sex Pistols were covered by the *NME, Sounds, Melody Maker, Record Mirror, Disc* and all the national tabloids, something that would be unknown now, in a world of PR 'exclusives'. One reason for this was that Rotten had insisted the journalists should pay their own way rather than sponge from the record company. Having done so, writers were doubly determined to get their money's worth.

As Sid gained confidence on stage he began to take a little of the spotlight away from John Lydon. 'No group is big enough for two front-men like that,' Julien Temple said in 2004. 'I think it works when you have a singer and a guitarist, which the Pistols already had, but Sid was another front-man. John was a big old friend of Sid's and it was John who brought Sid into the group, I think there was clearly friction when Malcolm started building up Sid and falling out with John. And as I say, I don't think the band could handle two front-men with that intensity.' Boogie would later cite the Pistols' frolics among the Nordic fjords as some of the biggest and best gigs that the group ever played. 'God Save the Queen' was riding high at No. 8 in the Swedish singles chart, which usually looked like an Abba *Greatest Hits* album tracklisting. The single had the added kudos of not actually being banned in Sweden. Dennis Morris' photos, which would later appear in his books *Rebel Rock* and *Destroy*, provided pictorial evidence that Scandinavia's youth was thrilled to welcome England's most notorious group to their homeland. The only flare-up came during a gig at Stockholm's Student Karen Happy House, which was invaded by the notorious 'Raggare', a fanatical group of Swedish Teddy Boys who, having read all about the Punks versus Teds battles on the Kings Road, were intent on going one better than their English counterparts. They even followed the group back to their hotel where the staff were forced to barricade the doors in order to prevent the Swedish rockers from gaining entrance. Upon arriving at the airport when leaving the country, Sid spotted Agnetha Faltskog and Anni-Frid 'Frida' Lyngstad of ABBA and, being a huge fan, ran across to get the girls' autographs. The girls were virtually speechless.

The tour was brought to a temporary halt when Sid had to return to London on Monday, 25 July in order to appear at Wells Street magistrates court. The charge dated back to his being caught in possession of a flick-knife on the second night of the 100 Club Punk Festival back in September. The glass-throwing charge had been dropped by the police, due to lack of evidence. In fact the hearing looked like a put-up job to get a Sex Pistol in the dock as the prosecuting council could only provide one solitary witness, and a policeman at that, which is probably why the case took ten months to reach the court. Witnesses for the defence included Anne Beverley, who arrived at the court on her new 250cc motorbike, journalists Caroline Coon and Jonh Ingham, as well as The Clash's Mick Jones and Paul Simonon. 'Mick was always a mate,' remembered Anne Beverley, 'but he and Paul were diamonds that day. They understood a storm in a teacup when they saw one, and stood by their mate.'

Sid, having begged, stolen or borrowed a suit, shirt and tie for the hearing, just wanted to get the whole thing over with so that he could rejoin the tour. He somehow managed to keep the smirk from his face during his solicitor's speech, which began by describing him as a 'fine upstanding young man' and ended with an impassioned plea that a custodial sentence might possibly jinx his future career with the Sex Pistols. The judge appeared to have been as equally bored with the proceedings as Sid was and snapped out of his lethargy long enough to give Sid a stern warning and a fine of £125. For Glitterbest this was a major result – after the events following the release of 'God Save the Queen', surely public hanging or flogging was just around the corner, so a mere £125 fine was an unexpected bonus.

A few weeks later, on 7 July, Sid was back in court with Nancy, who was being charged with carrying an offensive weapon. The weapon in question was a police truncheon, which Nancy claimed she kept in her handbag for protection, but this offence had inadvertently raised the question over her now-invalid visa. 'That was touch-and-go stuff,' said Anne Beverley. 'Illegal aliens? Oh yes, your honour, and they are in the Sex Pistols' camp.' Nancy was saved from being deported after Sid informed the court that he intended to marry her. It is perhaps just as well that the judge didn't choose to call Sid's bluff. He had made a similar promise to Nancy's compatriot, Chrissie Hynde, who was a vague acquaintance of Sid, when she had found herself facing possible deportation back to the USA, but had subsequently failed to turn up for the service. An engagement ring of sorts was bought not long after at Camden market – a silver band with Celtic markings.

⚜ ⚜ ⚜

Upon their return to the UK at the end of July the Sex Pistols headed into Wessex Studios to continue working on their debut album, which was still going under the working title of *God Save the Sex Pistols*. Sid's lack of musical ability brought up the question of whether he actually played on the album or not. In fact he did, but only on two songs – 'God Save the Queen' and 'Bodies'. The remnants of Sid's best efforts are hard to hear, however, as Steve Jones had to overdub the bass parts to bring them up to an acceptable standard. With little to keep himself occupied in the studio, Sid took to making his own entertainment. One incident saw him gate-crashing the adjoining studio where Queen were busy recording their album, *News of the World*.

'I was leaving the studio one night with Sid and Steve. When we got near the door, in walks Freddie Mercury and his bodyguard,' recalled Steve English. 'He took one look at Sid, grinned across the face and said, "Oh, Hello Mr Ferocious!" in the campest voice you've ever heard. We pissed ourselves.' Also while at Wessex Sid was caught performing daredevil cycle rides around the edge of the studio roof, seemingly oblivious to the fact that even one slip would result in serious injury or possible death. 'You know, if you fall from there you could kill yourself,' engineer Bill Price informed Sid. The response was typical of Vicious: 'And your point is what, exactly?'

Once the album was complete the band attempted another UK tour. After the earlier problems they knew they had to keep things under wraps so they booked dates under assumed names on what became known as the SPOTS tour (Sex Pistols On Tour Secretly). The six-show tour opened on Friday, 19 August 1977 at Wolverhampton's Lafayette Club. The tour saw the group play under names such as 'The Spots', 'The Hamsters', 'The Tax

Exiles' and 'Acne Rabble' in order to defy the collective council ban. This was something of a managerial masterstroke on McLaren's part. 'That had been some mix up,' reflects Nils Stevenson. 'Alright, so they were banned in some places by some councils, but by constantly telling the press it had finally backfired. By the late summer of '77 Malcolm had painted himself into a corner from which there was no obvious return – the only option of playing in the UK was the undercover tour, and Rotten hated the idea.' The plan was as simple as it was brilliant. The group would arrive at a designated venue hoping that the authorities hadn't tumbled to the scam, while also relying on word of mouth to ensure that said venue would be filled with kids that were into the group. The Sex Pistols were like a terrorist cell furtively travailing the country, stopping off at hurriedly arranged venues to unleash their devastating wares before moving on to their next intended target. In fact, it is fair to say that the SPOTS tour was a precursor to the rave scene of the late 1980s and the 'guerrilla gigs' of the twenty-first century.

The SPOTS tour was Sid's 'coming out party'. Unlike Rotten, whose performances were beginning to suffer as a result of his ever-increasing paranoia following the attacks, Sid was now in his element on stage and his confidence seemed to grow with each performance. 'When I saw the *Filth and the Fury*, the one thing that really angered me was John collapsing into tears over his best friend Sid,' remembered a clearly upset-looking Alan Jones. 'Now that really annoyed me because they hated each other. John hated Sid, he really did, because he was definitely becoming the face of Punk and he was being sidelined from it. Look now at the photographs of Sid and you really see that iconic poster man, in the way that James Dean or Che Guevara were. I think John felt very threatened by that, and as a result he was really dissing him and really slagging him off.'

Lydon's growing hatred of Sid was devastating to Vicious' psyche. He'd always looked up to Lydon and wanted to be a part of his gang, but that vision was dissolving before his eyes. A journalist had once described the Sex Pistols as consisting of 'three middle-class art students and a real-live dementoid', and although Steve and Paul were neither academically minded nor born to parents of affluent means, Sid recognised the need to even up the score for the dementoids. Unfortunately from this point on, the Sex Pistols now had two front-men because Sid realised that a microphone means an audience will listen to you, and he made it his mission to 'present' the show. 'At one of the gigs,' says McLaren, 'Rotten was being his usual self and wouldn't soundcheck, so we've no singer, and Steve was about to step up, when Sid grabbed the microphone and effortlessly cruised his way through one of the numbers. I mean talk about choosing the wrong front-man!' In 2000, Steve Jones summed up the position. 'Sid was the face,' he said, 'not just of the Sex Pistols but of the entire Punk movement.'

The SPOTS tour was book-ended by the notable deaths of two of Sid's musical heroes. On 16 August Elvis Presley died and on 16 September Marc Bolan was killed in a road crash. Sid found himself being elevated, on notoriety if not musical ability, into the space vacated by his dead heroes. Vicious was now on the road to being exactly what McLaren and Westwood perceived to be the ultimate Sex Pistol and he was perfectly happy to allow the pair to monopolise him at every turn. In fact he was usually blissfully unaware of his being used.

'I don't think they [Malcolm and Vivienne] ever understood that they destroyed Simon,' Anne said one night. 'They took my son and they moulded him into this "icon" which was very much of their own making. I saw him a couple of times around that time and although he still looked and sounded like my Simon, he had changed, and not for the better. He used to have such a cheeky smile and a mischievous glint in his eyes, but by Christmas 1977 the boyish smile had been replaced by a snarl and the glint had all but disappeared.'

The Sex Pistols had relished the opportunity to play in front of an all-English audience again after an enforced eight-month

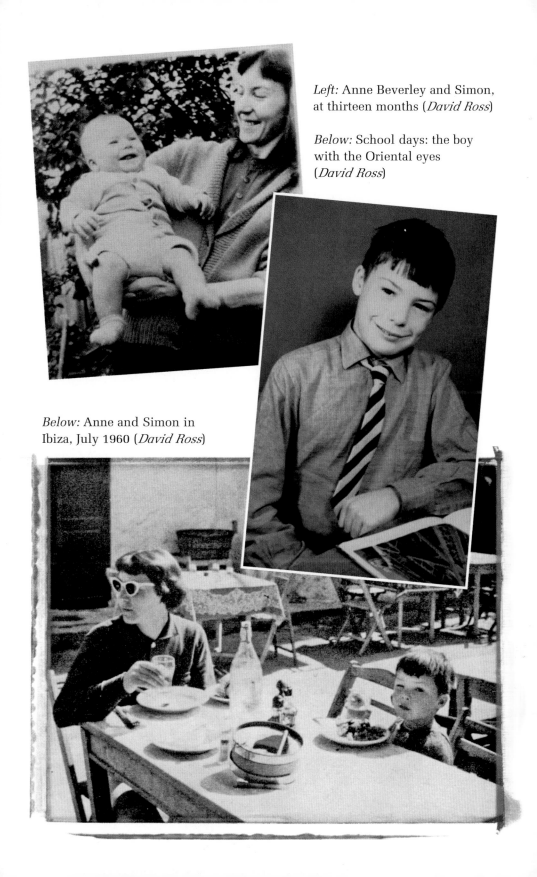

Left: Anne Beverley and Simon, at thirteen months (*David Ross*)

Below: School days: the boy with the Oriental eyes (*David Ross*)

Below: Anne and Simon in Ibiza, July 1960 (*David Ross*)

Marc Bolan fan at Hackney College, 1975 (*David Ross*)

Hackney College work by John Beverley, aka 'The Highwayman'
(*David Ross/Jane Dalton*)

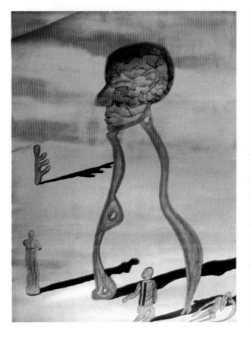

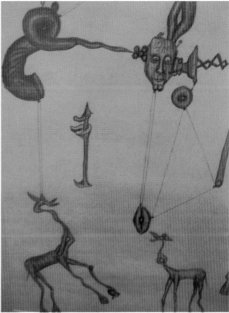

The four loveable spiky tops from Shepherd's Bush (*Richard Young/Rex Features*)

The master puppeteer: Malcolm McLaren in 1976 (*Mirrorpix*)

A first public viewing of the bondage suit: Rotten in Paris, 1976 (*Ray Stevenson/Rex Features*)

Vicious and Rotten:
two mates before it all went wrong (*Virginia Turbett/Redferns*)

Hotel bathroom hell: Paul Cook, Sid and Steve Jones (*Mirrorpix*)

Above: The A&M press conference. *Below:* six days later, having just been sacked by A&M (*Richard Youngs/Rex Features & Mirrorpix*)

Opposite: Punk's biggest icon: late summer, 1977 (*Mirrorpix*)

Below: The summer of '77: 'Kick one of us and we all limp.'
(*Virginia Turbett/Redferns*)

Right: An early Jamie Reid
poster for 'God Save the Queen'
(*Nils Jorgensen/Rex Features*)

Left: Taking a break during filming the *Swindle* (*John Tiberi*)

Below: Classic 'My Way' performance from the *Swindle* (*John Tiberi*)

Above: Sid and Paul meet the punters, USA style
(*Richard E Aaron/ Redferns*)

Below: Sid in his Paris hotel, April '78 (*John Tiberi*)

Opposite: Sid and Nancy at CBGB's
with Marky Ramone, late August 1978
(*Eileen Polk*)

Below: The Vicious White Kids: one gig
only, then off to the USA (*Sheila
Rock/Rex Features*)

The cheeky grin his mother loved so much (*Richard E Aaron/Redferns*)

Backstage at Max's Kansas City, 7th September 1978. Nancy, Sid, Jerry Nolan, Steve Dior, Arthur Kane and Mick Jones; Jones and Dior are still with us (*Eileen Polk*)

Left: Neon Leon, wannabe pop
star, 1974 (*Eileen Polk*)

Below: Sid's Rikers
Island ID (*David Ross*)

Left to Right: Unknown female, Neon Leon, Jerry Only and Michelle
Robinson – The New York Punk Gang, those at the centre of the 'Sid Affair'
(*Eileen Polk*)

Backstage at a New York Blondie gig: Sid and Michelle Robinson (*Eileen Polk*)

hiatus, but once again the tour was blighted by McLaren's total lack of interest in the group as a working musical unit. Although he had loved the chaos surrounding the Wolverhampton gig, Malcolm had found the group themselves somewhat disappointing, particularly Rotten, and his dissatisfaction was so great that he even refused to go backstage and meet up with the boys after the show. The relationship between Rotten and McLaren had been slowly disintegrating for several months by this time and, although Steve Jones would later succinctly suggest that the pair's constant butting of heads was due to their both being Capricorns, that particular slight had more to do with Rotten's exploits of the previous evening when the singer had almost single-handedly killed off the proposed film by purposely insulting Russ Meyer and scriptwriter Roger Ebert during a specially arranged dinner.

Russ Meyer's film, *Who Killed Bambi?*, came to nothing after 20th Century Fox dropped out. They had initially been interested in funding a film starring the group, but when they learned that the script was almost impossible to shoot and that 'Mr Skin-flick' himself was to be director, they pulled out. Meyer did travel to England in the end, but not only did he hate McLaren on sight, he really didn't understand the group. Meyer had worked with 20th Century Fox before and he blamed the fact that they had walked away on McLaren. Meyer's scriptwriter, Robert Ebert, had written a scene in which Sid was called upon to have sex with his mother (Marianne Faithfull was already signed on for the role) and then they would shoot heroin together. 'Well I don't mind balling her,' Sid told Meyer. 'But shooting up? Forget it!' Ebert would later tell the press in the USA that Sid was on about $14 a week wages (nothing like the truth) and thus, 'He had nothing to eat. Russ bought him two six packs of beer and a big can of pork and beans.' The group and Meyer were like two planets colliding, and so working together was never really going to be possible. In the end Meyer shot just one scene, which didn't feature any of the band.

Meyer's growing hatred of McLaren was such that he would later make the preposterous claim that if Sid had completed his film he'd still be alive today.

Sid continued to over-indulge in drugs and the stereotypical rock 'n' roll excesses on the tour. In Coventry he took it to the limit and everything that could be destroyed in one room was. The next morning he emerged with more scars on his chest – the lunacy had moved to new levels. The very nature of the SPOTS tour meant that the Sex Pistols would probably do far more travelling than they ever would performing, and two weeks of criss-crossing the country trying to keep one step ahead of the authorities resulted in the group suffering from saddle sores by the time their war wagon rolled into Penzance on 1 September. Sid, having gone at both ends of the candle, was definitely suffering the most. Following the gig, he approached the tour driver, Barbara Harwood (yet another matriarchal figure), who, when she wasn't behind the wheel was keen to nurture her interest in homeopathy. According to Harwood (who, because of Sid, would later work with drug-addicted teenagers), Sid came to her seeking help and wanted her to take him away from the whole scene and help him get cleaned up. Harwood, although sensing that the plea was genuine, was astute enough to realise that Sid was hopelessly caught within a 'sex, drugs and rock 'n' roll' image that was of his own making and which would just as surely prove to be his undoing. 'I've often wondered what would have happened if he'd been able to bail [out] at that point,' said Anne Beverley. 'Although I suppose none of it was meant to be.'

❀   ❀   ❀

On Friday, 28 October 1977, *Never Mind the Bollocks* was finally released by Virgin with advance orders of 125,000 – a figure which instantly qualified the album for a gold disc and sent it soaring to No. 1 in the UK album chart. This sort of success had not been seen in the UK since The Beatles. The Sex Pistols' renegade status meant that many of those advance purchases were made by kids that had yet to see the group perform live and so it mattered little that all but two of the album's twelve tracks were over a year old. The album was initially released containing eleven tracks with 'Submission' included as a free one-sided single. The album's opening track 'Holidays in the Sun' had been released as a single two weeks earlier, but despite it being a relatively new composition, the song failed to match the success of its two predecessors and stalled at No. 8 in the UK chart. The song's reference to the Belsen concentration camp meant that it was axed from most radio station playlists and its picture sleeve also sparked controversy when the Belgian Travel Service issued a summons claiming infringement of copyright of their summer brochure. This resulted in some 60,000 copies of the sleeve being removed from Virgin's offices.

It wasn't only the record's picture sleeve that brought controversy, however, as some people were quick to point out the similarity between the song's opening riff to that of The Jam's 'In the City', which had been released several months earlier. Although the descending chord sequence on both songs is identical, Steve Jones' chugging powerhouse guitar takes 'Holidays' in a different direction from Weller's composition. The sniping continued with Weller himself happy to point the plagiaristic finger, and when Sid happened upon the Jam frontman outside the Speakeasy one night he decided to exact revenge by head-butting him. Weller, although several inches smaller than Sid, retaliated. Today, Weller describes this as 'handbags at six paces'.

Virgin's original idea had been to release two versions of the album, one of which wouldn't include 'God Save the Queen' so that it could then be sold in Woolworth's, Boots and W.H. Smiths. But the idea came to nothing. The album's supposedly provocative title also ensured that it came under fire from the powers that be, who, not being satisfied at banning the group from playing live as well as blacklisting their songs from radio and TV, once again planted their standard upon the moral high ground and proclaimed the word 'bollocks' to be offensive. 'I remember first seeing a proof sleeve,' says Nils Stevenson. 'At that very point the penny dropped. I thought "You're not in this for the long haul, are you?", because no one could have kept up that kind of controversy. In the Banshees we were planning a career, but you couldn't help feeling that Glitterbest were playing a game.' During November the group attended signing sessions at Virgin record shops across the country. When they arrived in Liverpool, Nancy turned up. No one could understand how she had made it up from London. The answer was simple: she'd booked a black cab on the Glitterbest account, simply to be with Sid.

Many outlets were forced to keep the album's distinctive yellow and pink sleeve tucked away from view for fear of upsetting their customers, but Branson was showing no sign of restraint and ordered his chain of Virgin shops to go overboard in promoting the album. His advertising campaign had cost a reported £25,000, so, if no one else was using his posters he might as well make use of them himself. Chris Searle, the manager of the King Street store in Nottingham, took Branson at his word and practically redecorated his shop with album sleeves and promotional posters (along with the yellow and pink promo posters, another poster was given away free with initial copies of the album, containing a Jamie Reid image for every song on the LP, and a number of these posters were displayed in Nottingham too). This attracted the attention of an overzealous policewoman called Julie Dawn Storey who considered the posters to be contravening the Indecent Advertising Act of 1899.

The court date was set for Thursday, 24 November at Nottingham Magistrates Court, but Branson was not unduly worried as he had been prosecuted under the archaic act seven years earlier in 1970 over a leaflet produced by his Student

Advisory Centre. He simply engaged the services of John Mortimer, the QC who had acted for him on that occasion. Mortimer had created the fictional TV barrister *Rumpole of the Bailey*, and the case against Virgin was so ludicrous that Mortimer could have sent *Rumpole* actor Leo McKern into court to act on his behalf. The presiding magistrate was chomping at the bit to declare the album sleeve obscene and would have gladly ordered every copy of the album to be destroyed, but unfortunately for him the prosecution's case was weak and the case collapsed when Mortimer called upon James Kingsley. Kingsley was not only the Professor of English Studies at Nottingham University, but was also an Anglican vicar. He arrived in court wearing his clerical collar and informed the court that 'bollocks' was a fine upstanding Anglo-Saxon word meaning 'nonsense' and had first appeared in records dating back to the year 1000. The court case was a nonsense and 'bollocks' became legal. Branson had delivered McLaren a victory with the sort of backing they'd seen nothing of previously at either EMI or A&M.

By this time, Sid and Nancy had vacated the cramped confines of Chelsea Cloisters and set up home in a larger flat at No. 3 Pindock Mews, which was situated off Warwick Avenue in the heart of what was then a hotbed of London activity in Maida Vale. 'Pindock Mews was their only real home,' said Anne Beverley. 'They made it real, put up Simon's posters, moved in his jukebox and motorbike. It was a wonderful area and I had high hopes when they told me about the move. But my hopes were based on the two of them getting cleaned up and I didn't realise until years later that by then it was already too late for that. They had set themselves on a one-way course to oblivion and nothing anybody could do or say was going to change that.' Steve Dior also remembers Pindock Mews: 'I went round one day with a mate, and Nancy cooked for us, we had fish fingers and beans. I remember saying to my mate, I didn't know you could ruin fish fingers and beans, but she managed it.'

The lease was for an eyebrow-raising seven years, which was all the more surprising given that the inner circle were already sensing that the Sex Pistols' endgame was drawing to its inexorable conclusion. In the Glitterbest office there was a bet between staff members that McDonalds, which was going to open its first outlet on Oxford Street, would be up and running before the group completed any proposed US tour. The usually frugal McLaren was not worried about the lease's lengthy, and potentially costly, tenure and was overheard quipping that Sid would be dead long before the lease was due for renewal. McLaren's throwaway comment would prove horribly prophetic, but it is clear from having recently spoken to him at length about Sid that he did try everything within his power to get him off heroin, including a botched attempt to kidnap Nancy and send her on a one-way trip back to New York.

The Glitterbest hierarchy, having lined up mini-tours of Holland and the UK for December, as well as a seven-date tour of the USA in January, had decided that Nancy lay at the root of all the Sex Pistols' problems and would have to go. The final straw came following newspaper headlines reporting of 'Sex Pistol And Girl In Drugs Probe' The article in the *Sun* went on to describe how Sid and Nancy had been arrested following a bust-up at the Ambassador Hotel in Bayswater, where the pair had been staying while Malcolm sorted out the lease at Pindock Mews. The huge headline-grabbing 'exclusive' was another storm in a teacup.

The story reported that Sid had gone down to Denmark Street for rehearsals only to discover that he would be the only one doing so, then had returned to the hotel where he abused Steve Jones over the telephone before proceeding to drown his demons in a bottle of vodka. After some stronger stuff he then attempted to throw himself out of the third-floor room window and was only saved from catastrophe by Nancy, who managed to help her distraught lover by grabbing onto Sid's belt and clinging on for dear life. Having failed to harm himself, Sid then proceeded to take his frustrations out on both the hotel room's furnishings and Nancy in no particular order. The hotel manager, who had already been driven to the point of distraction by Sid and Nancy's constant fighting, feared that someone was going to get killed, so he called in the police. When the police arrived they found a variety of pills and drug paraphernalia littered among the broken furniture and duly arrested the pair. As soon as the police arrived, Sid and Nancy, as so many times before, closed ranks. They had nothing to say and nothing happened.

Malcolm McLaren decided he'd have to take drastic measures to get Nancy away from Sid. In order for his plan to succeed he would have to make sure that Sid was out of the way for several hours, and so with the unsuspecting bassist safely ensconced in a dentist's chair, and under gas, Glitterbest sprang into action. Sophie Richmond headed round to Pindock Mews and collected the equally unsuspecting Nancy under the guise of a shopping excursion into nearby Paddington, supposedly to purchase household items for the couple's new flat. Nancy did actually get as far as purchasing several things for the kitchen, but when she mentioned the name of a shop that she wanted to visit, Sophie informed her that the next and final shop on their girlie excursion would be of the duty-free variety at Heathrow Airport. Nancy must have thought she'd either misheard Sophie or that she was being set up for the following week's edition of *Candid Camera*. Upon realising that Malcolm's secretary was deadly serious, she became hysterical – not only at the thought of never seeing her beloved Sidney again, but also at the prospect of getting on an aeroplane without her equally beloved Methadone. Sophie, who was getting desperate, was left with no option but to call the Glitterbest office for reinforcements, but when Nancy saw Malcolm, Boogie and Roadent, who'd all arrived dressed in Seditionaries double-breasted, light-blue raincoats (the Glitterbest Mafia uniform), she set off running down Paddington High Street, screaming out to the startled passers-by that she was being kidnapped. McLaren realised that there was no way he was going to get Nancy to the airport without losing a testicle or an eye and began screaming at her that she was not only fucking up Sid's life but that she was also ruining the group. Nancy would later claim during an interview with *Record Mirror*'s Rosalind Russell that she herself had offered to return to New York for a couple of weeks while the Sex Pistols sorted themselves out, but whether or not this was true has never been established. The fact that McLaren was prepared to go to such lengths in order to help Sid suggests just how much he really cared for him, but needless to say, Sid saw things differently and the incident instilled within him a deep-seated hatred of his manager, which he would never quite shake. McLaren could have made things much easier on himself – all he needed to do was contact the Immigration Department at Heathrow and inform the relevant parties that Nancy was still residing in the country with an invalid visa.

'I'm sure that he thought his [Malcolm's] idea was perfect,' Anne Beverley reflected. 'But in truth it achieved only two things. Firstly, it brought Simon and Nancy even closer, and secondly, Simon's resentment of Malcolm grew so intense that he never shook it off.'

During the aforementioned interview with Rosalind Russell (which appeared in the paper's 8 April 1978 issue and featured Sid and Nancy together with equal billing on the cover), Sid would claim that he had threatened to leave the group over the attempted kidnapping shortly before the tour of Holland was due to commence because he wouldn't have been able to work with such slimy people. He finally relented and agreed to go on the tour since it had been the management who were culpable rather than his fellow Sex Pistols. When Russell asked Sid why the failure of the kidnap attempt had rendered it a lesser crime than had it actually succeeded, Sid side-stepped the question by claiming that he'd made it clear to Malcolm that if he tried anything like that again he would kill him. This statement would rear its head on more than one occasion in the summer of 1978, but to Malcolm it was simply more fuel to the fire.

Sid's decision to go to Holland may have prolonged the Sex Pistols' turbulent career by several weeks, but his on-going drug problems meant that he spent much of the tour feeling sick from withdrawal. 'I was sick all the time and the others were really unreasonable about it,' he told Russell, seemingly unwilling to apportion any of the blame for either his ills or the fractious situation within the group to his own behaviour. 'Malcolm and the band treated me like dirt. They even made me walk to the doctors in the rain, but the doctor wouldn't give me any valium. I was shivering and when I fell down Malcolm kicked me.' The idea of John, Steve and Paul showing little or no compassion for Sid's self-inflicted plight and their letting him wander the streets in the pouring rain in search of pharmaceutical relief is indeed believable, but Sid's claim that Malcolm physically assaulted him by kicking him when he fell down is stretching the boundaries of credibility. Despite the strained relations between Sid, Malcolm and the rest of the Pistols, the Holland tour was a great success with Sid going so far as to single out the opening night at Rotterdam's Eksit Club as being the best gig the group had ever played.

When Russell again questioned Sid as to why he chose to remain in the Sex Pistols after the group's callous treatment towards him during the Holland tour, he responded by claiming that his only motivation for doing so was because he still believed that Rotten would 'get his act together again' and 'stop playing at being the big star'. He went on to intimate that his threat to quit the group did initially bring about a change in Rotten's attitude, but that the singer had apparently fallen back into his old ways by the time the Pistols returned to the UK for their short pre-Christmas tour. This jaunt took in off-the-radar venues such as Coventry's Mr George's, Keighley's Nikkers Club and Cromer's Links Pavilion and culminated in a Christmas benefit show at Ivanhoe's in Huddersfield on 25 December. 'At first, in the 100

Club days, he [Rotten] was definitely the focal point, but after Sweden it was me and Steve,' Vicious informed Russell. 'The way he went on stage; he looked such a mess and even forgot the words to "Anarchy in the UK". I like everyone to look good, not just the central figure. I wanted him to look as good as me and Steve, but he looked ridiculous wearing a hunter's hat and doing that silly fuckin' skank dance to rock 'n' roll.

'He made us look foolish and that was what pissed me off. He'd lost all his charisma and me and Steve were the front-men. I hoped he'd still look good, instead of like a dirty old bum. And he looked shorter. He's quite tall you know, but when you let yourself go, you start to look shorter. He was a pain in the arse. He was such a prima donna.' These thoughts were weighed out by Nils Stevenson. 'There was a genuine change after they arrived home from Sweden,' he recalled. 'The friendship of Sid and John was called into question – you could see the cracks in the group. While both Steve and Paul told me that on stage Sid was fast becoming a focal point, to the outside world they had written just three songs since Glen left.'

The Christmas shows at Ivanhoe's were in aid of a local children's charity as well as a benefit for the children of the local striking firemen who, without the Sex Pistols' benevolence, wouldn't have had much of a Christmas that year. The afternoon was taken up with Sid, John, Steve and Paul joining the under-fourteens for a Christmas feast, which started out with them handing out food and presents and ended up with Sid engaging in a trifle fight with several kids who had been drawn to his childlike innocence and sense of fun, before ending with a matinee performance – with censored lyrics, naturally. Later that evening Sid unwittingly took to the stage to make what would prove to be his last appearance as a Sex Pistol on home soil and his penultimate UK live appearance. Julien Temple was once again on hand to capture everything on film, including Sid and Nancy's failed attempt to have sex atop a *Never Mind the Bollocks* poster spread out on the dressing room floor – S&M sex you understand, mistress and slave, none of your regular porn nonsense: Nancy seemed to think that was beneath them. Sid was clearly revelling in the festive atmosphere, so much so that he even enjoyed a solo spot, performing the two Heartbreakers' songs – 'Born To Lose' and 'Chinese Rocks' – which would later turn up on his one and only solo album, *Sid Sings*. 'I think Sid was the only person who didn't understand that there was no stars in the Sex Pistols,' John Lydon states. 'It wasn't about that. We weren't out for pop crowns. The only person in England who didn't understand. Poor Sid.'

It is a pity that the tabloids, while happy for any opportunity to castigate the Sex Pistols, chose to ignore the group's unsolicited show of generosity, presumably because putting supposedly nasty Punk Rockers in a good light does not make good copy. The British public may indeed have been curious about Punk Rock, but it was only interested when the Punk Rockers were doing outrageous things such as spitting and swearing, and a photograph of the supposedly tough and violent Sid Vicious being smothered in jelly and whipped cream by a bunch of gleeful seven- to ten-year-olds might have at least given the nation the chance to see Sid as he really was, rather than as the alleged girlfriend-murdering monster that would dominate the headlines ten months later.

CHAPTER 7

Anarchy in the USA: Taking Civilization to the Barbarians

America, like the UK, was slipping into economic turmoil at the end of the 1970s. President Jimmy Carter was losing the battle against unemployment and inflation was fast approaching 10%. This depression seemed to form the perfect backdrop for a Punk explosion, but the sheer size of the USA meant that outside the country's major media centres Punk acolytes were confined to small pockets across the land. The majority of the music-buying public were snapping up disco and middle-of-the-road rock albums. The *Saturday Night Fever* soundtrack was 1978's biggest selling album in the USA, following by Meatloaf's *Bat Out of Hell* and Fleetwood Mac's *Rumours*. Any Punk band wanting to tour the States would have been advised to stick to the likes of New York, Boston, Chicago and Los Angeles. Straying far from these cities would only bring out a combination of the curious and the angry.

When Malcolm McLaren decided that the time was right to take the Sex Pistols stateside he knew the paperwork would be a difficult obstacle to overcome. The criminal records of the band were always going to mean lengthy delays over the issuing of any visas. An internal memo from Warner Bros. (the band's US label) written by Alan Rosenberg shows what the label considered it was up against – personnel were briefed as to the band members' previous arrests. John Lydon had one Class B drug fine, Steve Jones a single fine for theft, Paul Cook had a couple of theft misdemeanours with a fine leading to probation, and Sid had a long list including assault of a police officer, criminal damage, attempted auto theft and carrying an offensive weapon. The memo ended with a list of the Pistols' birth dates below which read the typed message: 'I hope none of you try to figure out what signs these geezers were born under because, take it from me, they wuz [sic] all born under a bad sign.'

The US Immigration Department had plenty to pore over and finally acquiesced when Warner Bros. put up a $1 million surety bond. Even with this massive financial endorsement the authorities would only issue fourteen day working visas, which meant that the original itinerary had to be revamped. The nineteen planned shows, which were to have started at Pennsylvania's Leona Theatre on 28 December 1977, were reduced to just seven, and an appearance on the influential *Saturday Night Live* TV show was scrapped.

The Pistols eventually touched down at New York's JFK Airport at 7 p.m. on Tuesday, 3 January 1978, with the opening show scheduled in Atlanta, Georgia just two days later. This was the first time in almost a year that the band travelled without certain members of its support team. Steve 'Roadent' Connolly, Jamie Reid and Steve English were among those left behind – as was Nancy Spungen. English believes to this day that had they all travelled together the group might have lasted a little longer. However, Warner Bros. had its own plans and wanted to safeguard its investment by using a US crew. The in-house tour manager was Noel Monk (who would later go on to manage Van Halen) and a team of burly Vietnam veterans to make sure that none of the Sex Pistols stepped out of line while they were on US soil. They did not trust Glitterbest for one second.

Sid felt compelled to test the elasticity of the restraining leash placed upon him and – having falsely assumed that he was above reproach after getting away with groping a stewardess during the flight from New York to Atlanta – he repeated his lecherous antics with a Warner Bros. female publicist. He soon found out that he had overstepped the line – his actions resulted in a punch from the no-nonsense Monk.

Never Mind the Bollocks had hit the shelves in America a week after its UK release and although it failed to trouble the US Billboard Top 100 chart – stalling at No. 108 – it was rapturously received in both New York and Los Angeles. The US version was issued in a pink and green cover, not the yellow and pink one used everywhere else around the world. John Tiberi claims this was done to irritate Richard Branson, who wanted to keep complete control over every aspect of the album. 'It was simply another exercise in getting up Richard Branson's nose,' he says. 'Malcolm knew it would be imported in bulk, and he knew Virgin stores would have to sell them.'

McLaren had no interest in using the two weeks to preach to the converted and so had the band booked to play across the southern states, travelling from east to west. The opening show was staged at an established country music venue called the Great Southeast Music Hall, which was tucked away within a giant shopping mall located on the outskirts of Atlanta. Media attention surrounding the Sex Pistols' arrival in America meant that the group's reputation had well and truly preceded the band, and teams from the vice squads of both Atlanta and Memphis (where the group were due to play the following night) were interspersed with the 500-strong audience. Hiding themselves wasn't too hard as the group's US audience included everyone from cowboys and bankers to Punks and walking freak-shows. John Lydon looked quite normal in comparison, wearing a blue tartan Vivienne Westwood suit.

As always, whenever finding themselves under intense scrutiny, the Sex Pistols put in a woeful performance – the reason being that all four members of the group were suffering from jet lag, while Rotten was also suffering from a bout of flu. Teenager Peter Buck, a future member of R.E.M., briefly attended the Atlanta show. He managed to get in when a group of youths broke down a door, but he only saw the band play a couple of songs before he was ejected by security for not having a ticket. It was what he called the 'quintessential Punk experience'. Whether he saw Lydon change the words to 'Anarchy in the USA', while standing centre-stage with one clenched fist held above his head next to a bare-chested grinning Sid Vicious, is unknown. Footage of fan interviews after the show indicated the divisions that the band caused wherever they played. 'It was the greatest thing I've ever seen' said one girl. 'They're garbage, man!' snapped one man. 'I like it for me but I don't think I'd recommend it to anybody,' added another girl. 'I heard that they urinated on the audience one time. Why? I just don't know. It just sounds goofy,' added a final southern accent.

As with the pre-Christmas UK shows, the music was no longer the main attraction. The Sex Pistols' larger-than-life reputation guaranteed them an audience wherever they played. The circus was in town, with Rotten the caustic ringmaster and Sid the ever-willing pantomime clown. Vicious was never one to hang around for the post-gig inquests and he disappeared immediately after the Atlanta show with a group of female admirers that had driven the 2,200 miles from Los Angeles. One of these fans was Helen 'Killer' Keller, a spiky-blonde Punkette and super-fan of Sid, who would earn lasting fame for bloodying her idol's nose at the Dallas show five days later. Keller and her friends had lured their idol away from his keepers with promises of a good time – blow jobs, and, more importantly, good drugs. Sid's dependency on heroin by this stage had reached chronic proportions. By the time the group found themselves on US soil, he was already shooting up two or three times a day whenever possible. Now he found himself cut off from his usual suppliers and had Noel Monk on his back with a 'no hard drugs on tour' policy. '[Sid] went AWOL to get a feel for America with a group of fans that were straight out of *Ziggy Stardust*,' Boogie later recounted for Jon Savage's *England's Dreaming*.

It had fallen upon Boogie's shoulders to keep special tabs on Sid but the latter was near-uncontrollable and, with officers from two vice squads waiting in the wings ready to pounce at any given minute, Boogie had sensibly refused. 'Sid had his private life, and it wasn't a case of me looking after him, shaking his willy and putting it away afterwards,' he offered Savage by way of explanation. Although for Sid just having Boogie around was a bonus, unlike a lot of people in the group's inner circle he actually had time for Boogie. When Judy Vermorel told Sid that John Lydon and Paul Cook had referred to Malcolm McLaren as 'the fifth member of the group', Sid saw red. His reply was sharp and to the point. 'I feel he ought to turn up to every gig we do, if he's got any bloody interest in us,' Vicious ranted. 'If he's the fifth member of the group he should be at every fucking gig. Boogie's the fifth member of the band, if anyone. Boogie the fucking sound geezer, Boogie's a laugh. But Malcolm, no way. Boogie's the fifth member of the group. I wouldn't even call him that, but if anybody is it's him.' The task of keeping Sid on the straight and narrow was placed in the hands of Glen Allison, a 6'5", 250-lb ex-Vietnam vet who ran the Atlanta venue and, having lent Monk a willing hand during the show, was subsequently invited to join up for the remainder of the tour.

Upon introduction, Sid had confronted the bearded man-mountain standing before him and somewhat foolishly decided to question Allison's toughness. The bemused Allison obliged by grabbing Sid by the throat and lifting him off the ground as though he was a leather-jacketed broom handle. He proceeded to smack his spiky head against the ceiling several times before letting him drop to the floor. Sid, however, failed to learn his lesson and – after going AWOL for a second time shortly following the group's arrival at the local Holiday Inn – he received a second and more severe beating. Allison and the rest of Monk's team could have been forgiven for thinking that they had witnessed everything under the sun after years of pandering to the whims and excesses of America's most famous rock 'n' roll bands. These boys were seasoned road warriors, but Sid was quite literally 'something else'. While in Memphis, he took a shining to Monk's knife, but rather than test the blade's sharpness on an inanimate object, instead ran it across his arm. This made a deep half-inch gash, which required immediate attention. The gash would later become infected and was bleeding puss before the tour was over.

The tour soon proved to be a logistical nightmare for all concerned. The planning behind the shows seemed to indicate a woeful unfamiliarity with the scale of the distances involved between each venue. The people at Warner Bros. felt that they'd already over-spent on the band and were not interested in losing even more money. The band thus faced the prospect of spending nine days travelling back and forth across six US states in the midst of a gruelling winter on a tour bus with a bunch of surly, Punk-phobic war veterans. This prospect proved to be just too much for Malcolm McLaren to bear, so he and Sophie Richmond abandoned the bus in favour of flying to the next venue. Cook and Jones then decided to follow suit, which did little to improve the rapidly degenerating relationship between themselves and Lydon and Vicious. John had always known that wherever Steve went Paul was sure to follow, which had been the predominant reasoning behind his insistence that his best friend should replace Glen, but the problem facing John now was that Sid's drug-dependency meant that his friend was no longer recognisable to him. The problem now was that the Sex Pistols – a rock 'n' roll band who had managed to function since the previous February as two separate units – now had to face the prospect of being split into three camps.

On Sunday, 8 January 1978, after playing two days earlier in Memphis, the group and its seemingly ever-expanding entourage arrived in the largely blue-collar town of San Antonio, Texas, where the Sex Pistols were booked to play at Randy's Rodeo. The venue had once served as the town's bowling alley and the stage was mounted across where the lanes had once ended. The locals would once again find themselves hurling inanimate objects towards that end of the hall – the only problem being that the four Sex Pistols would be standing in as makeshift skittles.

The entourage now included *High Times* publisher Tom Forcade, who had invited himself onto the tour after being talked into financing a documentary film, *DOA: Dead on Arrival*, about the tour by a small-time director called Lech Kowalski. It had been Kowalski's idea to shoot a professional film of the group's first US tour but, having been given the bum's rush by both McLaren and the record company, he decided upon some guerrilla filming of his own. *Punk* magazine's illustrator John Holmstrom, who was being funded by Forcade, had also joined the tour in Memphis, but Forcade's paranoia that he was being followed by both the CIA and the FBI was so great that Holmstrom was under strict instruction not to let slip that he had any connection with the publisher.

Photographers Bob Gruen, Roberta Bayley and Joe Stevens (who was covering the tour for the *NME*) had all travelled down from New York to capture the Sex Pistols' inaugural US tour for posterity. Stevens, who would later cite the San Antonio concert as one of the greatest rock 'n' roll shows that he ever witnessed, hadn't seen the Sex Pistols with Sid in the line-up and was quick to realise that even though Rotten's flu had dissipated and the front-man was back to his vitriolic best, he was struggling to keep the spotlight from straying stage-right towards Sid. At Randy's Rodeo the 2,200-strong predominantly Mexican audience, although hostile throughout, could not help but be captivated by Sid's goofy on-stage antics, which included self-mutilation and using his bass to pole-axe some unfortunate bystander.

'That was totally insane,' remembers Roberta Bayley, who had cut her teeth photographing The Ramones, Blondie, New York Dolls and the other New York bands at CBGBs. 'All these rednecks were throwing bottles at the band and so when Sid hit the guy over the head with his bass guitar you definitely felt there was going to be a riot. The audience was made up of macho Mexicans who had come along to check out Punk Rock. I thought the Sex Pistols were absolutely amazing that night, but I wasn't getting up close, not even to take photos. No, sir, it was just too frightening.'

The third member of the New York picture posse, Bob Gruen, was an acquaintance of Nancy's through his involvement with the New York Dolls, and was therefore of special interest to Sid, who would while away the hours grilling the photographer about Nancy's time in New York. Gruen's recollections of Nancy's salad days in the Big Apple were not the only thing of interest to Sid as he had taken a shine to the photographer's heavy-duty black motorcycle boots (known in the USA as engineer's boots), because they were identical to the ones worn by his hero Johnny Thunders. Late one evening while Gruen was grabbing a few hours' sleep on one of the couches at the front of the tour bus, Sid 'borrowed' the boots and, after walking up and down the aisle several times in them to satisfy himself that they were a good fit, advanced upon the comatose Gruen and pressed a knife to the American's throat. 'If I kill him, can I keep the boots?' he furtively inquired of Rotten and Joe Stevens who were both still awake and watching on in bemused fascination. Taking the ensuing silence as a sign of their acquiescence, he pocketed the knife and returned to his own bunk, still wearing the purloined boots. Although Gruen's life was never actually in danger, he had unknowingly kissed goodbye to his boots forever.

Two days later the Sex Pistols arrived in Dallas where they were scheduled to perform at the Longhorn Ballroom, which in a previous incarnation had been the Carousel Club – owned by Mob associate and Lee Harvey Oswald's killer, Jack Ruby. For the second time in three days, the Sex Pistols were treated to a little Southern hospitality with the hostile audience constantly goading the group while pelting the stage with any missile that came to hand. A pig's snout among other things found its way onto the stage. Needless to say, the group's performance suffered as a result of their having to play dodge-ball with the projectiles. High above the stage were large head-and-shoulder portraits of country music greats that had played the venue. As their images looked down at the stage filled with British Punks, what must the lingering ghosts of Johnny Cash, Dolly Parton and friends have thought?

By now Sid's need to score was so great that even downing two bottles of peppermint schnapps a day was failing to subdue his constant cravings. He was in the grip of the sweats – alternately hot, then cold; needing to stand up, sit still, lie down, walk if off. Nothing was right. He would have probably sold his mother for a wrap of brown sugar, but with Monk's crew keeping him under twenty-four-hour surveillance and knowing that the rest of the group would veto his request to perform a solo rendition of 'Chinese Rocks' as he had done in Huddersfield on Christmas Day, he would have to find other ways of getting his message across. That evening he took to the Longhorn stage with the plea 'Gimme a fix' scrawled across his chest in black marker pen. The fans had never seen anything like this before, although for Sid it wasn't a first. He'd taken to doing it on occasion since the group had toured Sweden.

The words 'moderation' and 'restraint' never featured in the Sid Vicious lexicon. Although the 'live fast, die young, and leave a good-looking corpse' credo was as old and careworn as rock 'n' roll music itself, it was as though Sid was on a one-man mission to become rock's uber-martyr. He would attempt to out-Glam David Bowie, out-loon Keith Moon, and out-Stone Keith Richards, before taking his place beside Iggy in the rock 'n' roll mortuary. When he laid out his master plan to Roberta Bayley, the photographer thought it prudent to point out to him that Iggy was still very much alive and fast-approaching his thirtieth birthday, but Sid elected to airbrush this glaring anomaly from what was an otherwise glorious suicide scenario.

It was in Dallas that Sid was reacquainted with Helen Keller who – having once again driven from Los Angeles with the express intent of livening up the proceedings – head-butted her idol on the nose. Rather than make any attempt to stem the blood that was now gushing from his nose, Sid allowed the blood to flow free and smeared it across his face and chest as though he was undergoing some ancient tribal ritual. 'Sid just reeled back,' says Bob Gruen. 'He had all this blood pouring out of his nose and had the biggest smile on his face. He thought it was so hilarious.' A few days later Sid told listeners to Radio K-SAN about the incident. 'I got a full beer can right in the face, like this, smash, right in the face, and it cut my lip open,' he spouted. 'I'm illiterate and I don't know what you're talking about.'

The blood-letting had not satiated Sid's appetite for self-destruction, for he proceeded to smash a beer bottle against his amp and then set about slashing his concave chest. This circus of horrors was cut short by Monk, who bounded onto the stage and knocked the bottle from Sid's hand before admonishing the errant Sex Pistol over his foolishness. Sid just shrugged his shoulders and leapt into his 'Dee Dee meets Johnny Thunders' stance. But when he hit the strings of his bass, nothing happened. It seems that when he had broken the bottle he had also accidentally hit the amp's on/off switch.

Bob Gruen was witness to another of Sid's self-mutilation parties, which occurred at a nondescript truck stop while the bus was on its way to Tulsa, the tour's penultimate stop. 'It was around 3 a.m. when we pulled into this truck stop,' remembers Gruen. 'Everyone else was asleep, so I suggested that me and Sid should get off and grab a burger and cup of coffee. The place was all but deserted except for some cowboy and his wife and kid. I don't know whether they had been to the Dallas show but the cowboy recognised Sid and invited us to join them. The guy was definitely looking to impress his kid and says, 'Sid Vicious, huh? If you're so tough, can you do this?' And the guy stubbed his cigarette butt out in the palm of his hand. Sid glanced up from his plate of steak and eggs, nodded, and then took out his knife and sliced his hand open. The blood was running down Sid's hand and onto the plate and he just carried on eating. The cowboy grabbed up his wife and kid and fled.'

The next stop on what now looked very much like the first and last Sex Pistols tour of America, was Thursday, 12 January 1978 at Cain's Ballroom in Tulsa, Oklahoma. In the dressing room before the show, one of the crew was showing Sid a pair of knuckle-dusters he'd been carrying with him on the off-chance. Sid took the knuckle-dusters, placed them on his hand and smashed a hole in the door. While a lot of venues might have called the police at this point, the management at Cain's simply removed the piece of wood from the middle of the door – it's now framed in the manager's office – and boarded up the other side. Fast forward some twenty-nine years and the venue will now happily sell you a T-shirt bearing a photo of Sid's handy work, along with the sort of advertising by-line that money simply can't buy – 'Cain's Ballroom: not just another hole in the wall.'

Perhaps the most bizarre on-the-road tale featuring Sid occurred immediately after the Tulsa show, which – being in the heart of America's mid-western 'Bible Belt' – had been picketed by the God-fearing local populace. Sid had been making his way off-stage when he'd spotted a tall blonde standing out in the audience, and although he had promised Nancy that he would be faithful, he was missing the female touch. This again high-lights the contradictions in Sid's personality – he missed Nancy so much that he was on the look-out for a one-night stand. Sid instructed Monk to send the girl up to his room, where he subsequently discovered that the 'girl' in question was actually a guy who was still in mid-process of having bits added and others taken away. 'I didn't know whether to suck her cock or her cunt,' he informed Monk the following morning. Sid's sexual exploits had not ended there. Later that same night, Monk had come across Sid receiving a blow job from a girl who was on her knees in front of the Sex Pistol while the girl's boyfriend stood by, casually watching. The girl was a huge fan of the group and the boyfriend had asked Sid to 'give his girl something to remember him by', whereby Sid duly obliged by voiding his bowels over the unfortunate girl. Well, she wasn't going to forget that one in a hurry, was she?

By the time the Sex Pistols' weary wagon rolled into America's hippy capital, San Francisco, on Friday, 13 January 1978, there was precious little love to be found within the divided camp, and the fragile peace was but a matter of hours away from a terminal implosion. Later that afternoon, after a visit to a local sex shop where they purchased several leather garments and studded accoutrements, Sid and John participated in a radio interview with K-SAN FM's resident DJ, Bonnie Simmons. Each was presented with brand-new leather motor-cycle jackets. If Simmons and the station's bosses had been hoping for a repeat of the no-holds-barred interview from the previous evening – in which a slightly intoxicated Steve Jones and Paul Cook had called upon good old English humour and sexual innuendo to bamboozle the show's listeners during a Q&A session – they were going to be disappointed. John appeared subdued and informed the startled Simmons that he didn't like Rock music and didn't know why he was in it. Sid did offer some insight into the Punk act of 'gobbing' and the now famous pogo dance. 'If they wanna gob they can gob – we don't mind it,' he said. 'Just as long as they don't mind being gobbed back at. People have been calling us Punks since we were about fifteen. We haven't jumped on any bandwagon. Pogo-ing started 'cos when I first saw the Pistols I couldn't dance and the only thing I could think of was leaping up and down, and I used to do it really good – it was a great dance, the way I used to do it and the way John used to do it. These arseholes that do it now, they're just pathetic, and I walk into clubs and I see these people and it's just disgusting.' He also talked about the problems that the band had had to face. 'Most of our records are banned because we're telling the truth,' he said. 'For a year we've been banned everywhere because we're saying things that the straight cops and grown-ups . . . that's unacceptable to them – they can't take anarchy, they want everything ordered so that life is nice and safe, and they're closet cases. They haven't ever been out of their closet since the day they were born.'

The following evening's show at the 5,000-capacity Winterland Ballroom had sold out in a single day and would be the largest audience that the group had faced to date, but back in the UK, however, it would seem that the tide was beginning to turn and the group's popularity was on the wane, because that same day the *Record Mirror* published its 1977 end-of-year readers' poll, which listed the Sex Pistols as being fourth best group and only seventh best in the 'Best New Wave Artist/ Group' category. They were also voted 'Bore of the Year'.

The Winterland Ballroom was a large tubular barn run by the legendary West Coast promoter and entrepreneur Bill Graham, who had a total monopoly on the city's live music scene. Graham, who was killed in a helicopter crash in 1991, was unmoved by Punk Rock and took an instant dislike to Malcolm McLaren after learning about his intention of turning the sell-out show into an 'open stage' by inviting local groups to turn up and play for free. Perhaps not surprisingly, given Graham's standing in the Bay Area, Malcolm's scheme came to nothing. At the soundcheck they made some effort to run through two new Rotten-penned numbers 'Religion' and 'Public Image', both would surface later in 1978 via Rotten's new group Public Image Limited. The doors opened at 5 p.m. and local Punk groups The

Nuns and The Avengers put in sets before the already pumped-up audience were given a taster of what was to come with a screening of the *Sex Pistols No. 1* film.

The Sex Pistols took to the stage at midnight, which had been pre-planned to coincide with a live simultaneous broadcast on K-SAN FM. The atmosphere inside the venue had reached fever-pitch, but by this point it was obvious to everyone involved that the Sex Pistols' *Gotterdammerung* was fast approaching. As had been in the case at earlier shows on the tour, the band was faced with an inadequate PA system, which rendered John's lyrics almost indecipherable. Lydon, like Steve and Paul, was merely going through the motions – judging by the trio's collective body language they looked as though they were wishing themselves anywhere else but there. Sid, although there in body, was in another mental dimension completely. The reason for this was that upon their arrival in San Francisco, Monk and his team, who had succeeded in keeping Sid away from heroin, considered their babysitting duties to be at an end and had allowed him to wander off freely and score some drugs.

The Sex Pistols ended the set as they had done on numerous occasions with their own version of the Stooges' 'No Fun', but never before had Iggy's lyrics proved so resonant than that night at Winterland as no one on-stage, especially John, was having any fun at all. He brought the shambolic proceedings to a close by famously inquiring of the audience, 'Ever get the feeling you've been cheated?' Later, Rotten would confess that his question had not been solely aimed at the audience but also at himself and his fellow Sex Pistols, with the possible exception of Sid. He believed that they *had* been cheated – cheated by Malcolm, who had created a myth surrounding the Sex Pistols so that they believed they were banned from playing in the UK, and who had also, allegedly, been cheating them out of their rightful earnings.

'In America,' Steve told Jon Savage for *England's Dreaming*, 'what fucked it up was that they treated us like rock stars. They don't know any different. They treat anyone who comes over from England the same way. At Winterland, I had a cold; Sid wasn't playing a note and wasn't even plugged in half the time.'

The atmosphere backstage after the gig was more akin to that of a wake than a celebratory party at the conclusion of what had been a relatively successful tour, with only Sid choosing to play at being a Sex Pistol for the gathered Warner Bros. hierarchy. Once again Helen Keller and her L.A. Punkette coterie were in attendance and having managed to find their way backstage they immediately surrounded their wayward hero. John Holmstrom, along with his *Punk* partner-in-crime, Eddie 'Legs' McNeil, was also in attendance and was feeling incredibly underwhelmed at the Sex Pistols' lethargic performance, with Legs going so far as to cite the Winterland show as the worst rock 'n' roll show that he'd ever seen. He had also gone backstage after the show hoping to gather a few choice sound-bites from Sid for the magazine but left empty-handed because Sid only had eyes for his female fan club. 'Which one of you is going to fuck me?' Legs heard him inquire of Keller and her crew. The *Punk* pioneer didn't stay backstage long enough to see whether any of the girls actually took up Sid on his offer, but he'd been around enough junkies to know that Sid's penis would probably be as lifeless as his bass playing.

Sid told Rosaline Russell during the *Record Mirror* interview that after the Winterland show he had returned to Haight Ashbury with Keller and her friends to score some more heroin, and that he had still been there when Malcolm McLaren had arrived early the following morning to take him to the airport. The manager had hastily arranged a trip down to Rio de Janeiro where he'd had the idea that the group would play a show and meet up with the fugitive Great Train Robber Ronnie Biggs. It was planned that he would read his own poetry as the support act. Biggs had been sunning himself on Copacabana Beach since fleeing Australia, where he had set up home under an assumed name after escaping from Wandsworth Prison in 1964.

McLaren, possibly with the proposed Sex Pistols film in mind and knowing that Warner Bros. was contracted to provide the Sex Pistols with plane tickets to the destination of their choice, had arranged the jaunt to Rio as a means of replacing a cancelled show in Finland. The group had been scheduled to play Helsinki's Worker's Hall on the 18th before then flying onto Stockholm for a show in the Swedish capital on the 19th before then returning to the UK. 'A friend of mine worked on the *Daily Express*,' remembered Boogie. 'So once the Swedish thing fell through, he had a contact number for Biggs, and we thought it would help the film anyway, given that Warner Bros. hadn't fulfilled their contract until they flew us to a destination of our choice.'

The following morning's 7 a.m. Pan-Am flight from San Francisco to Rio de Janeiro departed on time, but of the four Sex Pistols, only Steve and Paul had made it to the airport. Sid was out of his gourd in Haight Ashbury, while Rotten had purposely chosen to defy Malcolm in the knowledge that his doing so would bring matters to a head. Although Rotten was willing to carry on with the group, albeit with a new bass player, there was also no way that he would continue to work with Malcolm. The singer's bargaining power was seriously reduced in that Malcolm was still controlling the band's finances, and Steve and Paul had come too far to switch allegiances now. The Sex Pistols were finished.

❦　❦　❦

Sid's explanation for missing the Rio flight is bizarre to say the least. He told Rosaline Russell that he had gone off with McLaren and that during the car ride to the airport he had voiced his disinterest in flying down to Rio to play to a bunch of 'Pakis' that didn't understand the group and therefore would have no idea what they were about. He also claimed that he'd lambasted Rotten over his shoddy stage performances and that

McLaren had agreed with every word and had told Sid that Rotten had turned into Robert Plant and was letting down the group. Sid then claimed to have ordered Malcolm to take him back to Haight Ashbury, where he'd spent a couple of hours mulling things over before telephoning Rotten to inform his one-time best friend that he was 'useless' and a 'failure'.

'When I first heard about Sid Vicious he was just one member of a great band,' remembers Eileen Polk. 'In 1977 there was only one place in New York City where you could buy British Punk singles hot off the presses and that was Bleecker Bob's record shop. You had to find out in advance when a shipment was expected and arrive early, like 10 a.m., because they would sell out immediately. During this time most of the American music press was still touting the superstardom of dinosaur rock acts such as Kiss, Queen, Rod Stewart and the Rolling Stones. The New York Punks had stopped going to rock shows because they were overpriced, and all the good seats were reserved for music industry insiders and mainstream press. We had to be satisfied with the gossipy *Rock Scene*, or if you could find them, British journals such as the *New Musical Express* for any information on British Punk. At the time, it was rumoured that the Sex Pistols weren't even playing on their records. Some people said that it was really Jimmy Page or Chris Spedding who laid down the Sex Pistols' tracks in the studio and that the band couldn't play at all. But we didn't care who was playing, whether they could play or not, or how cute they were, because they made great records. So nobody knew much about Sid or why he replaced Glen Matlock. The "face" of the Sex Pistols was Johnny Rotten, with his dumpster dive clothes held together with sharp implements. The best article of the year was the *Rolling Stone* cover story "Punk is sick and living in London" by Charles M. Young. I read that in October of 1977 and chopped all my hair off the next day. As soon as British Punk was publicised in the US, the British press began saying "It's over, Punk is dead, becoming commercial, losing its edge." We had been going to Punk gigs in New York since 1975, but it didn't become a fashion thing until the Sex Pistols. The driving beat and feeling of getting ploughed by a locomotive had originated with the Ramones, but the Sex Pistols gave Punk its look and political edginess. So at that time Sid was just one of the members of a great band. Sid's wisecracks about being a "sexless monster" and his general self-destructiveness added to his mystique, but we really didn't know much about him. When the Pistols finally came to America everyone was disappointed that they only played gigs in the south, because unfortunately this meant that just as it was before in the stadium rock scene, only people with money or connections could afford to travel to see the band. Malcolm made the same mistake with the Pistols that he had with the New York Dolls – dragging them through the south, when all their real fans were in the industrial north. They may have sold Punk records in Atlanta, but not in Texas. Even the L.A. scene was way behind New York. If you want to see just how embryonic it was, watch Cheech and Chong's *Up in Smoke*.'

❋   ❋   ❋

Sid's story to Russell turned out to be fictitious. In fact it was Boogie and Steve Jones, not Malcolm, who arrived at the Haight Ashbury shooting gallery in response to one of Keller's distraught friends having called the MiYako to inform anyone willing to listen that Sid had overdosed. 'He was lying on a grubby mattress in the corner of the room turning blue when we arrived,' says Boogie. 'He was pretty lifeless but I picked him up and began walking him around the room until he came round. We then drove him to Marin County to see an alternative doctor who gave him acupuncture and a bed for the night.' Sometime the next morning, Sophie collected a revitalised Sid from the doctors and drove him to Los Angeles where the pair spent the next twenty-four hours together before Boogie arrived the following morning to take Sid back to London. 'I don't want to be a junkie for the rest of my life,' Sid would confess to Julien Temple. 'I don't want to be a junkie at all.'

The first task, however, was to get Sid to another doctor who would be willing to supply him with Methadone in order to get him through the next couple of days. Having secured the Methadone tablets, Boogie then booked himself and Sid on the next available flight to New York, during which Sid managed to pull a fast one on Boogie by slipping a few valium tablets that he'd put aside for a rainy day and overdosed for the second time within as many days, lapsing into a drug-induced coma. His condition was so poor that upon arrival at JFK he was immediately rushed to the nearby Jamaica Hospital, where he was placed under observation. Unfortunately for Sid, a raging blizzard descended upon the Big Apple, which brought traffic in and around the city to a complete standstill.

'The overdose was an accident,' Sid told Rosaline Russell. 'I'd drunk too much and I'd got some Methadone from a doctor there. It was stronger than the stuff you get in London. I was only supposed to take a bit, but I took it all. I was tired and I went to sleep and then I woke up two days later in the hospital.'

Sid was alone in a strange hospital, with a drip-feed attached to his arm. Although Rotten was also stranded in the city, Sid's fellow Sex Pistol made no attempt whatsoever to contact him. The only contact Sid did receive from the outside world was a phone call from Roberta Bayley on the evening of 20 January 1978 during which Sid bemoaned his enforced isolation, chastised Boogie for returning to London with his prized Marvel comics, admitted to taking the valium during the flight to New York, and pondered the possibility of getting himself clean so that he could put a group together with Johnny Thunders back in the UK. Bayley, although having seen all but one of the US shows and therefore au fait with Sid's musical prowess, was happy to fuel the fantasy by telling Sid that he was a better bass player than Billy Rath of the Heartbreakers and even made light of Thunders' own drug problems by pondering how the guitarist somehow managed to remain in pretty good health despite his questionable habits. Sid responded by informing Bayley that the difference between his own health problems to those of Thunders' was that the American had never contracted Hepatitis. He went on to explain that when he'd got out of hospital after recovering from the disease he'd set out on a mission to 'fuck himself up as badly as possible'. He hadn't known why other than it was his basic nature. Bayley tried to inject a little seriousness into the conversation by warning Sid that his basic nature was likely to get him into trouble. 'My basic nature is going to kill me in six months,' was Sid's earnest reply.

CHAPTER 8

Regrets, I've Had a Few . . .

'They sanctified Sid, till he puked up his life, a prick for an idol, what a very strange sight, now everyone wants to touch the golden boy.'

(From 'Golden Boy' by The Stranglers)

When Sid Vicious was finally returned to the UK it was a case of 'out of the frying pan, into the fire'. London meant a return to Nancy where the pair shut themselves away within their Pindock Mews love nest. Here they became hopelessly mired in a heroin tailspin from which neither would fully emerge. 'I rang them one Sunday,' said Anne Beverley. 'I said to Nancy, "I'll come over and cook you both a nice Sunday lunch. We can get together and make a day of it." Nancy responded by saying that it was a really great idea but that she and Simon were still in bed and could they call me back later. That was the last I heard from them until around 10 p.m. that evening when Simon called me wanting to borrow £20 because he needed to buy food for Sunday lunch.'

DOA director Lech Kowalski arrived at Pindock Mews during the early spring with a film crew looking to conduct an in-depth interview with Sid for his work-in-progress, but if Kowalski was hoping to gain a telling insight into the day-to-day life of an ex-Sex Pistol then he was to be left sorely disappointed. Nancy demanded extra cash from the bemused director before allowing him access to Sid and she was the one doing most of the talking. The footage he did manage to obtain shows the couple lounging on their bed. Sid, wearing sunglasses, is barely conscious and on the rare occasions that he does manage to string a few mumbled words together he nods-off in mid-sentence, clutching a scotch and coke like his life depended on it. Nancy, in-between completing her lethargic lover's sentences, fusses over Sid as though he was a semi-retarded child; lighting his cigarettes and bringing him a 'cup of cwoffee', which he subsequently spilt over her and the bed sheets (which were black so as to match the walls, ceiling and carpet of the flat's master bedroom). 'We're partners in crime, we help each other out,' she informed Kowalski. She then stripped off her coffee-soaked top and exposed her breasts, perhaps thinking that this might somehow make amends for the non-interview. The couple later signed a release form, although their signatures barely resemble either of their autographs from little more than a year before.

The Sex Pistols were over, but Malcolm McLaren still talked about them as though they were a going concern to aid his next project. With Julien Temple he'd started work on his long-held aim of a rock 'n' roll film. By keeping the Pistols' name at the forefront of things he was managing to get some financial backing from Virgin for the project, which was called *The Great Rock 'n' Roll Swindle*. As part of this project, Temple invited Sid to Hyde Park for a filmed interview. Sid was certainly more animated than he had been for Kowalski, but he was still a physical wreck. Set against the gloriously sunny London day, Sid's pallor was akin to that of a dead carp and when he removed his leather jacket he revealed skinny alabaster arms, which were scarred with the tell-tale marks of the long-term intravenous drug user. His gaunt face was a battle zone with a fresh blood-smeared cut on his left cheek and his right eye was all but closed after a recent one-sided encounter with an off-duty US marine. The boy who couldn't fight still believed he was Superman after enough drinks. 'Rules were meant to be broken, right?' Sid told the camera. 'When there are no more rules or categorisations, when there are no more niggers or whites, when there are just people, when there's no more Punks, when there's no more dirt, that's when things are gonna be OK.' Vicious unceremoniously plonked himself into a rented deckchair, oblivious to the disbelieving stares that his dirty swastika T-shirt was attracting from passers-by. He went on to provide a chilling insight into what it was like to suffer the agonies of heroin withdrawal. 'You can't get comfortable and you sweat,' he told Temple. 'You're boiling hot and you pour with sweat, and your nose dribbles and all of a sudden you get the colds and the sweat turns to fucking ice on you. So you put a jumper on but then you're boiling hot again and you take it off and then you get cold again. You just can't win. You lie down, and then you sit up. It drives you insane.' The monologue was offered with such heartfelt conviction that it seemed as though he was hoping that by confessing his sins he might one day be granted absolution, or at least a temporary release from his living hell.

'Sid just fell into the rebel role,' Nils Stevenson said. 'I mean lots of kids go through a phase where they say they're not going to live past a certain age but most of them are still around, married with kids of their own and working a regular nine-to-five job because they got past the point of rebellion. They recognise that the red light spells danger and pull back, but for Sid there was no red light, it was green for go all the way. He bought the whole "live fast, die young" ethos and in the end he ended up destroying himself because he thought that was what people expected of him.'

The lifestyle was also having serious effects on Nancy's health. In June 1978 she was admitted to hospital with an infection in her fallopian tubes. She was also having trouble with her kidneys and was in a great deal of pain but was refusing to see a doctor. During the *Record Mirror* interview with an increasingly concerned Rosalind Russell, Nancy, in-between visits to the bathroom, explained that she had damaged her kidneys in a car accident. She also said that the police had confiscated her pills during the fracas at the Ambassador Hotel and had not returned them despite their being prescribed medication. Only the second claim was true.

       ❂   ❂   ❂

Although Steve, Paul and even John would all come to realise that the sum of the Sex Pistols was far greater than its individual parts, Sid was harbouring no such thoughts, largely because in his fragile mental state he still saw the band as a viable entity. Even as late as May 1978 Sid arrived at the door of one-time SEX employee Alan Jones with a birthday card which read 'From the Sex Pistols'. Sid also thought he could have a continued life in the music industry as he was serious about putting a group together with his idol Johnny Thunders. The dream became a brief reality one night in April at the Speakeasy when Sid was invited to sit in on Thunders' latest project, the aptly named 'Living Dead'.

Only Ones' front-man, Peter Perrett, was invited to jam with the impromptu combo and later informed Thunders' biographer Nina Antonia that for the soundcheck they had rehearsed a cover of The Monkees' classic 'Stepping Stone'. The song had also been a staple feature in the Matlock-era Sex Pistols reper-toire, but had been forced to a stop on several occasions because Sid's playing had been so inept. 'Stepping Stone' was in the key of 'E' but Sid apparently didn't know, or couldn't remember, which string was which on his guitar and so Perrett was forced to come to his rescue by moving his fingers to the prerequisite frets. Thunders wasn't feeling quite so charitable as he himself was a junkie but could still function on stage. Perrett, knowing that Sid would be devastated if he lost the gig, stepped in at the eleventh hour. He suggested a compromise whereby Sid could join the group on stage but with his amp switched off. To add insult to injury, Thunders insisted that a topless Nancy should introduce the group onto the stage. Whether Thunders was gaining revenge on Nancy over some long-harboured slight or just attempting to titillate the audience isn't known, but Perrett believes that Sid was really hurt, which is perhaps ironic given that Nancy's breasts had already been viewed by so many people. If Sid was unhappy at having his girlfriend's body on gratuitous display then his humiliation was complete upon realising, several songs into the set, that his amplifier wasn't switched on. When he called upon a roadie to rectify the problem, an anxious Thunders rushed across to the microphone and thanked Sid for his efforts, leaving the latter crestfallen as he slinked off the stage.

While Sid was happy to inform any reporter who would listen that he was going to form a group with Johnny Thunders and Dee Dee Ramone (although the latter never seems to have been privy to this), there was another, bigger problem with his plan. Thunders had informed a friend one night prior to a visit to the Speakeasy not to tell Sid where they were going because Sid and Nancy were just too much to handle. While a lot of this problem could reasonably be seen as Nancy's fault, if a piece of junkie low-life on the level of Johnny Thunders was going out of his way to ignore Sid, where did that put him on the ladder of social standing?

      ✻   ✻   ✻

Sid still had some support – McLaren was holding on to the idea that he might be able to replace Rotten as the Pistols' lead singer. With this in mind he managed to coerce Sid out of his bolthole and accompany himself, Julian Temple and Boogie to

Paris in order to shoot some footage for the *Swindle* film. 'He was very difficult to get to do things, but he used to say "if you plug me in I can do anything". But the problem was plugging him in,' says Julien Temple. 'Especially with his girlfriend being around in Paris. It was unfortunate in Paris because for some reason we chose to film in a Jewish ghetto, which was a very picturesque area, but he insisted on the swastika emblem on his T-shirt, which was fair enough but it caused horrendous problems on the streets. We had old ladies coming up in tears, on the cameraman's shoulder saying, "Why are you involved with this?" and Sid would be having a go at people who were looking at him. The cameraman would say, "I've worked in Vietnam and the Congo but it was nothing. Sid Vicious is the worst I've ever come across."

'The idea originally was to go and record, "Je Ne Regrette Rien", which he completely dismissed as a joke. Strangely there was this record executive from the French record company Barclay Records called Jean Fernandez, who was an old resist-ance fighter who used to sit outside the studio, tuning in his radio to the old resistance connections that he still had, and exchanged very surreal messages with them. He came up with the idea of "My Way", because the record label owned the rights to the Claude Francois song "Comme D'habitude", which is "My Way". Again Sid dismissed it out of hand. 'Malcolm was insistent that he did it though, and we spent probably a month in the studio in Paris with him, basically going in every night and listening to him trying to learn Ramones riffs really and nothing much else. We flew Steve Jones over to try and get him more interested. I changed the lyrics with him as he wouldn't sing the lyrics as written. In the end he started getting interested in changing things to "I ducked the blows", rather than "I took the blows". He just he wanted to do it like the Ramones, but we tried to convince him to do the opening bit like Sinatra and then kick in to the Ramones bit, which in the end is how it happened.' The new lyric 'For what is a prat when he wears hats?' was aimed squarely at Johnny Rotten and his huge hat collection.

The first session, according to Phil Singleton's God Save the Sex Pistols website, and backed up by testimony from Malcolm, Julien and Boogie was booked at Studio des Dames on the Rue de Stockholm towards the end of March and in early April. Much to Malcolm's chagrin the session had to be abandoned on account of Sid's refusal to work with the hired session musicians. A second attempt was booked for the evening of Friday, 7 April 1978 at Studio Aquarium, which was situated on the Rue Lecourbe, but once again the scheduled session had to be abandoned when Sid failed to arrive. With both time and money, not to mention Malcolm's patience, swiftly running out a third session was booked for Monday, 10 April at Studio de la Grand Armee in Porte Maillot.

Resident guitarist Claude Engel, who had been present at both of the previous studios, was forced to take a back seat when Steve Jones arrived, but if Engel thought Steve's presence would result in a productive session then, according to Boogie, he was sorely mistaken. Finding themselves reunited, Sid and Steve spent several hours of expensive recording time getting drunk, which, perhaps not surprisingly, resulted in yet another cancellation. The session was postponed until the following afternoon. 'He was worse than I'd seen him before. It was very depressing, the decline of Sid – he was a shell physically of himself at the end, as a result of smack,' remembers Julien Temple. 'It was depressing, he had said he was going to die before he was twenty-one and everyone laughed about it at the time, but it became increasingly clear towards the end that that was on the cards.' Even then, neither Sid nor Steve appeared any more willing to co-operate with Engel, with Sid being particularly obstinate by refusing to work with 'fucking froggies'. The French people in question, apart from Engel, were bassist Sauveur Mallia and drummer Andre Dehan and although Sid and Steve were trying their damnedest to ensure that yet another session would have to be cancelled so that they could resume with their drinking, Engel took the bit by the teeth and pressed on without them. The three French musicians succeeded in laying down the backing track within two hours, but yet again Sid was proving difficult and unwilling to listen to Engel's suggestions and so another two hours were wasted before the vocals were finally captured on tape.

With the session finally at an end, the studio's resident engineer, Manu Guyot, made just one solitary copy of the rough mix before then sending the twenty-four-track recording to Virgin's head office in London, where Steve Jones was brought in to add his signature chugging guitar sound and the Penguin Cafe Orchestra's Simon Jeffes added the strings overture. 'They didn't actually inform me until much later,' Jeffes told *Record Mirror*, 'that I was playing for Sid Vicious. The session was all very top secret.' The resulting footage of a tuxedo-clad, emaciated Sid sneering and snarling his way through Paul Anka's classic became not just one of the highlights of the finished film, but also one of Punk's most defining images.

Sid was also filmed wandering through the Jewish quarter where he purchases the gun which he would whip out at the end of the 'My Way' video and shoot his stand-in mother as well as several supposedly prominent members of Parisian society, assaulting a prostitute with a slice of strawberry gateau and brandishing a knife at any unsuspecting Parisian foolish enough to stray into his path. 'The other funny thing was shooting the video because we shot it at the Olympia Music Hall in Paris, which is a very famous, mythic place in Paris,' recalls Julien Temple. 'But they were shooting a variety TV show there and had a lit-up staircase just sitting there for this variety show, so I had the idea of him coming down that staircase as it was there. They gave us an hour at lunchtime between recording the acts for this variety show to shoot Sid singing 'My Way', and you know, it was a succession of really French *chanson*-type variety acts, ending just before lunch with Serge Gainsbourg, who sang a song about following a train girl on the Metro, changing trains and following her, and as she changed trains he would follow her. And I remember he had a walking stick as he'd hurt his leg, and he came down the staircase singing that. Then they broke for lunch and Sid appeared, and I remember Gainsbourg just flipping out – he'd never seen anything like this as Sid came down, he was just hypnotised.'

'Malcolm rang me one night,' recalled Anne Beverley. 'He said that he wanted Simon to shoot me in the film. I told him that he could go and fuck himself. They used someone else in the end, an actress that didn't look like me at all, but because no one had seen me, they all believed that it was me. Years later at Virgin Records, someone said, "You've changed a bit since the film." I said, "I was never in the bloody film!"'

It was quickly becoming impossible to even get Sid to agree to disagree and Julien Temple, who was normally one of Sid's staunchest supporters, would later admit that he was extremely difficult to work with during the Paris trip. By his own admission the Sid that arrived in Paris was not in great shape. 'I'm on Methadone at the moment though,' he said. 'Eventually I'll come down off the Methadone, like, weekly they bring you down five milligrams. I'm on 100 milligrams a day, which is the maximum you can take, 'cos I've got a three quarter of a gram habit. I do that in one shot.'

Malcolm's decision to allow Nancy on the Paris trip would come back to haunt him. She'd spent the weeks leading up to the trip cajoling Sid into letting her become his manager and as soon as they arrived at the Hotel Brighton on the Rue de Rivoli (not the Charles 5th which Malcolm happily informed all the press they were staying at: 'Well he would do,' says Boogie with a grin, 'cos that's a good story, never let truth come in the way of a good story'), she set her plan into action. She told Sid to refuse to do any filming unless Malcolm agreed to sign a piece of paper relinquishing his rights to act as his manager. Not surprisingly, this made for unhappy bedfellows and matters finally came to a head during a heated telephone conversation when Malcolm informed Sid that he was 'just another fucked-up junkie with no future'. While Malcolm was busy berating Sid, unbeknownst to him Sid had handed the phone to Nancy and was bounding his way up to Malcolm's room on the next floor dressed in nothing more than his biker boots and a pair of grubby swastika underpants, and having kicked in the door leapt upon a startled Malcolm and proceeded to pummel him into submission.

❧   ❧   ❧

On 30 June 1978, Virgin Records issued the first post-Rotten Sex Pistols single, a double 'A'-side featuring the Cook/Jones collaboration 'No One is Innocent' (also referred to as 'The Biggest Blow' in its 12" edition) with Ronnie Biggs on vocals, along with Sid's rendition of 'My Way'. If McLaren had been anxious about the Sex Pistols' popularity following Rotten's departure then he need not have worried – the single shot up the charts, reaching No. 7 and equalling the highest placing of 'Pretty Vacant'. This was especially impressive as 'No One is Innocent' received no radio airplay or TV exposure due to Biggs' involvement. The powers that be at Virgin hadn't failed to notice that it was Sid who was picking up all the airplay.

By early August Temple had filmed and recorded Sid's versions of Eddie Cochrane's 'C'mon Everybody' and 'Something Else'. The first of these showed Sid riding a motorbike from central London to the countryside – no helmet, all attitude and sneers – but the bike for close-up scenes was mounted on a flat bed wagon so he could be as brave as need be, and the long shots down winding country lanes were filmed with a mixture of Sid and a stand-in.

The promo clip for 'Something Else' was filmed at Boogie's flat, showing Sid in his underpants tipping bottles of beer around the place and singing to himself in a full-length mirror.

Sid fulfilled his final obligations as a Sex Pistol by recording two more scenes for the film. One of these was an unused Jubilee kiosk scene, a ramshackle piece of filming at best, in which a clearly drug-blotted Sid hands out free 'God Save the Queen' memorabilia to a bunch of Punks, before he begins abusing them. The second was the audition scene, which was filmed at the Duchess Theatre in the heart of London's West End. Here, a host of young hopefuls, including the obvious winner Eddie 'Tenpole' Tudor, vied for the role of Rotten's replacement as the Sex Pistols' front-man. The first applicant even appears complete with Seditionaries bondage suit and 'Rotten' face mask. This would be the last time that Sid, Steve and Paul would appear together on the same stage and although Sid, who for some unknown reason is fumbling with a red Rickenbacker bass rather than his trademark white Fender Precision, is happy to swap instruments, he appears uncomfortable with what's going on around him. Then again, he could just have been wondering when Rotten was going to turn up.

Late in the summer, Sid made moves to rekindle his friendship with Rotten, who had by now reverted back to plain old 'John Lydon', in the hope that the two might be able to work together again. Lydon had not been totally adverse to the idea, but there were two major obstacles blocking the prospective collaboration – drugs and Nancy. Sid may have been willing to at least try and give up the needle but there was no way that he was ever going to give up his heroine. Nancy was also happy to allow her Sidney to work with Lydon again, but only on the proviso that Sid would be the front-man in the latter's new musical venture. 'And what would I do, dearie?' inquired Lydon upon hearing this. 'You can play drums,' came the collaboration-killing reply.

Several days later Sid and Nancy were making their way from Bowden House, the private hospital in Harrow-on-the-Hill where the pair had registered for yet another soon-to-be-abandoned Methadone cure, when they found themselves outside Lydon's flat at 45 Gunter Grove, just around the corner from Malcolm and Vivienne's shop. Although the couple could hear noises coming from the upstairs room, neither Lydon nor any of his regular nocturnal guests were showing any interest in responding to Sid's pounding on the door. Having failed to gain entrance Sid and Nancy wandered off into the night but returned again several hours later. Jah Wobble, who was in attendance that night, remembers answering the phone to find an extremely irate Sid on the line. Wobble was disorientated owing to the cocktail of uppers and downers that he'd taken during the course of the evening's festivities, and was less than impressed with being abused down the phone, so hung up. But Sid was not going to go away quietly and, finding his calls ignored, returned to the flat and proceeded to kick in the front door. He made it half way up the stairs before someone purportedly attacked him with an axe. Wobble has always denied that it was he who attacked Sid with the axe and even goes so far to claim that the assault was a figment of Sid's addled imagination.

'Someone may have threatened Sid with the axe,' Wobble recounted for Mark Paytress' *The Art Of Dying Young*, 'but I mean, if you hit someone with an axe, you split their fucking head open.' Wobble believes that Sid was either pushed or possibly even fell down the stairs and smacked his head against the metal boot-scraper, which accounted for his injuries. It would be the last time that either Lydon or Wobble would see their old Kingsway friend, but the axe incident would subsequently be revived for the sleeve of PiL's eponymous debut single, which shows a manic-looking Wobble brandishing a hatchet, and the slogan 'I was wild with my chopper until I discovered PiL'.

❀   ❀   ❀

'I went along to the studio when Simon recorded "C'mon Everybody",' recalled Anne Beverley. 'He seemed really happy that day because it meant everything to him, being a rock star, but as I watched him I suddenly realised that nobody was going out of their way to hire ex-Sex Pistols so I did begin to panic. I thought, beyond this, what is there for him? But of course by that time, Nancy had already concocted her little plan.'

Nancy's 'plan', now that she had replaced Malcolm as Sid's manager (although the wily fox McLaren had failed to sign off on everything, which would prove very useful over the next few months), was to return to New York where she hoped to turn him into a star on a scale that the other Sex Pistols could only dream of. Just how Nancy – who had no previous experience of the music industry – was expecting to transform Sid's fortunes when all she had to offer by way of a portfolio was a collection of dog-eared newspaper cuttings chronicling his rise to the top of the Punk pile, is anyone's guess.

There was also the problem of how they were intending to get to New York as the couple were virtually destitute by this stage. Although Sid was still receiving his £60-per-week wages from Glitterbest this was not even enough to feed his and Nancy's joint £80 heroin habit let alone buy food or other such essentials, so there was nothing at all in the Vicious kitty to pay for flight tickets. If self-delusion was a marketable commodity then Sid and Nancy would surely have been multi-millionaires, but if Nancy's scheme was to come to fruition then they were going to need help. With Sid having seemingly now outlived his celebrity, there were few people willing to offer financial assistance. It is therefore ironic that the one person who was willing to stand up and be counted was the man that he had replaced in the Sex Pistols – Glen Matlock.

Glen was living in Maida Vale and would occasionally bump into Sid and Nancy on the street as well as in their shared local pub, The Warrington (located on Warrington Crescent). It was here that the initial seeds were first sown of the ad hoc combo which became the legendary Vicious White Kids. Glen not only agreed to sign up as bass player for what was to all intents and purposes a one-off fundraiser, but also offered to provide other musicians to act as Sid's backing group. The music press had portrayed Sid and Glen as enemies, but the pair had never actually worked together and were on little more than nodding and waving terms while Glen was still a Pistol. Glen's fellow soon-to-be-ex Rich Kid, Steve New, was recruited on guitar while former Damned tub-thumper Rat Scabies, who at the time had his own outfit The White Cats, agreed to occupy the drum stool. Nancy appointed herself as backing singer, but come the night of the gig – which was staged at the Electric Circus in Camden Town on 15 August – she would suffer the Sid treatment when a canny Irish roadie named Frank (at the time in the employment of Thin Lizzy) decided after the soundcheck to disengage her microphone for that evening's performance.

Several years after the event, Glen was having lunch with Rob Dickens, who was then head of Warner Bros., and was shocked when Dickens informed him that the Vicious White Kids, and not the Sex Pistols, had been the best group that he had played in. 'So how come you didn't offer us a deal, then?' groaned Glen. 'Because you were all so out of it,' was Dickens' reply. The Warner boss, who obviously had an eye for talent, had believed Sid to be a 'natural', but had shied away from offering the group a contract because he'd been in the industry long enough to recognise a walking suicide when he saw one, and doubted that Sid would be around long enough for the ink to dry.

As the gig was intended as a one-off, there was no need to write any new material. It was reluctantly decided that Sid would belt out his recent chart hit 'My Way', as well as his other two as yet unissued *Swindle* offerings, 'C'mon Everybody' and 'Something Else', plus 'Belsen Was a Gas' and a few well-worn standards such as 'Stepping Stone', Dave Berry's 'Don't You Give Me (No Lip)' and The Stooges' 'I Wanna Be Your Dog', which Sid dedicated to his 'Honey, Nancy'.

The makeshift combo booked a couple of afternoons of rehearsal time at John Henry's Rehearsals in Islington. It is, and always has been, a time-honoured tradition among musicians to never appear on time for rehearsals, but although Glen, Rat and Steve ensured that the tradition continued by turning up one hour late, they still had to rouse Sid from his lair. When he did eventually appear, the others saw that he was limping and – upon inquiring as to what mishap might have occurred to account for the injury – were informed rather matter-of-factly that he had been forced to shoot-up into his foot on account of the veins in his forearms having collapsed.

Upon arrival at the rehearsal space, Sid had spied a brand-new Fender Mustang leaning against the wall and – suffering a sudden rush of blood to the head – decided to help himself to the instrument. It was obvious that the guitar belonged to the studio but although Glen and the others tried to steer him away from this course of action, Sid tucked the bass under his arm and nonchalantly walked past the portakabin office where the studio's owners were watching on with bemused interest, and placed the Fender in the boot of Glen's car.

Although the owners had offered no resistance the previous afternoon, it was a different story when the time came to pack up the gear at the end of the second day's rehearsals. Not only were they waiting by the door but they had also parked a van in the entrance in order to thwart any mad-dash escape. The message was simple – the group's gear wasn't going to be going anywhere until the Fender Mustang had been restored to its rightful place. All eyes turned towards Sid who, to everyone's amazement, flatly denied having had anything to do with the guitar's disappearance. 'He was that convincing,' remembers Glen Matlock, 'that if you hadn't seen it with your own two eyes, you'd have believed him.' It was therefore left to Glen to take Sid to one side and explain the situation. If the Fender wasn't returned pronto then they would have to forfeit their own gear. If that was allowed to happen then they wouldn't be able to do the show, and if there was no show then there was no money for New York. With the penny having finally dropped,

Sid called Nancy and told her to put the bass in a cab and send it to the studio. The cab duly arrived and the purloined bass, which was wrapped up within a black plastic bin liner, was restored to its rightful owner. To Glen's horror, Nancy had taken it upon herself to customise the Fender and Sid's call had obviously caught her in mid-flow. 'The guy's face was a picture,' says Glen, 'because Nancy had painted the bass with black emulsion and it was still dripping wet.'

●   ●   ●

The Clash's road manager, Johnny Green, whose girlfriend Lindy Poltock lived in New Court at the same time as Sid, was serving as stage manager for the show and remembers being blown away by Sid's dynamic performance. Or at least he was blown away by Sid's performance during the soundcheck. When the time came to do it for real he had resorted to form and was stumbling about the stage, smacked off his head. The capacity crowd included the likes of Viv Albertine who is rumoured to have filmed the gig on a Super 8 camera, although to date not a second of this performance has surfaced anywhere in visual form. American Punkettes Debby Harry and Joan Jett were present, as was Captain Sensible. The after-show party was held on Joan Jett's rented houseboat, which was moored at Chelsea Reach. Here, Sid – aided and abetted by Glen, Rat and the Captain – proceeded to get even further out of his head and ended up picking a fight with someone he shouldn't have. Once again he found himself at the wrong end of another beating.

Several days later, Glen and a bruised Sid met up for a farewell beer at the Warrington. 'He thanked me for the Camden gig and then told me that I probably wouldn't see him again,' says Glen, shaking his head at the memory. 'He said that he wasn't going to make it past twenty-one, but I didn't really pay all that much attention because he'd been saying pretty much the same thing for the past twelve months. I remember asking him why he was going to New York and he said that he was going there to "find himself a new life". But I knew that wasn't likely to happen. Not with Nancy around, at any rate. I think he just fell for Nancy's claptrap that she would make him a superstar. What did I think of his singing? Well, he didn't have the gift of the gab like Rotten did, but he was, or could have been, a really decent front-man.'

'I was invited to the Camden gig,' said Anne Beverley. 'I wasn't all that sure of what to expect so I stayed away. Besides, I knew that Simon and Nancy would be using the funds raised from the gig to go to New York, so it made it a very sad time for me. I was so sure that I wouldn't be seeing at least one of them again but having said that, I never would have imagined that things would turn out the way they did.'

Sid and Nancy's hedonistic lifestyle ensured that their circle of friends was as much at risk as they were. A drug buddy of theirs called John Shepcock, a promising sound engineer, spent an evening partying with Sid and Nancy before overdosing on a lethal cocktail of cocaine and heroin. Such was the couple's state that it wasn't until late afternoon of the following day that they realised they were sharing their bed with a corpse. 'That was their wake-up call,' Anne Beverley said. 'I knew there and then that they had to get away from London. Things were getting out of hand and a young man, who was no older than my Simon, was dead. The police would never have left him alone after that.'

CHAPTER 9

Who Killed Bambi?

'I've done a lot of things I wished I hadn't
There's other things I never hope to do
But sliding off the map in both directions
Is the sorry mess I've made of knowing you
I've seen a lot of things I wished I hadn't
There's other things I never hope to see
But no one left alive can paint the picture
Of the mess that knowing you has made of me.'

(From 'Bed of Roses Number 9' by Ian Dury)

Sid and Nancy arrived in New York on 23 August 1978 and they immediately checked into the Chelsea Hotel at 222 West 23rd Street under the names Mr and Mrs Ritchie. 'The Chelsea was a beautiful old building with nineteenth-century charm although it was a bit rundown,' remembers Eileen Polk. 'It had marble and wrought iron staircases and the walls were covered in art pieces done by some of its more famous residents. The lobby was filled with antique furniture and some beautiful stone carvings that people used to sit on. There were always some interesting, crazy people in the lobby. The restaurant on the first floor, Don Quixote's, was always cool and dark and served great margaritas.

Some people say it was a haven for artists and musicians, while others say it was a cheap hotel full of low-life junkies and prostitutes. The truth is that it was both. Like most hotels in New York the small cheaper rooms that rented by the week, were on the first three floors, and the larger expensive rooms were on the top floors. Some of the rooms that were rented by long-term residents were lovely suites with grand pianos and full balconies.'

The Chelsea had first opened its doors in 1884 and until 1902 had been the city's tallest building. It had started out as the city's first artist's co-operative but had gone bust after just ten years. When it re-opened its doors as a hotel in 1905 it catered for the city's literati. Mark Twain, Thomas Wolfe, Brendan Behan and Eugene O'Neill all stepped through its doors but by the late 1970s the eleven-storey red-brick-fronted hotel's register was bereft of writing luminaries and had instead become the reserve of down-at-heel musicians and actors, low-life characters and junkies. Now and then they got lucky – as in 1975 when John Lennon and Yoko Ono stayed while looking for somewhere to live in Greenwich Village. Rolling Stone Keith Richards had once joked that the Chelsea's bellhops were registered drug dealers, and if truth be told it wasn't that much of an exaggeration.

Before flying out from the UK, Nancy had called her mother and told her that she and Sid had married in an attempt to get her family to send some money over. When she returned to the States she was quite different to those who remembered her. 'Nancy returned twenty pounds thinner and a platinum blonde, with Sid Vicious on her arm and a fake British accent,' remembers Eileen Polk. 'I thought this was hilarious because it gave her license to be nasty to everyone who had made fun of her before. She wouldn't let anybody who had been mean to her get near Sid. She was like the kid who gets bullied and beaten up in the schoolyard and eventually becomes vengeful. At first she had tried to buy friends with money and drugs but that didn't make her any more popular, so she just turned mean. Then she used her meanness to make money as a dominatrix, which was much more lucrative than just actually having sex for money. Finally she had her moment of glory with a Sex Pistol boyfriend and showed them all that living well is the best revenge. But she was not well. Her appearance was armour, a disguise, to hide a deep insecurity. The insidious thing about heroin addiction is that at first it makes you look great, for about six months. And then it destroys you. Neither Sid nor Nancy had the slightest clue how to be in a relationship so they fell into a destructive co-dependency. I think they really thought that destroying themselves was what was expected of them.'

The couple set up residence at the Chelsea and unpacked their meagre possessions. These included Sid's gold records, a soon-to-be-blood-splattered *Never Mind the Bollocks* poster (which would later be used to empty needles onto) and an innocuous-looking Fairy Liquid bottle within which was stored the couple's stash of Methadone and Nancy's scrapbook, which was in fact a Sex Pistols promo folder filled with cuttings of what amounted to their legend. The dream of a new life quickly turned into a nightmare for Sid as New Yorkers tended to take him at face value. The greater American general public was ignorant of the fact that a tabloid-filling limey was now walking among them. In the USA the Sex Pistols still didn't mean much to many people.

Eileen Polk had heard through the grapevine that Nancy was back in the city. 'I was working in a second-hand clothes shop called *Revenge*, when in walked Sid and Nancy,' says Polk. 'I'd heard on the street that she was back in town with her famous rock star lover and the word was that she wasn't letting anyone who had previously been mean to her anywhere near Sid, so I was quite surprised to see them as we were never what I would call friends. She introduced me to Sid who was unable to get a word in edgeways as Nancy was babbling on about the Max's shows as well as some shows at a place called The Hive in

Philly for the end of October, and how she was gonna turn Sid into a huge star. They stayed about twenty minutes and when they left, I purposely waited a couple of minutes before following them out onto the street and stood watching them from the corner. It was really funny to see people purposely going out of their way to avoid coming into contact with them.'

The New York Punk scene, still bemused at having watched its London counterpart steal its thunder, was hostile towards Sid, but Nancy, with the aid of the odd sexual favour, did at least manage to secure several dates at Max's Kansas City. The legendary restaurant-come-nightclub on Park Avenue South had been the favoured watering hole of Andy Warhol and his Factory crowd. David Bowie, Lou Reed, Iggy Pop, Elton John and the New York Dolls had all taken tea here in the early 1970s, along with a cast of thousands.

Dead Boys guitarist Cheetah Chrome encountered Sid and Nancy at Max's in manager Peter Crowley's office while he was also looking to book some shows at the club. Sid's reputation was such that news of his imminent arrival in New York had brought a mixture of both fear and an air of expectancy among the Lower East Side crowd, but if anything, Chrome was under-whelmed at meeting the notorious ex-Sex Pistol, who appeared anything but Vicious. While Nancy was occupied with final-ising Sid's bookings the two musicians struck up a conversation during which the subject of them possibly working together was broached. Having discovered that it was Sid's first night in New York and with the business end of the meeting over, Chrome invited Sid and Nancy to join him at the bar for a few drinks before then heading back to Chrome's apartment in order to sample some of Chrome's dope. Chrome shared the apartment with fellow Dead Boy Jeff Magnum, and the bassist must have got the shock of his life upon being roused from his drug-induced slumber to find a skinny, lope-eyed, spiky-haired scarecrow wanting to challenge him to a fight. 'What annoys me is the speed at which people will tell you something bad about

Nancy,' Steve Dior says. 'I remember when they first arrived in New York, I was walking down Canal Street wearing thin little black Chinese slippers, and they were worn out – my toe was sticking through one of them. I bumped into Nancy and she took me off and bought me motorcycle boots.'

Between shooting up and swapping tour anecdotes the subject once again turned towards the three of them putting a group together. Having enlisted the services of another Dead Boy, Jimmy Zero (who was also living at the Chelsea and was one of the hotel's more colourful habitués) and ex-New York Dolls drummer Jerry Nolan (who knew Sid from his year-long stay in London while in the Heartbreakers), a rehearsal of sorts was hastily arranged. Before heading to the rehearsal space, however, the four decided to meet up at Max's for dinner in order to lay out a stratagem. In fact, the meeting had to be abandoned on account of Sid falling asleep at the table. With the Fairy Liquid bottle having been drained of its illicit contents, Sid had sought compensation by downing four Tuinols, which rendered the meeting, and the planned rehearsal, obsolete.

Zero and Chrome were in the process of booking a second rehearsal when they were summoned to a meeting with Nancy at Max's. Before passing out in her salad, a stoned Nancy informed the pair that their services were no longer required. Zero still maintains that he and Chrome were sacked for being too musically proficient and for not being English. Nolan, although equally guilty on both counts, was spared the axe on account of his having been in the Heartbreakers. 'It just goes to prove what I've always believed,' Zero says today. 'Rock 'n' roll was dead as an art form because the poster boy [Sid] couldn't play a fucking note, which in a way was kinda perfect.'

❋   ❋   ❋

After getting settled in at the Chelsea, Nancy decided it was time that Sid met his prospective in-laws. They travelled south for a week-long visit to Frank and Deborah Spungen's two-storey colonial house in the Philadelphian suburb of Huntingdon. Their stay proved to be somewhat less-than-idyllic because in the eighteen months since Nancy's departure, the Spungens had found time to achieve some semblance of normality. Both Frank and Deborah had steady jobs in New York, while Nancy's nineteen-year–old sister Suzy had recently been accepted into the Philadelphia College of Art and was in the process of moving into an apartment in the city, and brother David had just returned from summer camp where he had worked as a councillor and was about to enter his senior year at high school.

There is no question that Frank and Deborah loved Nancy. It was just that they had become accustomed to loving her from afar. The news that Nancy was returning to New York came as something of a relief to Deborah as she worked in the city and would now at least now be able to visit Nancy occasionally, but the news that Nancy was coming home and bringing Sid along for the ride filled her with apprehension. As she later admitted in *And I Don't Want to Live This Life*, the prospect of Nancy's return had stirred up a whole host of memories, none of which were particularly heart-warming. Nevertheless, Frank and Deborah put aside their anxieties and were waiting on the platform at Trenton Station to meet their wayward offspring. The train was running late, which provided the already-nervous Deborah with an extra twenty minutes to dwell on her anxieties. When the train finally arrived and began disgorging its passengers, Frank and Deborah watched as their fellow Philadelphians greeted or bid farewell to loved ones but they themselves failed to recognise their first-born. The peroxide-headed, leather-clad, blanched-skinned woman tottering along the platform in a pair of hooker's heels – and dragging what seemed to be Frankenstein's monster behind her – sounded like their Nancy but, beyond that, was totally unrecognisable from the girl they had waved off eighteen months earlier. In fact, Deborah likened Nancy's appearance to that of a Holocaust victim – not an attractive sight for a Jewish family. Her first impression of Sid was equally uncharitable – dressed in his by-now trademark leather motorcycle jacket and boots and black jeans, he looked as though he'd just stepped off stage at Winterland.

In a bid to preserve the family's sanity, Deborah and Frank suggested that Nancy and Sid might be more comfortable staying at the nearby Holiday Inn, where they would take them after dinner (Frank had turned Nancy's old bedroom into an office but Suzy's room was available). Deborah had been expecting a typical Nancy outburst upon hearing that she and Sid were being dumped in a hotel, but surprisingly she had accepted her parents' offer.

David was standing in the hallway as Nancy dragged Sid into the house and such was Nancy's excitement that she failed to notice her brother's bewildered expression. David had been about to leave in order to pick up Suzy from Bethayres Station and was stunned when Nancy volunteered herself and Sid to ride shotgun. Also on the train were Nancy's 'Aunt' Susan and her daughter Holly. Susan had achieved 'aunt' status through being one of Deborah's closest and oldest friends rather than through blood and had met up with Nancy during a visit to London the previous year in order to hand over the money that Deborah was sending her daughter. Nancy's appearance had degenerated to such an extent that Susan had failed to recognise her.

Later that evening, after a family meal that Sid and Nancy barely touched, Sid treated the bemused Spungens to a little musical entertainment with the aid of David's acoustic guitar. Although the bass was Sid's instrument of choice, he was not totally unfamiliar with the workings of a six-string guitar. He struggled to string together two chords, however, let alone play a recognisable tune. To make his humiliation complete, David – who had only been taking guitar lessons for six months – took the guitar off him and played the Beatles' classic 'Eleanor Rigby' from start to finish. By this time, however, Sid had dozed off. Frank seized the opportunity to get Sid and Nancy out of the house and volunteered to drive them to the Holiday Inn. Nancy was having none of it, at least not until she had shown her parents her 'portfolio' of newspaper cuttings and photos of her and Sid. Some of the photos, however, predated her time with Sid – a photo of the family's cats triggered Nancy into digging out her baby photos. Sid, having been roused from his slumber by Nancy, expressed particular interest in a snapshot of a seventeen-month-old Nancy curled up naked on her parents' bed and asked if he could keep it.

The rest of the week passed without incident and when the time came for Sid and Nancy to return to New York to prepare for Sid's up-and-coming New York debut at Max's, Frank, Deborah and David saw them off. During the car ride to Trenton Station, Nancy had delivered a chilling monologue on how she was 'going to die very soon'. She didn't ever want to be old and ugly and having already crammed a lifetime of living into her twenty years she stunned her nearest and dearest, who had now come to think of themselves beyond being shocked by anything, by casually informing them that she would be dead before her twenty-first birthday, which was a matter of weeks away. Deborah, Frank and David were probably waiting for Sid to step in and chastise Nancy for being silly, but Sid had remained silent and Nancy's soon-to-be-prophetic words were left to float around the car like a bad smell. Deborah would later admit to being relieved at seeing them off, while Frank could have had no idea that he would never see his daughter again.

❀ ❀ ❀

Sid played three shows at Max's during the first week of September 1978 with a backing group comprised of Jerry Nolan and Arthur Kane (who borrowed Sid's bass for the shows), plus Steve Dior on guitar. 'Sid was supposed to be doing a gig or something with the Dead Boys, but that came to nothing so him and Nancy turned up at our rehearsal space, Sunset Sound, offering us the gig,' Arthur Kane recollected shortly before his death from leukaemia in July 2004. 'We didn't rehearse as such because it was never my style; it's all about human emotion rather than perfection. We did maybe three shows in all and by the last show there must have been 4,000 people trying to get into a venue that only held around 600.'

'I was getting excited at the whole prospect that lay ahead of me,' remembers Steve Dior. 'I did want to appear confident that we were going to pull this off. Sid and Nancy sat on the sofa stoned. Arthur "Killer" Kane stood in the doorway chatting to anyone who would listen. Jerry Nolan, dressed up for the occasion, sat quietly smoking in a corner. I had to get high before the show but decided afterwards was a better idea. There was, after all, a possibility that it could end in disaster.'

Those New Yorkers curious enough to go along to Max's to see what an ex-Sex Pistol had to offer were woefully disappointed as Sid either clung on to the microphone stand as though it was his only anchor in a sea of uncertainty or lumbered about the stage in a near-sleeping state, barely able to remember the words to the same set-list he had performed at the Electric Circus only a month previously.

'Sid's solo gigs were very crowded. I photographed Sid and Nancy backstage,' recalls Eileen Polk. 'It was so crowded that the band couldn't get to the stage so we all had to go down the two flights of stairs, out the front door, into the alley and up the fire escape, which was directly behind the stage. Sid was very crabby and sullen that night. I think he was really high and he looked very unhealthy. Nancy was in all her groupie glory. The club was totally packed. The crowd was the same as it was for Johnny Thunders gigs. They were all hoping for really good music, but would have been just as happy if Sid croaked on stage right in front of everybody. It was a Punk scene happening! All the groupies were there. To distinguish themselves from the groupies, the band's wives and girlfriends sat on stage, which is what they sometimes used to do when the Dolls played. The band was very loud and sounded pretty good, but not really tight. They obviously hadn't rehearsed very much and played the standard Punk anthems – 'I Wanna Be Your Dog' dragged on forever. Sid fell down a few times and read the words to 'My Way' from a piece of paper. He was pretty out of it, but managed to crack a few jokes and insult everyone in the band and everyone in the audience. The photographer Stephanie Chernikowski has a book called *Dream Baby Dream*. On the cover of that book you can see me on the side of the stage taking photos.'

'It was really kind of pathetic because Sid didn't finish any of the songs,' adds Bob Gruen. 'Some people thought it was funny that this guy was so out of it that he couldn't do the show, but the general consensus among the audience was, "What's the point?" He didn't seem to have much awareness of what he was doing or where he was while Nancy was sat in the corner saying, "It's OK, Sid, just do the next one." Nancy said to me, "We're staying at the Chelsea, Bobby, why don't you come round and take some pictures of us?" I told her that she looked terrible, that she and Sid should get some sleep and that I'd happily come over in a couple of days. Nancy was a friend of sorts and there was no way that I would take pictures of my friends looking like that.'

For the third and final show on the 7th, the ad hoc combo was supplemented by a special guest in the form of The Clash's Mick Jones. 'Mick and I spent a couple of hours listening to the record ['My Way'], trying to work it out,' says Steve Dior. 'We gave up after the first chorus where it seemed to change key mysteriously. "Just tell them you've forgotten the rest," I told Sid, thinking that was typically Punk.' Mick happened to be in New York with Joe Strummer mixing the second Clash album, *Give 'em Enough Rope*, and upon being sequestered, had initially baulked at the idea but finally acquiesced after being cajoled into doing so by Joe. Mick certainly gave the performance added impetus – although he was no stranger to drugs, he regarded himself as a professional musician and took to the stage sober.

Mick would later lament that his one-time friend, Sid, and the rest of the group were 'as out of it as you could be without actually being dead'.

'You could hardly move in there,' says Eileen Polk. 'People came from all over town to see the show because New Yorkers have always had a fascination for someone who could self-destruct at any moment. The band was pretty good but Sid was too far off the radar to make much of an impact.'

Despite Nancy's promptings, Sid could think of little beyond his next Methadone fix. Unlike London, where he could acquire the drug on prescription, in New York Sid and Nancy were forced to stand in line outside the Spring Street clinic with New York's low-lifes, who would often as not pass the time by picking fights with the celebrity standing in their midst. At the behest of concerned friends and associates, including Peter Crowley, Sid purchased a knife with which to protect himself. By now, however, Methadone was no longer Sid and Nancy's sole drug of choice as they were also hooked on barbiturates such as Tuinols and Dilaudid, a synthetic morphine given to cancer patients. When added to large quantities of alcohol they blotted out the world, which, perhaps unsurprisingly, made them extremely popular among the city's drug-dealing fraternity and brought them into contact with some decidedly dubious characters.

'When Simon first arrived in New York I used to receive the odd phone call, but then everything went quiet,' said Anne Beverley. 'I thought to myself, well, you know, he'd told me that they would be visiting Nancy's parents in Philadelphia and that he had some gigs to do so they were going to be busy and that I might not hear anything for a while. But the "while" came and went and I still hadn't heard anything. My son was 3,000 miles away and I had no way of getting hold of him so I started to get worried. It sounds strange looking back now but I didn't realise at the time just how worried I should have been.'

❋   ❋   ❋

On the evening of Wednesday, 11 October 1978, Sid and Nancy were in their room, number 100, at the Chelsea Hotel. They had only recently moved into room 100 after the mattress in their previous room caught fire. What exactly happened over the next twelve hours will never be clearly understood and the events have become shrouded in mystery. Many things are unclear – they might have visited one or more of the other rooms on their floor, they had an uncertain number of visitors, and they went out together or alone at unconfirmed times. By the morning, a large amount of cash was missing from their room, Nancy was dead of a stab wound and Sid couldn't remember much of anything that had happened.

When Sid eventually came to – sometime around 9.30 a.m. on Thursday, 12 October – he found the bed sheets and mattress covered in dried blood. The bloody trail led from the bed to a tiny en-suite bathroom where Nancy's body, clad in black bra and panties, lay slumped between the toilet and washbasin. She had been stabbed once in the abdomen sometime during the night and had crawled into the bathroom where she'd bled to death. According to doctors' reports at the time, a single opening such as this would have meant that the victim had survived between two and three hours before she died.

Who murdered Nancy and why are questions that have never satisfactorily been answered. The most important witness, Sid, had swallowed a large dose of Tuinol and medical reports showed clearly that he'd been out cold for the best part of five hours. Another unsolved mystery is what happened to almost $20,000 in cash that the couple had deposited in the bedside cabinet. Virgin had recently paid Sid the money for royalties due on the 'My Way' single and the couple hadn't had time to spend much of it yet.

Several people had, or claimed to have had, contact with Sid and Nancy during the night in question. One of them was Neon Leon Webster, an aspiring singer/songwriter and drug addict who was in room 119 with his girlfriend Cathi O'Rourke when

Sid and Nancy are said to have visited them at 9.45 p.m.

'The first person I knew at the Chelsea was Neon Leon,' says Eileen Polk. 'When I met him in 1974, he had a nice room. It was clean and bright and very reasonably priced at under 100 dollars a week. The Chelsea was a great place to meet up before going out to the discos, because you could do whatever you wanted and as long as you didn't disturb anyone else, the management didn't care. The place reeked of pot smoke. As the seventies wore on the Chelsea became known as the best place for "entertainers" who wanted to be in New York for short-term stays. This meant that it not only appealed to musicians on the road. It also appealed to strippers, and strippers who were really hookers. Thus the Chelsea was the place for the perfect marriage of sex industry and music industry. The posh life for musicians was to get a stripper to pay your rent so you could party all day and all night and not be impinged on by work. Unfortunately being a New York rock scene Mecca, the Chelsea became more associated with hard drugs as the white powder infiltrated the scene. By 1978, the place was so full of junkies it became depressing and I stopped going there.'

Webster would later sell his version of events in room 100 to two leading publications, the *New York Post* and *Soho Weekly News*, within twelve hours of giving a statement to the NYPD. The police statement and two press stories give a total of three completely different tales. It's therefore safe to believe that at least two, or possibly all three, are totally fabricated.

In the *Soho Weekly News* dated 19 October 1978 Webster claimed that during the visit Sid had sat on the bed leafing through Nancy's portfolio, pointing out photos from the Pistols' US tour and lamenting his having lost his good looks. He also dismissed himself as a 'nothing', a 'nobody' and said that he had 'no future'. Nancy, meanwhile, was pacing the room in a highly agitated state, demanding of no one in particular that they should be looking for drugs – good drugs. Webster would also claim that Nancy's death was part of a suicide pact as Sid had gifted him with his possessions, including his newspaper clippings, gold records and his beloved motorcycle jacket.

Webster had already told the police that Sid and Nancy had left around midnight to return to their own room when Cathi went off to her go-go dancing job in New Jersey and that he went to Max's. However, none of the club's staff or punters could verify his being at Max's that night, which seemed strange given that he'd been practically living at the club for a number of years. A friend of his, who preferred to remain anonymous, did however vouch that Webster was at another Punk hangout called The Nursery.

Webster claimed to have returned to the Chelsea at around 3.30 a.m. with a go-go dancer called Kelly, another hotel resident, and that at 4 a.m. he had received a call from a highly stoned Nancy asking him if he had any pot. He and Kelly also claimed that an unknown person was pounding away at the door, but that they ignored the mystery caller.

Not one person has been able to corroborate Webster's story that Sid and Nancy visited them that evening, or that their relationship was strong enough to merit Sid bequeathing him all his worldly goods. Further doubt is cast upon Webster's story as one of the Chelsea's staff recalled having seen Sid and Nancy chatting to an unidentified New York Punkette in the hotel lobby at around the same time that he claims the couple were in his room. Malcolm McLaren later revealed that Sid told him the couple had actually left the Chelsea around midnight, but where the couple supposedly went has never been confirmed.

At around 2.30 a.m., Nancy contacted local drug dealer, occasional police informer, wannabe actor and face about town, 'Rockets Redglare', whose most prominent acting role was playing a cab driver in Madonna's 1985 film *Desperately Seeking Susan*. The son of a junkie and an abusive step-father, Michael Morro, to give him his real name, was sometime bodyguard and drug dealer to Sid Vicious. Redglare confirmed to the police that

Nancy placed an order for forty Dilaudid capsules which were known on the street as D-4s and cost $40 each, as well as some new hypodermics. Redglare further explained that he'd arrived at room 100 at around 3.15 a.m., which means that if Sid woke at 9.30 a.m. as the police report claims, he could not have been far from a state of total black-out at this point in the morning. Redglare's eyes must have lit up when Nancy, who was dressed in a long T-shirt over black underwear, reached into her bag and pulled out a wad of $50 and $100 bills to pay for the Dilaudids. When police asked him why he went to the hotel even though he didn't have the drugs for Sid and Nancy, Redglare (who was himself a Methadone addict), replied that he had done so to be 'comforting'. He claimed that he stayed with the couple until around 4.30 a.m. – by which time Sid would have been out cold, according to later tests – before then heading out onto the street to try to purchase the Dilaudids for them.

Redglare also told the investigating officers that as he was leaving the Chelsea he had encountered another known dealer, Steve Cincotti, whom he recognised as being Sid and Nancy's regular Tuinol and Quaalude dealer. Cincotti, who was known to be highly unstable and would later sell to the *New York Post* what has to be the most bizarre account of the tragedy, claimed that he sold Sid and Nancy some Tuinol capsules but then left immediately after. Redglare's account is thrown into question as Leon Webster's manager, Wayne Skip, reported seeing Sid and Nancy in the hotel lobby at 3 a.m., but Skip would later make several conflicting statements to the police, suggesting that anything he says might need to be viewed with suspicion. Like his client, he was a man of many statements.

In his book, *Pretty Vacant*, Phil Strongman states that Redglare murdered Nancy while stealing Sid's stash of money and that the next day he was seen in a bar with blood-stained bank notes. Redglare died in 1999, and in the twenty-one years between Nancy's murder and his own demise he told a number of people, including underground filmmaker Nick Zedd, that he had killed Nancy in order to get his hands on the couple's cash. This is backed up by the fact that on the day of Nancy's murder, he was seen in the Chelsea residents' bar bumming dollars for beer from his fellow barflies, yet just twenty-four hours later he was strutting around the bars in the East Village with a wad of cash while sporting a pair of brand-new leather jeans and an equally brand-new pair of cowboy boots. He talked that day of starting up a record label and seemed to have undergone an amazing transformation from the figure of the previous night. It is also worth noting that two years before his own death, he tried on more than one occasion to sell a snuff film of Nancy's death. While it is thought that such a tape no longer exists (if indeed it ever did), it seems certain that he was trying to cash in on the murder. Redglare later told Gene Gregorits, 'I know that Sid did not kill Nancy. Nancy's murder was videotaped, while Sid sits there on the couch, completely out of it, practically in a coma. This was the tableau I had left them in.'

Sid and Nancy's next-door neighbour, Lisa Garcia, who lived in room 103, had returned to the Chelsea around the time that Skip says he was in the lobby, but did not see Sid, Nancy or anyone answering Skip's description hanging around in the lobby. Garcia also reported that an unknown male had pounded on her door several times while demanding to be allowed in. It is possible to speculate whether this could have been Cincotti mistaking her room for that of Sid and Nancy. Kenny, the bell-hop on duty that night, muddied the waters further by telling the police that he hadn't seen Sid or Nancy in the lobby and that no one had come into the hotel asking to see the couple following Redglare's departure.

At 5 a.m., Kenny the bell-hop received a complaint from room 228 saying that someone was banging on their door and that when he went up to investigate he found an unruly and belligerent Sid wandering up and down the hallway. Kenny later told police that he had tried to reason with Vicious, but that when Sid swung at him, he had defended himself and got the better of Sid. 'He had a bloodied mouth and there was blood on his face, nose and T-shirt,' Kenny later told the police. 'When I was leaving to go back downstairs, [Sid] was heading for the stairs. I don't know if he went to his room but I got back to the desk at 5.15 a.m.'

Sid's beating at the hands of the no-nonsense Kenny must have affected his in-built navigation system – a female resident, who refused to be identified, later claimed that the bloodied Sid had staggered into her room at about 5.30 a.m. that morning. It is worth keeping in mind that the official medical statement states that Sid would still have been out cold at this point.

Another neighbour, Vera Mendelssohn, who lived next door to Sid and Nancy in room 102, reported having heard moans coming from room 100 at sometime around 7.30 a.m. The moaning sounds, which she described as 'coming from a person who was alone', had frightened the forty-eight-year-old sculptor, which was the reason she gave for not going to investigate. The moaning had eventually ceased and Mendelssohn had fallen back asleep. Were these moaning sounds Nancy's final death throes?

The biggest clue that Sid and Nancy hadn't been alone in room 100 came from Herman Ramos, the Chelsea's deskman who reported receiving a telephone call from someone outside the hotel informing him that there had been some trouble in room 100. Ramos sent Charles, who had recently relieved Kenny on bell-hop duties, up to room 100 to see what was going on. Before Charles returned to Ramos the hotel received a call from Sid who told him 'someone is sick – need help'. Ramos decided that this was serious and called for an ambulance and the police.

At around 10.30 a.m. Sid was spotted coming up the stairs and onto the hallway by NYU student Rob Braden, who was on his way to school. Where Sid had been has never been disclosed. The ambulance, closely followed by a squad car from the nearby 10th Precinct, arrived shortly thereafter and upon discovering Nancy's body in the bathroom placed a call to the Third Homicide Division. Mendelssohn, having been wakened by the police's arrival, went out into the hallway to see what was happening and, surprisingly, was allowed into the room – potentially a crime scene – where she saw Nancy's body. Sid, meanwhile, was out in the hallway surrounded by police officers. 'His face looked battered,' Mendelssohn informed reporters, 'and he was saying, "Baby, baby, baby" over and over to himself.' Mendelssohn claimed that Sid, having recognised his neighbour, said, 'I killed her. I can't live without her.' The sculptor also claimed that she may have heard him say something about Nancy having fallen on the knife and that he was 'very high on Tuinol'.

Nancy's body was taken away to the morgue at around 5.30 p.m., by which time Sid, having been the only person in the room and owner of the murder weapon – a large folding Jaguar hunting knife – was sitting in a holding cell at Third Homicide Division's headquarters on East 51st Street charged with second-degree murder. Homicide in the second degree is the most serious murder charge in regard to the death of a civilian in the USA. First-degree murder is reserved for the killing of a police or corrections officer in the line of duty. Sid is supposedly said to have 'confessed' to the murder by saying, 'I did it because I'm a dirty dog.' He is also known to have told the arresting detectives that they couldn't arrest him because he was a 'rock 'n' roll star'. In subsequent interviews he would stringently deny having made a confession and told one reporter, 'When the fuck did I make a confession, mate? I was well out of it!'

Not surprisingly, the news spread fast. Within hours the pavement outside the Chelsea was teeming with people, most of whom stuck around long enough to see Nancy's body being removed. 'On the afternoon of Thursday the twelfth, I was writing my American chapter, *Taking Civilization to the Barbarians*,' recalls Malcolm McLaren. 'I got a phone call from a tabloid journalist. He had come across the name of John Simon Beverly:

"John Simon – that's Sid, isn't it, Malc?"

"Yes."

"He's just been arrested at the Chelsea Hotel in New York – for murder."

"Murder?"

I hung up the phone. I wasn't about to believe a story told to me by a tabloid journalist, so I immediately phoned a photographer in New York [Joe Stevens] to confirm it. Yes, he said, it was true. Sid had been arrested and charged with the murder of his girlfriend, Nancy Spungen. It was already on television.' Every newspaper, TV and radio station was convinced that the police had their man and had already tried and sentenced Sid.

McLaren's next call was not easy: what thoughts must have been running through his mind as he waited for Anne Beverley to pick up the phone? 'The phone rang and it was Malcolm,' Anne said. 'I could tell by the sound of his voice that something was wrong. He didn't know how to break the news so he just came out with it. My mind went completely blank because at that moment my whole world collapsed, and the worst thing about it was I knew the story wasn't going to have a happy ending.'

'There were five of us in my cramped management office that afternoon, and we were stunned,' says McLaren. 'Sid was capable of a wide range of self-destructive acts, but none of us thought that he could kill someone, especially his girlfriend. Sid's trouble was usually over drugs. Now there would be a trial, a murder trial in New York, and it was going to cost a fortune. Even though I was technically no longer managing Sid, I wanted to help. I'm still not entirely sure why. Maybe because I felt that there was no one more fun than Sid. He never saw a red light; he saw only green. He was chaos incarnate, and he made my blood flow. And I suspected that if I didn't help him, no one else would. I rushed off to Heathrow for the next flight to New York. Press people were everywhere. One of them wished me luck, and spotting my holdall, said, "Got the cash, Malc?" When I landed in New York, I went straight to the court. It was packed with journalists, who all turned around as I entered. The proceeding had already begun. Sid was in the dock with his familiar black spiky hair and wearing a black suit. But he was frightened; he looked pale and fragile. Bail had just been set: fifty thousand dollars. I needed to do something and raised my holdall in the air as if it were loaded with money. I wanted to let the lawyers know that I could guarantee bail. But there was no money in my holdall, and I couldn't guarantee the bail, and Sid, vulnerable and dejected and confused, was escorted from the courtroom and taken to Rikers Island.'

Being the most notorious member of arguably the world's most notorious band, Vicious' arrest made front-page news around the world. Deborah Orin, writing in the 13 October 1978 issue of the *New York Post*, reported that 'Sid Vicious, bass guitarist of Britain's spitting and stomping Sex Pistols Punk Rock band, yesterday was arrested and charged with stabbing his sultry blond girlfriend to death in their room at Manhattan's famed Chelsea Hotel. His face pale and scratched, the dazed-looking Vicious muttered curses and "I'll smash your cameras" as he was led from the hotel.' Orin also wrote that 'a distraught young man in a brown checkered shirt and cowboy boots who refused to give his name but was identified by hotel employees as a friend of the couple' said that Sid 'beat her with a guitar every so often but I didn't think he was going to kill her'.

In London, the next day's issue of the *Sun* carried the Vicious story on its front page. 'VICIOUS IN A TRANCE' it proclaimed. 'SEX PISTOL IS NEAR COLLAPSE AFTER "I DIDN'T STAB HER CLAIM"'. Reporter Leslie Hinton continued: 'Sex Pistol Sid Vicious almost collapsed in court yesterday when he was accused of murdering his blonde girlfriend Nancy Spungen. His body shuddered periodically as he spent the rest of the ten-minute hearing with his head resting on a table. Throughout, he seemed oblivious to the proceedings as he was formally charged with murder under his real name, John Simon Ritchie.'

With such media scrutiny and pressure on the NYPD to clear this up as soon as possible, Sid was going to all the help he could muster. 'I was going to have to find some money fast,' said Malcolm McLaren. 'And I needed to get Sid a very powerful lawyer.'

CHAPTER 10

Give 'em Enough Hope

Many questions were being asked in October 1978. Who killed Nancy? Where was the missing money? 'After Nancy died I asked Sid point blank whether he had killed her,' says Steve Dior today. 'He said, "I didn't do it! I didn't kill her! I didn't kill Nancy!" I still believe him.' On Monday, 17 October she was laid to rest following a private service for family members at St David's Jewish Cemetery on the outskirts of Philadelphia. She was buried with her hair dyed back to chestnut brown, in her green high-school prom dress. Rather than a headstone the Spungens chose a metal plaque, which reads: 'Your odyssey is over – sleep in peace, Nancy Laura Spungen'. Inscribed beneath her Hebrew name were the dates 'Feb 27th 1958 – Oct 12th 1978'. 'Although I do believe that Nancy was on a collision course,' Deborah Spungen later told the press, 'there's still part of me that believes that had the right person come along, she could and should have been saved.'

Meanwhile Sid was biding his time in Rikers Island prison, New York City's largest jail. Malcolm McLaren was searching for the right man to defend Vicious. 'I had to find a serious lawyer,' he says. 'I contacted my London solicitor, Steven Fisher, and asked him to come over to New York, even though I knew that he was involved in the legal case about the ownership of the Sex Pistols, which seemed to be escalating by the day in its complexity. But this was a murder trial and Sid needed help. The only asset I had was the soundtrack that was being made for *The Great Rock 'n' Roll Swindle*. We asked around town for the names of good lawyers and began our search. Roy Cohn was our first stop.' Cohn was a powerful lawyer who had worked with the notorious Senator Joseph McCarthy during his infamous anti-communist witch-hunt of the 1950s.

'[Cohn] was sitting at his desk with an authoritative calm, wearing bright-coloured suspenders and a loosely knotted tie,' recalls McLaren. 'Steel garters held up his sleeves; the impression was of an uncompromising dedication to work. This, it was clear, was a man in control. Cohn, imperious in his bearing, invited us to understand that he was an Olympian within the legal profession, one who sold justice for shit-loads of money. He greeted us brusquely, "I don't wanna know," he said straight off, "whether he did it or not. What I wanna know is whether Sid wants to live." I assured him that he did. "He's gotta know what it's like in a United States prison." I pointed out that he was in Rikers Island. Cohn snorted. "Rikers Island is for beginners. The first thing we have to do is to show this young man what life in a New York prison is all about. Then he'll be more co-operative. We gotta make him understand, in no uncertain terms, that the last thing he wants is to be locked up in one of those hellholes."'

Cohn had already come up with a basic storyline which he was confident would provide enough doubt regarding the case of the prosecution to leave Sid a free man. A lack of fingerprints on the knife would contribute to this doubt. 'According to Cohn's strategy, Sid had got involved with a bunch of low-lifes, and on the night of the murder a fight had broken out, during which the foul deed was committed by any number of roving criminals,' explains Malcolm McLaren. 'Sid was a victim of circumstance. There was, of course, the legendary reputation of the Chelsea Hotel and, according to Cohn, its first three floors were reserved exclusively for junkies, prostitutes and their drug dealers – all of them otherwise known as artists. Cohn, I could see, was a hood lawyer, and there was no way he was going to sympathise with Sid's angst: the boy needed discipline – if only to insure that he behaved – and for two hundred and fifty thousand dollars Cohn virtually guaranteed victory. I looked at Steven and he blanched at the price and at the impossible confidence radiating from this booming, impatient man. We knew we had to move on.'

The first bail hearing was on Friday, 21 October and the legal team certainly knew what they were doing because they were able to get their client released on $50,000 bail. Strong objections were raised by District Attorney Kenneth Schachter, who argued that Sid might try to flee because of the strong likelihood of a conviction.

'I met Allen Ginsberg in a night club,' remembers Malcolm McLaren. '"It was a set-up by the police," he suggested, concerned, interested, and he then added, following a brief spasm of doubt, "He didn't kill her, did he?" But it was a statement, really, not a question, and I heartily agreed, keeping my own unexamined doubts to myself. Ginsberg, determined that Sid should get justice, introduced me to William Kunstler, the legendary left-wing lawyer who defended the Chicago Seven [a group of anti-war protesters at the Democratic convention of 1968]. We met Kunstler at his home in Greenwich Village, wearing jeans and an open-necked shirt, his hair dusted with cigarette ash. We were led to a study carpeted in kilims, where Kunstler made points about the politics of the culture and started to roll a joint. The eyes of my London solicitor widened behind his spectacles. Kunstler asked, deep concern in his voice, "Tell me. Is Sid still on drugs?" "He's going cold turkey at Rikers," I replied. "He's on vitamin pills." "Has he ever had psychiatric help?" I shifted nervously at this. The

implications of the question, and the prospect of Sid, unrecon-
structed London lad, expounding on the intimate details of
childhood trauma for the benefit of a New York therapist, struck
me as ludicrously improbable. "Umm," I said. "I don't believe
so." Kunstler was an impressive figure, and the most sympa-
thetic lawyer I'd meet, and I could see that his politics were
grand and serious, although it was unlikely that they would
ever match Sid's. And Kunstler wanted to help. He tried desperately hard to understand Punk Rock and listened patiently to
our explanations. His music, I suspected, was Bob Dylan or Joan
Baez – possibly even Joni Mitchell. This was a concern. How
would he ever understand the Sex Pistols? We knew we had to
move on again.'

Once bail had been set, McLaren made a flurry of transatlantic calls to Richard Branson in London and managed to
secure a promise from the Virgin boss that the $50,000 bail
money would arrive by Monday at the latest.

During an interview about his new band, Public Image
Limited, John Lydon was asked by the *Melody Maker* what he
thought of the whole Sid and Nancy affair. 'I don't see why I
should have any feelings about it at all,' he replied. 'You see Sid
decided quite some time ago that he was going to become an
arsehole, and he did. All that fucking heroin shit, it just got on
my nerves. I mean people take it once in a while, but not every
fucking day. And then that decadence trip that he got into, you
know, cutting himself and ugh! It's nothing.'

Anne Beverley had flown into New York the previous
afternoon, on the back of some cash pulled together by her sister
and some close friends. Given that her latest boyfriend Charlie
was a cocaine dealer, one might have thought money was freely
available, but once again Anne was struggling. Armed with a
sleeping bag, and a reported $10,000 payment from the *New
York Post* – although if this were true the money disappeared
very quickly – Anne cleared customs and immediately headed
for the hospital wing at Rikers Island. Sid was in the wing

undergoing his cold-turkey drug withdrawal treatment. 'I tried to keep my distance from her,' says Malcolm McLaren. 'Sid's mother was a disenfranchised flower child and trouble tended to accompany her everywhere. I wasn't able to avoid her and the next day three of us, me, mom and a journalist from the tabloid went out to Rikers Island to get Sid. I had managed to secure bail from Virgin, which advanced money against the soundtrack of *The Great Rock 'n' Roll Swindle.* Sid emerged in impressively good spirits: healthy, clear, and elated to be free. He actually had some colour in his cheeks. I was thrilled: maybe he did want to live. Maybe he could be an F. Lee Bailey client after all. He'd been moved from a cell to the hospital, where he'd been detoxed and given heavy doses of vitamins. He was animated, and talked about the friends he'd made inside. His pockets were filled with pieces of paper – fan mail from the inmates, along with phone numbers of people to contact in New York. We got into the car and headed back to the city.'

'Everybody we knew came together,' Anne Beverley said. 'Money came in from various sources so that I could do my best for Simon. Malcolm held everything together and talked to all the right people.' Eileen Polk met Anne in New York. 'I really liked Anne,' recalls Polk. 'I met her at Max's one night. I recognised her from her photos in the paper and went right up to her and said "hi". She was a lot of fun considering her circumstances. I thought the press was demonizing her just like they had done with Nancy. I also thought she was a far more intelligent and ethical person than the way she was portrayed by the press.'

Malcolm McLaren continued to search for the right lawyer to take the case, but more and more of them seemed to be disinterested as to whether Sid was guilty or not. They just wanted to know how much he wanted to get off. 'I began to ask myself, "Well, did he do it?"' says McLaren. 'I wonder now if Sid actually told me, but if he did I've shut out whatever it was that he said. Did he do it? I don't know. I know only that I didn't want to know. I wanted to get Sid out of trouble. Finally, the question became immaterial. Sid, my Sid, did not deserve to die in jail. But I still didn't have a lawyer. Why not, Steven suggested, try for the very best? Why not F. Lee Bailey? F. Lee Bailey had a practice in Boston. I phoned and spoke to his secretary.' McLaren was informed that Francis Lee Bailey, now regarded as the most successful defence lawyer in US history, was actually in New York taking part in a book signing on Wall Street.

'I got the address, grabbed Steven, and dashed to the bookstore, picking up a copy of the *Post* en route,' says McLaren. 'Sid, once again, was on the front page. But by the time we got there we thought we were too late. F. Lee, the star with this crowd, was surrounded by so many stockbrokers wanting an autograph that we gave up all hope of a meeting until we learned that when he was done he would be at a nearby bar. He'd taken the place over for the day. The bar was around the corner, F. Lee was at the back – his booth theatrically lit – quietly talking to a client. We were summoned and led to the table, and Steven briefly summarised our case. As F. Lee leaned into the pool of light, my first impression was of utter astonishment. F. Lee Bailey was wearing make-up! I was transfixed by this extraordinary man, whose rugged features were glazed in orange Max Factor pan stick. He wasn't effeminate, he was simply, from what I could deduce, someone who was always on stage. He wore a navy-blue pin-striped Savile Row suit with a fresh gardenia on his lapel.'

Bailey explained that he liked to do a lot of preparation including in-depth research and courtroom rehearsals, especially as Sid was a possible jail sentence of twenty-five years with an earliest release date of late 2003. Just as Roy Cohn had done, Bailey sketched out a strategy for the defence. 'He explained that we had to paint New York as a lonely, dark, miserable kind of place, rotten to the core,' says McLaren. 'We had to show that the hotel was not a hotel, but a place for degenerates bent on corrupting newcomers to the city. "How old is

Sid?" he asked. For a moment I'd forgotten. "Nineteen or twenty" I replied. F. Lee looked at Steven, "Here's this kid from London. An innocent, pleasant enough rock 'n' roll boy, right? What does he know?" he asked, spreading his hands. "What's more," he said, "in America we can virtually decide who'll make up the jury. We can argue who will be suitable to sit on this trial, and we'll want only those who'll really understand Sid. In other words, those from a similar working-class background." Leaning forward, F. Lee emphasised the point: "I want toilet cleaners! Road sweepers!" I glanced sideways at Steven. "They've got to be paid more to sit on that bench than they could ever make otherwise, a jury happy to have this trial drawn out for as long as possible. I want a jury that's on our side." He had an approach, a brilliant, deliciously anti-establishment one. "In order to win over the press, you're going to have to rework Sid's image," he continued. "You know. You're good at publicity." He looked at me steadily. "Get him jogging in Central Park. Dating librarians. I want to see him as a likable young man lost in New York." He caught my expression. "I know he's a rock 'n' roll kid, but he's got to have some other interests, doesn't he?" I flinched at the thought of reinventing Sid as a friendly jock. And a librarian to take the place of Nancy? F. Lee then told us that he wanted Sid to come to his house the following weekend, to relax, so that they could get to know each other. He wanted to see for himself whether Sid wanted to live. He asked us how we intended to pay – he wanted $50,000 up front. There was talk about the book and film rights. He explained that he had an assistant named Jim Merberg to whom he wanted us to report. He would try to check out who was at the hotel, the details of the evening Nancy died, the murder weapon, and the fingerprints on it. This was all going to cost a lot of money.'

❁   ❁   ❁

Upon being released from Rikers under $25,000 bail set by Judge Martin Erdmann, Sid and his mother booked into The Deauville, a low-rent welfare hostel on Madison Avenue. 'Anne had had a hard life and no one was giving her a break,' says Eileen Polk. 'When I heard from Joe Stevens that Anne and Sid were being evicted from the Deauville Hotel for not paying the bill I couldn't let that happen. I lent them $200 to pay their bill and Anne paid me back as soon as the check from the record company arrived. I still don't understand why they were in that place. It wasn't even as "nice" as the Chelsea, and being located in the hub of Manhattan made it easier for drug dealers and groupies to have access to Sid.'

On 30 October 1978, Sid made a phone call to Deborah Spungen. 'We always knew that we would go to the same place when we died,' Sid told her. 'We so much wanted to die together in each other's arms. I cry every time I think about that. I promised my baby that I would kill myself if anything ever happened to her, and she promised me the same. This is the final commitment to my love.' Sid had been forced to surrender his passport to the NYPD and each morning he was expected to report in at the local police station to provide urine samples to test for drugs. Sid told McLaren that he'd been something of a hero in Rikers Island. 'They thought I was Big Charlie Potatoes in there, Malcolm,' he told McLaren. 'I was on the cover of the newspapers every day. They had me pinned up on their walls. I was a pin-up. I was signing autographs! These big black guys, they fuckin' love the Sex Pistols, they knew everything about us.'

McLaren, Beverley and Sid had a meeting about Bailey's plans for the defence. 'Malcolm is going to help you, Simon,' Anne said to Sid. 'He's going to change your image.'

'I looked at Sid's mother,' recalls McLaren. 'Did she need to say that just now? I didn't trust her. I never trusted mothers. I still don't. I asked Sid, "What about it? Do you think you could start jogging in Central Park? Get fit? It's going to be a long trial."

Sid considered this, "I'm not looking like a prat. Suppose my friends see me running in the fuckin' park!" "Don't worry, Sid. I'll buy you a dog." I found him a hotel, the Seville, on 29th Street. I wanted his mother to be with him. I was hoping that she'd behave responsibly. I didn't want him hanging out at clubs and rock 'n' roll shows. "Get him reading," I said to her. "Take him to the library. If he needs companions, maybe he'll find a new friend there." I paused. "A librarian perhaps. It would be awfully helpful if Sid fell in love with a librarian." I told Sid that he had nothing to worry about: he now had F. Lee Bailey. "He's the best. He's going to get you off. In two or three months, you'll be singing in Las Vegas on the same fucking stage as Elvis Presley." "If Sid plays Vegas," I told Steven later, "It'll cover the trial. Sid will work hard. He's going to have a new life.'"

The Seville hotel was described by Eileen Polk as 'some dump in midtown where every junkie and drug pusher in town knew where to find them'. Sid started sinking into depression. At the Seville he attempted suicide by slashing his wrists with a broken light bulb, but Anne was on hand and called McLaren.

'That weekend I was supposed to take Sid to see F. Lee Bailey in Boston,' says McLaren. 'Before setting off, I stopped by the hotel where Joe Stevens was still staying and Sid's mother rang, sounding weak and vague. "Come immediately to the hotel," she said. "I can't control Simon anymore." Stevens and I sped across town to the hotel and raced to Sid's room. His mother opened the door and then shrank away into the bathroom. Sid was screaming, his arms extended, his hands reaching out toward me, dripping with blood. "I want to die," he was shouting. "I want to go to Nancy now! Get me out, get me some pills. I don't wanna carry on. I want to be with Nancy." I said, "Sid, please don't do this to yourself." I looked at his mother. She pointed to a broken light bulb in the toilet, which he had used to slash his arms and wrists. I tried to sound calm. "You were supposed to be coming to Boston with me today, Sid. To see F. Lee Bailey." Wrong move. Sid screamed, "Just get me something – anything, anything! Get me some pills! Please, Malcolm." I told him I'd get him some Quaaludes. He was very frightened, his mother was in bad shape. She appeared to be bruised around the face; they'd obviously been fighting. Steven and I left the room. We went down to the lobby and sat trying to figure out what to do. I felt terrible. I had no intention, of course, of getting Quaaludes. I called an ambulance, even though I knew that it was going to make for news, and that the news wasn't going to help our case. It didn't. Within ten minutes, the police arrived, and a team of officers rushed upstairs, their guns out. I followed them, thinking, "My god, what are they going to do to him?" They smashed open the door and rushed toward Sid, terrifying him. He moved toward the window and looked as though he were going to leap – we were nine or ten floors up. Nothing I shouted had any effect. They grabbed him, slapped him, strapped him up, and dragged him out of the room and took him to Bellevue Hospital. We followed the ambulance in a cab. When we reached the hospital, we could hear Sid screaming. Then he started singing "C'mon Everybody". It made me laugh. They had bandaged Sid's wounds and put him in a straitjacket. This was rock 'n' roll pushed to the limit. And then it occurred to me: Sid's mother. She had been, I suddenly just knew it, scoring for Sid. Their argument had probably been about drugs. It didn't take her long. Perhaps Sid should remain in the hospital, just to be kept safe. Later, as I stood on the street outside the hospital, I realised that I was going to have to return to London. My [own] trial began shortly. I felt uneasy leaving Sid behind, especially with his mother here to look after him. How, I remember thinking, would any of this turn out all right?'

News of the attempted suicide was leaked to local journalists, who all assumed that this was further evidence that Nancy's death was a suicide pact gone wrong. Stevens quizzed Sid about the events of 12 October. 'Let me tell you something, Joe

Stevens,' Sid had retorted angrily. 'I'd never kill her. I loved that woman. I want to be with her now, and I'll be with her soon.'

With Sid tucked up in Bellevue Hospital and hopefully out of harm's way, McLaren brought in a team of private investigators in order to provide a more accurate and more convincing account of events than the police had been able to find.

❦   ❦   ❦

Back in London, Vivienne Westwood was cashing in on Sid's increased notoriety by selling a newly designed T-shirt featuring a photo of Sid surrounded by blood-splattered roses and the tasteless slogan 'She's dead, I'm alive, I'm yours,' and the Seditionaries logo in inverted brackets underneath. 'When I got home to London the next morning, I found Vivienne and Joe making Sid Vicious dolls,' says Malcolm McLaren with a sly grin. 'Every detail was in place: the swastika T-shirt, the padlock around his neck, the black spiky hair, the long legs, the permanent sneer. The dolls were extremely accomplished. Vivienne didn't spare a thought over the death of Nancy. Vivienne loved Sid. She'd been a fan even before he was a member of the group, and she was very upset.'

London's Punk fraternity descended upon Seditionaries in their droves to buy one of the shirts, no doubt believing – falsely, as it turned out – that the proceeds from their sale would be put towards their idol's legal costs. The Kings Road was also awash with rumours of a Sex Pistols reunion gig in order to raise money for Sid. In fact, John Lydon had well and truly washed his hands of Vicious – he was now busy with Wobble, promoting PiL's eponymous debut single, which had been released the day following Nancy's death.

Lydon and Wobble weren't the only ones to turn a blind eye to Sid's plight and only The Clash, following a meeting with Anne Beverley, agreed to help out by playing a benefit gig at the Music Machine in Camden Town on Tuesday, 19 December

1978. On the night, they played an instrumental version of 'My Way'. 'Mick [Jones] always came through for him [Sid],' Anne said of the ex-Clash guitarist. 'You have to say "God bless Mick Jones" because he was a real mate. Anyone can talk about friendship, but it's only when the chips are down that you find out who your real friends are and Mick came through for him. I just wish sometimes that Simon could have been more like Mick as a person, but I'm not one for dreaming.'

❀　❀　❀

Any trial for Sid would have brought the NYPD's investigation under close scrutiny. The Forensic Crime Unit team, which arrived at the Chelsea around 1 p.m. on 12 October, had been guilty of a dereliction of duty. Amazingly, the team failed to find a bottle of Tuinol tablets – the drug Sid claimed to have taken the previous night and which was thought to have rendered him unconscious. They also failed to spot some 'brown flaky powder' and three hypodermic needles, all of which were lying in plain view on a bedside cabinet. These items lay undiscovered for a further two hours until the arrival of Associate Medical Examiner Dr Geeta Natarajan, who collected these items and took them, along with Nancy's body, back to the Chief Medical Examiner's mortuary at 520 1st Avenue. The autopsy, toxicology and serology tests were carried out later that afternoon. The autopsy, which wasn't completed until around 8.30 p.m. that evening, concluded that Nancy had died from external and internal haemorrhaging caused by a one-inch stab wound that was compatible with the blade of a Jaguar K-11.

James O'Conner, the Chief Medical Examiner's administrative assistant, told *Soho Weekly News* reporter Lesley Vinson that the reason for the lengthy autopsy was due to the celebrity status of the accused, and that the Chief Medical Examiner (CME) would be called upon to testify in court. Apart from the fatal stab wound, Nancy's autopsy also revealed track marks, contusions and eccymoses – black and blue bruises, which were relatively fresh at the time of her death. Two of these eccymoses were of particular interest to the CME because they happened to be on Nancy's face and corroborated Leon Webster's claim that Sid and Nancy had been fighting on the night she died. One of the bruises was on the right side of her chin and was the size of a quarter, while the second and larger bruise was on the right side of her face next to the eye.

Although the cause of death was clearly the large stab wound, the autopsy had been anything but straightforward due to the deteriorated condition of Nancy's internal organs, and Dr Natarajan would not commit herself to providing an exact time of death until the toxicology and serology tests had been completed. It was generally assumed, however, that Nancy had been stabbed between 6–7 a.m. and had died sometime between 8–10 a.m.

The Forensic Crime Unit's report should have been a cause for concern in Third Homicide Division's HQ. The team's inventory of all the items they had found within room 100 listed inconsequential items such as Nancy's scrapbook and a plastic Harrods carrier bag stuffed with black hosiery, but the report made no mention whatsoever of the $18,750 that several of the couple's friends and acquaintances had reported seeing stuffed in the bottom drawer of the bedside cabinet in the days leading up to Nancy's death. This could also have been corroborated by Virgin's accountancy department, who still have records of a large payment to one Mr J. Ritchie (only two weeks prior to 12 October) and Peter Crowley at Max's Kansas City, who had paid for his recent gig at the venue.

❀   ❀   ❀

Once the initial rush of publicity over Nancy's death had passed, the manager of the Chelsea Hotel, Stanley Bard, had further problems to contend with. Room 100 had remained closed long after the NYPD's forensic team had finished their investigation, but Bard quickly realised that this would not be enough to deter the coterie of black-clad teenage girls that had begun sneaking into the hotel and holding all-night séances outside the room. This was upsetting the residents, and although Stanley knew he wouldn't be able to eradicate Sid and Nancy's connection to the Chelsea, or stop them from being hailed as Punk's own Romeo and Juliet, what he *could* do to deny the ghoulish girls and anyone else wanting to a get kick from gawping at the murder room was to remove the room altogether. If you walk along the Chelsea's first-floor landing today you will notice that the room numbers jump from 98 to 102. Where room 100 once stood there is now an emergency stairwell, with a laundry room to one side of it. The old room 100 occupied a little of both but has now been wiped from existence.

CHAPTER 11

Too Fast to Live

'Well you're the coolest thing in town, with your face flat on the ground, friends went through your pockets as the coffin went down, you overdosed at last, spike stuck in your head, now you're dead . . . dead! Dead! Dead!'

(From 'Too Much Junkie Business' by
Johnny Thunders & Walter Lure)

'I kept in touch with Sid through his mother who phoned daily,' says Malcolm McLaren. '"Sid is fine," she said each time. "Just fine." After a while the calls reported progress. Sid was now more than just fine. He was better, much better, but dead bored. Was there any way we could get him released? Sid's mother promised to look after him.' McLaren had no trust of the woman Virgin Records would later christen 'The Widow Beverley'. He began to panic. In his own words: 'I rang Jim Merberg in Boston. "Can we trust her?" I asked. I was frustrated that I couldn't be there. Merberg said he would visit every day and, he admitted, it would be helpful if Sid were out. A defendant in a loony bin wasn't building a better image. Also, F. Lee still hadn't met Sid and there was the evidence to collect. Sid could direct Merberg to informers and people who might be able to testify on his behalf.'

Sid finally left the Bellevue Hospital on Monday, 29 October 1978 after passing a rigorous psychological examination. He had little to do except wait for his next court appearance, which was scheduled for late November. On 28 November, Sid gave what would be his last UK television interview to Bernard Clarke, a reporter on the BBC programme *Nationwide*. Anne Beverley was present and in the footage her hand is visible, stroking Sid's leg. Sid is seen wearing a new padlock and chain, which was a gift from Dee Dee Ramone in lieu of the original one being in an NYPD evidence bag. The short interview clip found the former Sex Pistol incredibly low.

Clarke: 'Why did it happen?'

Vicious: 'It was meant to happen. Nancy always said she'd die before she was twenty-one.'

Clarke: 'What would you like to do over the next year or two?'

Vicious: 'I'd like to have fun, any kind of fun just fun, that's my object in life.'

Clarke: 'Are you having fun at the moment?'

Vicious: 'Are you kidding? No, I'm not having fun at all.'

Clarke: 'Where would you like to be?'

Vicious: 'Under the ground.'

Clarke: 'Are you serious?'

Vicious: 'Oh yeah.'

Around this time Sid went to see a Blondie gig at the New York Palladium. This was possibly the same night as the *Nationwide* recording because Sid was photographed backstage hanging out with Johnny Thunders, Richard Hell and Jerry Nolan, wearing the exact same clothes as in the interview. In the few weeks since Nancy's death Sid had met and become an item with a twenty-year-old 'actress' and wannabe socialite called Michelle Robison, who was also pictured with Sid at the Blondie show. Despite his obvious grief over Nancy, Sid and Michelle found that they both had more in common than could have been imagined, and both seemed emotionally vulnerable to a 'rebound' relationship, should the chance come about.

Robison has always been a bit of a mystery character in Sid's life, starting with the fact that she has been called 'Robinson'. Like Sid, it was reported that she had recently lost her partner to drugs. Other false claims said that she was a pole dancer, a heroin user and a porn star. Sid had been introduced to Michelle by Joe Stevens at Max's Kansas City while out cele-brating his recent release from Bellevue. Stevens has good cause to remember the evening in question for he had been the one hitting on Michelle, but saw his amorous advances crushed in a heartbeat when the famous Sid walked through the door.

'Some people have said that Michelle Robison was a groupie or "super-groupie", but this is not true,' recalls Eileen Polk. 'I had been going to rock clubs since 1970 and if she was a groupie I would have known about it. I did not meet Michelle until 1978 when she began going to Max's Kansas City. She was a well-educated girl from an upper-middle-class family. She had a nice mother, whom I met, and a really nice apartment in a brown-stone on Bank Street. She said that she was an "actress", but New York was full of actresses like Michelle who could not find work. However, I never knew Michelle to have to go to a job everyday, so I assumed that she had some support from her family. She was not a junkie. Michelle liked guys who fell into one type: tall, dark, thin, black-clad, English rockers, preferably with some money. She never supported a guy – she was too classy for that. The only guy I ever saw her with besides Sid, was Dave. She gave him short shrift as soon as she met Sid. Of course conspiracy theorists would say "Dave! He was there the night Sid died!" and make something out of that, but it was all coincidence. Our group of scene people was small and inces-tuous, and there were only a few English guys of that type available at the time.'

'We bumped into each other in Max's Kansas City,' remembers Peter Kodick. 'There was a bunch of people who knew him and there was a lot of back-slapping, it was a bit shocking to see him. That particular night he was on pills, God knows what, probably Secanol, some sort of downer. Take a couple of those, have a few drinks and you're OK. I can't remember him looking for smack that particular night.'

Part of Sid's stringent bail conditions were that he remained in the care of Anne Beverley at the Seville, but within days of meeting Michelle he'd moved into Michelle's West Village apartment at 63 Bank Street. With Robison on his arm, Sid reintroduced himself to New York nightlife, but wherever Sid went trouble was sure to follow. 'Michelle was really not very tough,' says Eileen Polk. 'She was emotionally fragile. Some would say that she was a "drama queen" and "hysterical", but I did not judge her for that. Being with someone like Sid Vicious meant that every day and night was spent fighting off groupies and drug fiends, and eventually she cracked. She ended up in St Vincent's hospital psych ward because she couldn't handle it. Then she regretted that decision because the doctors removed the numerous headlines about Sid from the newspapers. Michelle had very limited time with her new flame. The whole Sid Vicious affair was, for Michelle, a repetition of a previous traumatic event in which her boyfriend, also an English rocker, was killed in a terrible motorcycle accident. I felt very bad for her because she was maligned in the press; all the while she was being so kind to Sid and his mother. By the time she was released from St Vincent's, Sid was back in Rikers again for the Todd Smith incident.'

The 'Todd Smith incident' happened during the early hours of Tuesday, 5 December 1978. Sid was attending a Manhattan disco called Hurrah's when he became embroiled in a fight with Patti Smith's brother Todd, who had taken exception to Sid supposedly having attempted to chat up his girlfriend. 'We go into the club and it was empty and you have good nights at Hurrah's and you have bad nights. This wasn't a particularly good night,' remembers Peter Kodick today. 'The band's playing, the music's really loud, so we walk around the club and Sid starts talking to some girl. The next thing I know there's screams, and this guy has come over and Sid just smashed this glass in this person's face. It was just stupid. Todd Smith was this meek, mild little guy. Why Sid turned round and smashed a glass in his face I'll never know. But he did it. It was stupidity, maybe it was the wrong combination of pills with drink and this person said something. I dragged him out and we took a taxi downtown and I dropped him off. They arrested him the next day. It was pointless – they obviously knew who it was who had done this.' Steve Dior remembers the night all too well: 'Peter saved us that night – he grabbed Sid and made a human chain behind him, and that's what got all of us out, before the police arrived.'

Eileen Polk's diary, Friday, 8 December 1978:

Anne said that Sid had returned home late on Wednesday night with cuts on his hand, which he claimed had come from falling on broken glass. But, Anne could tell that he was worried about something and there must have been more to the story than that. They reported to the police station as Sid was supposed to do and then to the Methadone clinic on time. The next day, when they reported to the police station Anne waited in a cab while Sid went into the station. She waited a long time and then a detective came out to the cab and told her that Sid had been arrested. He did not report to the Methadone clinic and on that technicality bail was revoked.

Punk Rock star Patti Smith's brother Todd Smith had received five stitches in his face at Roosevelt Hospital. He claimed he was assaulted and the police were called. Todd Smith claimed that Sid had pinched his girlfriend on the behind and that Todd had said something 'protective'. According to Todd, Sid broke a Heineken bottle and jabbed him in the face. According to Sid, it was Todd who provoked the fight and it was in fact Todd who had the

Heineken bottle and Sid had a glass from which he had been drinking. According to Sid, Todd went to hit him and during the scuffle the glass broke in his hand and Todd's face was cut from shattering glass. Eyewitness to this event so far are; Danielle Booth, David, an English photographer and someone named Pete. They said that they are ready to give statements to the police supporting Sid's story. David, the photographer, had a camera with him that night and whether he has pictures of the fight is not known.

When the news reached London, Malcolm McLaren's heart sank. So much for putting Sid in a better light and increasing his public image before the trial. 'Just as I feared when Sid left Rikers, he went straight to one of the clubs downtown and beat some guy over the head with a bottle,' says McLaren. 'Smith was pressing charges. Merberg was concerned; Sid was back at Rikers. There was more bad news; a woman was involved. A friend phoned me to fill me in on the details, "Sid *was* with a girl that night – Michelle Robison." Alarm bells rang in my head – not another Nancy! "And Sid's mom seems to like her too." "What?" "And they're both giving interviews to the *Post*." More details were to come. "And Sid's mom has now got green hair!" "What?" "And she's wearing Sid's clothes. She's, you know, dressed like a Punk. And do you want to know something else?" "No," I said. "Don't tell me any more!" Everything I hated about mothers came to the surface. I was so angry but I couldn't leave London. I still had my film to finish, my court case to face, and money to raise. Vivienne was haranguing me to finish with it all. Things were closing in on us in the most menacing way. Couldn't I just quit? I went to see my lawyer.'

Eileen Polk's Diary, Friday, 8 December 1978:

Conversation at Hurrah's on 7 December with Danielle Boothe, Rockets Redglare and the two English guys, Pete and Dave. This was the first time I met Peter Kodick and his assistant Dave. I didn't realise at the time that they were both photographers, and I didn't know their last names. I don't know if Pete and Dave ever talked to the police. I told them that they should call Sid's lawyer. I didn't really know Rockets that well either, but he had achieved some notoriety by being one of the last people to see Nancy alive. Sid didn't seem to have anything against Rockets, except that he was really annoying, and he called Sid and Anne at the Deauville almost every day.

Sid's story about the glass shattering in his hand makes more sense than Todd's story about the Heineken bottle because Sid didn't drink beer when he was out at the clubs. He was beyond beer and with all the free drinks he was offered everywhere he went, it seems more plausible that he was drinking hard liquor from a glass. It's ironic that with his Methadone maintenance program and the daily drug testing, Sid began hitting the bottle even harder!

Whether Smith would have pressed charges or not was a moot point, for the club's manager had already called the police and that meant Sid was on his way back to Rikers Island via the courtroom of Judge Herbert Altman. Again Sid did well at the prison and avoided falling prey to the population of gang-bangers, armed robbers and murderers. Sid's cellmate was 'Jimmy' – the NYPD weren't prepared to supply his surname and it's not listed in any of Merberg's files – a large man with a string of charges against him who was more than able to look after himself. Jimmy soon realised the benefits of a celebrity cellmate and within days of Sid's second incarceration the pair were selling signed visiting orders at three dollars a pop, an incredible income by any prison standards. The cash paid for drugs and the odd glass of prison hooch.

Sid's next hearing came three days after the incident at Hurrah's and the prison authorities decided that he should be switched from the main cells to the prison's hospital wing where he would undergo yet another detoxification programme. Although Sid would spend the festive season locked up, he was also getting cleaned up. A further hearing was postponed until Thursday, 1 February 1979 so that the hospital's psychiatrists could compile their reports. During his time in the detoxification programme Sid wrote two very deep and hugely understanding letters to Deborah Spungen. In her book *And I Don't Want to Live This Life* – its title taken directly from Sid's own writing – Deborah explains how she was shocked to receive the letters but even more surprised by their content. The second letter, which explained that Nancy was the love of his life and that he couldn't possibly continue without her, also contained the following poem:

You were my baby girl,
And I shared all your fears.
Such joy to hold you in my arms,
And kiss away your tears.
But now you're gone, there's only pain,
And nothing I can do,
And I don't want to live this life,
if I can't live for you.
My beautiful baby girl,
our love will never die.

This certainly changed Deborah's opinion of the person she had met only months earlier. 'Sid was back in Rikers, and Merberg now had to let him out of there,' says McLaren. 'The man was indefatigable. I assured him that I would be in New York myself. It was only a matter of days, then I'd personally be able to look after Sid. I was terrified of his mother's influence. I had to get to New York as quickly as possible, and I was confident, after the Virgin meeting, that we'd reach a settlement. This wouldn't go to trial. Merberg went back to the courthouse and, evidently, made a brilliant plea – possibly too brilliant. He was able to get Sid released almost immediately. I wasn't able to get back to New York so quickly.'

●　　●　　●

Nancy's death couldn't have come at a worse time for Malcolm McLaren – he was fully occupied with preparing for the impending court case with Johnny Rotten, who had instigated high court proceedings to wind up the Sex Pistols partnership. The court case, No. 1152 in the 1978 list, duly opened on Friday, 10 November 1978, but owing to Sid's situation, the case was immediately adjourned for three months.

Instead of preparing for his legal showdown with Lydon, Malcolm found himself having to think of a means to bolster Sid's bail fund for the up-and-coming hearing. Richard Branson had already informed him that there would be no further cash input from Virgin unless there was a viable Sex Pistols product in the can. McLaren had previously been planning to release 'Something Else' as a new Sex Pistols single but Virgin understandably baulked at the timing, which would have seen the record come out in the third week of October. McLaren needed another way to raise some money. He came up with a plan that included flying to New York with Steve Jones and Paul Cook, then heading down to Miami with Sid to record an album containing cover versions of rock 'n' roll standards. He informed Branson that he would deliver ten finished songs, although by his own admission he was already counting Sid's three finished *Swindle* numbers as part of the project.

Harvey Goldsmith had also been in contact with Glitterbest to talk about setting up some New York shows, but with the impending murder case lifting Sid's profile, there was no reason to stay in small clubs such as Max's. The offer included Radio City and The Palladium, along with talk of hotel shows in Las Vegas.

McLaren, Jones and Cook had planned to fly out to New York on Sunday, 4 February 1979. They had it on good authority from the legal team in New York that Sid would be granted bail at the hearing, although the plan rested on the hearing lasting until late on Friday, whereby Anne Beverley could be counted on to keep Sid out of trouble over the weekend until the trio arrived. Unfortunately for McLaren, James Merberg had been busy collating evidence that suggested several major inconsistencies in the police's case and his impassioned plea saw Judge Betty Ellerin allow Sid back on the street by Thursday lunchtime.

Sid had been released into the care of his mother Anne, girlfriend Michelle, photographer Eileen Polk, and several members of the New York drug fraternity. 'They bring in the prisoners from Rikers or wherever he was, and his mother's down there, and I think I waited about fifteen minutes and then he arrived,' says Peter Kodick. 'It was: undo the cuffs, sign all the papers and out of the court-house. But here you were looking at some guy with black jeans, T-shirt, plain jacket, no studded belt, no studs on his shoes, you know, it had all gone a bit meek and mild. The first thing we did, we walked out, obviously it was February, freezing cold in New York, walk out of the court-house he didn't have a coat or anything, and we walked eight or ten blocks to his mother's place. I remember as we were walking along the way he was like, "Did you get it? Did you get it?" His mother was supposed to pick up something for him. We go back to Anne's place, he takes this stuff, he shoots it up, and nothing. It was complete crap. He asked me if I could find anything for him, and I said I'll see what I can do, I'll try. I find something for him, and I call him up that evening and get the address or whatever and go over to Michelle's place. I must have arrived at about 8 o'clock that evening. We're talking a small apartment in Greenwich Village, and he's dying for the stuff, he's a junkie, you know, so the first thing he's asking is, "Did you get it? Did you get it?" OK. So I gave him the stuff. There's Anne Beverley in the living-room watching TV, there's Sid and Michelle in her bedroom. And that was the way it was the whole evening.'

Eileen Polk remembers Sid's exit from the courthouse rather differently. 'I met Anne and Michelle at Michelle's apartment early in the morning so that we could be at the courthouse for Sid's hearing by 8 a.m.' recalls Polk today. 'When we arrived at court there were dozens of reporters and cameras following us around. Anne told us not to say anything to them and we didn't. This really pissed them off because if we didn't do or say something obnoxious, or anything at all, they really couldn't use much of the video. Anne, Michelle and I went in the courtroom and they went up to the first row of seats, while I stayed in the back. I could see the judge saying something to Sid's lawyer, but the crowding of reporters made it difficult to understand what was happening. Then the crowd made a big gasp of surprise, and I realised that the judge was letting Sid out! Anne, Michelle and I left the courtroom and a female reporter shoved a microphone in my face and shouted aggressively at me, "Are you from England?" I said nothing and the woman became angry. We went outside and waited for Sid. By the time he and his lawyer came out, the press had all left and we had a moment to talk. Joe Stevens was there too and snapped a few pictures of Sid and his lawyer. Then Sid and Anne told Michelle that we should all meet at her apartment. I shared a cab with Michelle who was very happy and Sid and Anne took the next cab. Sid hated riding in a crowded taxi because his legs were so long. The thing that really irks me is the assumption by some journalists that Sid was "taken to a party at Michelle's" by his mother instead of "taking him home" and how "irresponsible" that was. That was his home! The morons!'

Sid seemed to be in good spirits and talked endlessly about the friends that he'd made in jail and how he also believed that his lawyers would get an acquittal or at least a reduced conviction. 'Michelle and I arrived at Bank Street and Sid and Anne arrived shortly after,' says Eileen Polk. 'Then Howie Pyro and

Jerry Only arrived. It was now close to noon. We all sat on Michelle's bed and listened to Sid's stories about Rikers Island. He said that the other inmates had taught him a lot about fighting the system and he seemed more confident than ever that he just might beat the murder rap. Then Jerry Nolan and his girlfriend Esther arrived. This made me a little nervous because Anne had told me that her goal was to keep Sid from taking drugs and also to keep him from going out and getting into trouble. I hadn't been told that Jerry Nolan was expected, and he was the only junkie, besides Sid, in the room. Sid and Jerry began pestering Anne for money. They were both acting like little children, "Pleeeease mum can I have some money, I promise to be good." I knew they were lying, especially when Jerry said, "We're just going to get a little cocaine, for the party." This was really ridiculous. Coke was the kind of drug rich people used to impress each other and was definitely out of our price range. I knew they were really interested in heroin, so I was surprised to see Anne hand Sid a one hundred dollar bill. Then Jerry and Sid left Michelle's place. I thought we would never see them again. So, I was surprised when they returned about an hour later and they didn't seem high on anything. We all decided to go ahead with our dinner plans and I went to the Jefferson Market to buy food. I bought round steak, spaghetti, fresh vegetables and all the ingredients to make spaghetti sauce plus two six-packs of whatever beer was on sale.'

If everyone who claims to have been at 63 Bank Street on the night Sid died had indeed been there, then the apartment would have needed to be vast. The number of guests who were really there that night numbered nine and even that relatively small number would have brought a sense of claustrophobia to the tiny apartment. While the food was being prepared Sid put on some New York Dolls albums and strutted around playing air guitar.

'The dinner took forever to cook because Anne insisted we use home-made sauce,' says Eileen Polk. 'Finally we all sat down and ate and the phone started ringing a lot. Just before midnight, two of Sid's friends from London arrived. I recognised them, because I had met Pete one night at Hurrah's right after Sid was arrested for the fight with Todd Smith, and remembered that he said he and his friend Dave had seen the fight and claimed that Sid was innocent. I already knew Dave because he had worked at Bleecker Bob's record shop and he was friends with Michelle. Sid introduced Pete to Anne as the photographer that would be doing his solo album cover. They seemed to be pretty tight with Sid. Then the atmosphere of the party changed pretty quickly. People were rummaging around the kitchen looking for spoons and heading off to the bathroom. It didn't take a rocket scientist to figure out that drugs had arrived. Apparently Sid had ordered the drugs to be delivered like a pizza! This was not the kind of party Anne had planned, and Howie, Jerry Only and I met in the living room and decided to leave. But, before we could get our bags and coats, there was a funny noise in the hallway. I went down the hall to Michelle's bedroom to see what had happened and saw Sid lying on the bed surrounded by the party guests. I thought at first he had fallen asleep, but then noticed how blue he was and realised that he was overdosing. Anne had wrapped Sid in a blanket and was rubbing his shoulders and shaking him. All of a sudden he came out of it and I'll never forget what he said; "Oh, I'm sorry I scared you all." I thought it wasn't like him to apologise, so he must have been pretty wasted. Howie, Jerry Only and I took off our coats and decided to stick around to make sure Sid was OK. I had never seen an overdose before and didn't know what you were supposed to do, but the others seemed pretty competent. I pulled Anne aside and said, "Do you think we should take him to the emergency room?" St Vincent's hospital was just a few blocks away. Anne said, "We can't do that the press will make a circus out of it and Sid will be back in prison tomorrow." By that time Sid was walking around and drinking a cup of tea. He had lost his good mood and was just as sullen as he was when he was with Nancy. The last I remember of him alive was the nasty look he gave us for even thinking of taking him to the hospital. He would not have gone anyway. He was carrying a cup of tea into Michelle's bedroom. Howie, Jerry and I finally left at about 2 a.m. We took a cab to Hurrah's and danced off our anxiety.'

'He'd been detoxing for the time he'd been inside,' adds Peter Kodick. 'Usually the time anybody's going to have problems with heroin, with deaths occurring with heroin, they happen in the period after people have been doing heroin for a long time. They stop, they clean up and then they go back doing it and they do too much and they're greedy. "Oh I shouldn't do too much, I'm clean, or supposedly clean, but a little bit more, a little bit more." So he does this stuff and he's sick as a dog and he's throwing up and everything, and I'm like "Oh shit, he's taken too much, this is awful." And I stayed there for four or five hours and left at about two in the morning, and he didn't do any more stuff in that time. We were keeping him awake and Michelle is making him tea and we're drinking tea and smoking cigarettes and hanging around. It was during this period that I got to talk to him a little bit. He had come round, so to speak. He didn't do a bunch of heroin and pass out, pass out and die, OK? No. The heroin I gave him, I'd only given him so much. When I left the apartment I gave the rest to his mother and said, "Don't give him any more, give him the rest in the morning, but don't give him any more tonight." And I told Sid that there wasn't any more.'

New York Police Department records show that almost all of the heroin seized on the city's streets between Christmas 1978 and Easter 1979 was cut down to between 32% and 36% pure. In a rare quirk of fate, however, the Rolling Stones were in town, and Kodick knew that Keith Richards didn't entertain anything that wasn't nearly pure – or practically uncut. He'd long since stopped using New York street gear. The wrap that Kodick purchased for Sid that cold winter evening was nearly 100% pure. After Sid and his fellow addicts had pushed the spaghetti around their plates long enough to give some pretence that they'd actually eaten something, they headed down the corridor to the bedroom to do a little cooking of their own. When they returned to the living room Anne couldn't help notice that Sid had an unusual rosy pink glow about him. 'Jesus, son,' she later claims to have said to him. 'That must have been a good hit.' Eileen, Howie and everyone else present also remember that Sid looked elated, but Sid was no 'one hit wonder' and returned to the bedroom, with Michelle in tow, to shoot up again. 'He knew the smack was pure and strong, and so he took a lot less than usual,' Anne Beverley later told reporters.

Michelle returned to the living room some twenty minutes later saying that Sid had collapsed on the bed and that she couldn't wake him. Everyone rushed into the bedroom and found a semi-naked Sid turning blue and began to panic. Sid was dragged to his feet and walked around the apartment until he eventually came around. Anne naturally fretted over her son's accidental overdose and after berating him for giving her a scare she took the remainder of the heroin from him for safe-keeping until Sid had checked in at the local police station the following morning.

What happened next proved fatal for Sid. Anne's version of events was that Sid must have woken sometime during the night and crept into the living room, where she was sleeping on the sofa. After surreptitiously reclaiming the heroin, he had returned to the bedroom to cook up another fix, which – either intentionally or inadvertently – would be his last. 'The next morning Michelle called me and cried, "Sid is dead, can you come right over."' says Eileen Polk. 'I thought, "She's being hysterical again – he's probably just sleeping." In the cold dawn I ran over and when I saw the crowd of reporters in front of 63 Bank Street I knew it was true. He was really dead.'

The first police officer on the scene at Bank Street was Sgt Richard Houseman, who had attended more than his fair share of drug-related fatalities. Houseman entered the flat to the sight of two women. The younger of the two was clearly hysterical, as though her world had just ended. The second woman sat calmly in a chair sipping larger – she seemed to be almost in a daze at first, but soon became vocal. When other officers arrived and things started to be logged or moved, she told them in no uncertain manner that the items they were holding belonged exclusively to the 'estate of Sid Vicious'.

Sgt Houseman was happy enough with the explanation he'd received regarding Sid's overdose, and made a note to write off the whole thing as accidental death. Once he got back to the precinct, he couldn't figure out why the girl, who seemed to have known Sid for two minutes, was more hysterical than the older woman whom he worked out was the mother of the recently deceased. Otherwise, Houseman was satisfied until the arrival of Dr Michael Baden – New York's Chief Medical Examiner from 1978 until 1979 – who would perform the autopsy on Sid. Before he entered the bedroom, Dr Baden was informed of the circumstances by Sgt Houseman.

According to Houseman, Dr Baden informed him a few minutes later that the recently deceased had taken the drug that killed him more recently than the night before. Dr Baden believed that a second or third dose had been the one that killed Vicious. The mystery was how someone recently brought back from a near-overdose could have possibly cooked up the heroin, tied a belt around his own arm, found a vein and injected himself without help. At this point, according to Sgt Houseman, Anne Beverley started to become hysterical and entered into a mantra about her being the estate of Sid Vicious and how her son, who would never have survived the harsh US penal system, was now in a better place – and, more to the point, with his Nancy.

Houseman was angry enough to consider charging Mrs Beverley with aiding and abetting, but as with many aspects of the case there was little to support this in court.

'I heard it on the news,' John Lydon later confirmed to the UK press. 'Nobody bothered to tell me. I felt nothing at the time. It's like the information of anyone's death. It doesn't hit you at first. In a curious way, I felt almost relieved.'

'I was sitting outside my favourite coffee shop in Greenwich Village,' Joe Stevens remembers. 'They had the radio playing in the background and I heard them saying that Sid Vicious had been found dead in his girlfriend's apartment in the West Village. Well, Bank Street was nearby and I had a good idea where No. 63 was. Michelle's apartment was on the first landing and the cops weren't for letting me pass, but Michelle spotted me and I got inside. The blinds were still drawn so the place was in darkness and crawling with cops and Sid's mum was freaking out. I took Ma Vicious to one side and said to her, "You know how these rock 'n' roll stories get out of hand. This one will be embellished within the hour. You trust me right?" I had never shafted them on anything so I said, "Why don't you give me the true story and we'll get it out through the *NME*." That's pretty much how it happened. We went into the bedroom and she sat in a chair while I sat on the bed, but I kept slipping off the edge and it wasn't until my eyes adjusted to the bad light that I realised that Sid was still lying in the fucking bed. He had a piece of tape across the top of his mouth and a plastic tube going up under the tape to his nostrils. He wasn't covered or anything. He was naked.'

Elsewhere in the village Peter Kodick was woken to the breaking news. 'I didn't get up too early the next day, and I was sharing a place downtown and the other person who was living in the place came in: "Oh, that friend of yours, man, that friend of yours is dead." "What friend. Who's dead?" "That Punk guy, man." So I ran out to the street, and I saw all the newspapers saying "Sid Vicious is dead". I couldn't believe it. This was not a person committing suicide, no way. This was misadventure.'

In her later years Anne Beverley revealed that Sid's death came as something of a relief as she knew her sensitive son wouldn't have survived one year in an American penitentiary, let alone twenty-five.

'Sid's mother made one of her daily calls,' recalls Malcolm McLaren. '"Sid was out." That was good. "Thank you, Malcolm." But there was a problem. He was dead. "There's nothing you can do, Malcolm. He passed away with a smile on his face." "Where are you?" I was desperate. "What do you mean, 'dead'? Get an ambulance. It's possible that he's just passed out." "Sid's gone away. He's happy now." "Where are you?" "I'm at Michelle's." I covered the receiver and told my assistant to call the NYPD, to get an ambulance over there. "I don't know. I found Sid dead. I've been sitting here looking at him, wondering what to do. Then I decided to call you." I could hear noises in the background. The ambulance and the police had arrived. "He's fine, Malcolm. He looks so happy." Sid was dead. The mother, I was to learn, had been buying the drugs for him since the moment she got to New York. A private detective I later hired, trying to find out what really happened, told me that the mother had been with Sid all along. He was left there for hours before the ambulance arrived. The mother just sat looking at him.'

The Clash had arrived in the Pacific Northwest to start a tour on 30 January 1979. As they began working their way down the coast they stopped off to visit the grave of Bruce Lee. The morning afterwards they heard the news that Sid was dead.

Back in London The Pretenders were about to take the stage for their first ever gig, at the Moonlight club in West Hampstead. 'Someone came up to me and said, "Wow, what about Sid?"' Chrissie Hynde later told reporters. 'I looked at him and said, "What about Sid?" Then I realised no one had told me about Sid because they were afraid it would bum me out before the gig. Instead, I found out right before I went on.'

BBC newsreader Martyn Lewis opened the evening news with the following statement: 'Sid Vicious is dead, after taking an overdose of heroin last night. Police say his death was an accident. Vicious, real name John Simon Ritchie, left a New York prison only yesterday. He was released on $50,000 bail, charged with the murder of his girlfriend Nancy Spungen last October. His mother met him at the prison gates, Vicious went to a party to celebrate his release, then – according to police – he took the heroin. He'd been having treatment to give up his addiction. Apparently last night's dose was too potent.'

❀   ❀   ❀

On Wednesday, 7 February 1979, John Simon Ritchie was cremated after a low-key private service in New Jersey. 'After Sid died I was pretty torn between Anne and Michelle,' says Eileen Polk. 'Nancy had usurped Anne's place as the primary woman in Sid's life for a while, and Anne didn't want to give that spot to Michelle. When we all came to Michelle's apartment on 2 February, she was hysterical, so Anne didn't really want Michelle at the funeral. I didn't think it was a good idea to exclude Michelle, but I was also trying to be nice to Anne and let her have her way. Michelle called me and asked where the funeral was going to be held and I told her the truth, that Anne didn't want her there. Michelle asked me to at least tell her the name of the funeral home and I told her Walter B. Cook.'

The funeral was held at the Garden State Crematory and Michelle was resourceful enough that she showed up there with one of her girlfriends. Others at the funeral were Anne's sister Renee (who had come from London and was staying with Anne at Eileen Polk's mother's house on West 11th Street), Jerry Nolan, Esther, Danielle Booth, Howie Pyro and Jerry Only. 'We rode in a black limo behind the hearse with Sid's coffin,' says Polk. 'All the traffic stopped for us on our way to the funeral. I remember thinking, "I wonder if they know it's Sid Vicious?" The people at the funeral parlour were really kind. After it was over we went to Jerry Only's parents' home, and then on to Philadelphia so that Anne could fulfil her promise to Sid that his ashes would be laid to rest with Nancy. He wasn't buried with his boots and leather jacket. Anne never meant to disrespect Nancy's family. We were surprised that the cemetery where Nancy's grave was located was behind walls and guarded by security.'

The party thought that it would be a quiet cemetery in the countryside, but it was a huge community place with large gates. They had to go through security and have people escort them to the graveside, so Anne wasn't able to take out the ashes. Eileen remembers it as being very cold and depressing. Then it began to snow so they said a few prayers and left. Macabre as it might seem, they wanted to look at the ashes since none of them had ever seen cremated ashes before. As such, they went into a bathroom in a nearby shopping mall and prised off the urn's lid with nail-clippers.

They were walking back to the car when Anne suddenly decided that she had to honour Sid's wishes, so Jerry drove around to the back of the cemetery. While Eileen kept watch, Anne climbed over the wall and scattered the ashes on Nancy's grave. She came back crying but pleased that she had done what Sid wanted. 'At least they're together now,' Anne said. 'And no one can ever part them.'

In more recent years Sex Pistols fans have visited the cemetery and assumed that this story was untrue because there were no gates in place. In fact, the gates were removed in the mid-1980s.

Within months of Sid's death Michelle Robison seemingly vanished from the face of the Earth. Rather than cashing in on the events and selling her story, she changed her name and restored her life to some form of normality via her friends and family. She still lives in New York, where she is a successful businesswoman. Rumour has it that she once declined an offer of $20,000 to tell her story to *Rolling Stone* magazine.

'[Michelle] was really mad at all of us and probably still is,' says Eileen Polk. 'I sent her some photos of Sid, but I never heard from her again. I kept in touch with Anne 'til about 1988 and then I lost touch with her, too. I don't blame her for becoming a recluse after that. About two weeks [after Sid's cremation] Jerry Only and I took Anne to the airport for her flight back to London. Anne was not drunk and did not spill Sid's ashes there or at Heathrow. That is a lie.'

Malcolm McLaren remembers his final meeting with Anne Beverley. 'The next time I spoke to Sid's mother, it was to ask her to bring the body back to London,' he says. 'She didn't say much. I found out later that she had had him cremated in New York. On her return, the London drugs squad, tipped off by the New York police, followed her from Heathrow airport to a house in Notting Hill Gate. The house was raided. She was arrested – an appropriate homecoming.'

'Sid is now the iconic figure he is because he was despised at the time,' says Eileen Polk. 'Just like Punk Rock and Punk clothes, what begins as garbage is later venerated as gold. It's alchemical. From the darkness comes the light and vice versa. I don't think Sid killed Nancy. I think Nancy pissed off some dealer or groupie and the truth will never be known.'

CHAPTER 12

Fuck Forever

'I woke up to be told Sid Vicious had died. I couldn't eat my breakfast'

— Joe Strummer, The Clash

'In the 1920s, when I was living in the Residencia, there was a double suicide in Madrid. A student and his young fiancée killed themselves in a restaurant garden. They were known to be passionately in love; their families were on excellent terms with each other; and when an autopsy was performed, the girl was found to be a virgin. So why the double suicide? I still don't have the answer, except that perhaps a truly passionate love, a sublime love that's reached a certain peak of intensity, is simply incompatible with life itself. Perhaps it's too great, too powerful. Perhaps it can exist only in death.'

— Luis Bunuel 'My Last Sigh'

Today, if you were to ask a member of the public to name a Punk band, the most likely answer would be the Sex Pistols. Ask them to name a member of the Sex Pistols and they will almost certainly answer 'Sid Vicious'. The quintessentially Punk nature of Sid's enduring fame means that the most recognisable face of the genre was also one of the movement's least talented individuals. Vicious proved in the most obvious terms that anyone could be in a band. His legacy means that he is the face on a million T-shirts and posters. He possessed the attitude, the looks and the clothes to become a true icon. His early death and bloody reputation has raised his fame above that of his peers. He is the Sex Pistol who had a semi-fictional film made about his life, although numerous other films about Punk have now been screened. Books, documentaries and magazine features have mined every facet of the Punk legacy. Jon Savage covered the Punk movement beautifully in *England's Dreaming,* and *Mojo* and *Q* magazine offer Punk cover stories on a regular basis. More often than not, it is Sid that fills the full-page photos. The thirst for Punk is still strong and Sid is still perceived as being at its centre.

The deification of Sid Vicious began the very night he died, when Anne Beverley berated police for moving items from the 'estate of Sid Vicious' – an estate that would become lucrative and continue for the following three decades and beyond.

❀　❀　❀

When asked by film director Alex Cox, in the September 2006 edition of *Uncut* magazine, 'Who killed Sid?' Malcolm McLaren answered, 'I'm not certain, except to say that his mother was probably inadvertently responsible and felt guilty every day after.' Whether Anne Beverley was responsible for her son's death or not, the next move in the posthumous career of Sid Vicious came on 23 February 1979 when Virgin Records released the next 'Sex Pistols' single – Sid singing 'Something Else'. It was reported that first-week sales of the single were in excess of 100,000 more than 'God Save the Queen'. It went on to become the biggest selling Sex Pistols single of them all.

The record had presented a huge headache for Virgin – after delaying it in the wake of Nancy's sudden death the company toyed with the idea of a December release and the chance of an unlikely Christmas No. 1. Sid's second arrest put an end to those plans. 'After a few meetings and what with all the money we were pushing Malcolm's way for lawyers and bail, we had a meeting on the first Monday back in January 1979,' recalls John Denton, a former Virgin employee. 'You could see Richard was worn out by it all, and getting more frustrated. At the end of the meeting he said, "Right, and regarding 'Something Else' by the Sex Pistols, its release day is 23 February, and frankly I don't care if World War Three breaks out between now and then!" A couple of the lads were laughing. We had no idea what lay ahead.'

The fifth single by the Sex Pistols was not a record company's attempt to cash in on Sid's death, but a long-planned release which saw Vicious finally become the group's front-man and secure a No. 3 hit in the UK. In the same month Virgin issued the second Sex Pistols album *The Great Rock 'n' Roll Swindle* – a double album soundtrack featuring some twenty-four tracks. Although fans would be divided for years on the actual importance of this 'second' album, Rotten clocked up lead vocal on just eight of the songs, while other front-men included Jones, Cook, Biggs, Tudor Pole, disco dancers Black Arabs, Jerzimy (a French busker), McLaren himself and, of course, Sid Vicious. The album rose to No. 7 in the UK charts and without the support of the accompanying film, which was still being edited.

It wasn't just in the UK that Sid was starting to be big business. In France the Barclay Records label issued Sid's three lead-vocal performances on a 12" EP entitled 'Sid Vicious Heritage'. The record was housed in a picture sleeve featuring an Action Man doll of Sid lying in a coffin, while a photo of the real Sid looked on. Then the aptly named Cash Pussies released a 7" picture sleeve of a blood-stained Sid from the January 1978 Longhorn Ballroom gig. The music on the single was a rather bizarre disco-type song over which were excerpts of Sid talking in an interview.

Over at Virgin the next release seemed screamingly obvious. 'By that time everyone at Glitterbest was concentrating on the film, and to be fair almost all the soundtrack material had been delivered,' says John Denton. 'So we knew we had another Sex Pistols album, which was the main concern. It would have been very easy for us to just stick out the next Sid song as a single and be sure of another hit, but Steve and Paul were still signed to us and still operating as the Sex Pistols, so we decided to go with "Silly Thing", which scored us a chart hit anyway.' Written in the latter part of 1978 'Silly Thing' had originally been titled 'Silly Cunt' and was written by Paul Cook, about watching a friend slide into serious heroin addiction. Many assumed that the song had been written about Sid, but this was not the case. Despite having watched the Sid story unfold at close quarters, Steve Jones was also now suffering from a serious heroin problem, and it would be years before Paul Cook finally admitted to his old friend that the song was about him. 'Silly Thing' was issued by Virgin on 30 March 1979 and made it to No. 6 in the UK charts.

        ●   ●   ●

After serving her brief spell in jail, Anne Beverley was simply trying to go about her normal day-to-day business, although she was already well aware that she was now more than just the mother of a dead Punk Rock legend. She was, in fact, the estate of Sid Vicious. To this end, Anne started attending meetings at Virgin Records. 'That wasn't an easy time for anybody at the label,' explains John Denton. 'We didn't want to be rude to her, but we were also very aware of the fact that she had zero knowledge of the workings of a record company. It became very difficult while we were compiling the film sound-track. We'd get phone calls saying things like, "I don't like the order in which Sid's tracks appear," or, "I don't want Sid appearing right next to a Great Train Robber on the track listing." We really couldn't understand her problem.'

To buy some breathing space Virgin issued a new single on 22 June in the shape of 'C'mon Everybody'. Their third and final Sid track, this moved up the charts and scored them another Top 10 hit. BBC Television allowed *Top of the Pops* to show the promo clip from the film, which featured Sid riding a motorbike around London. The show's presenter that week was Jimmy Saville, who made a point of warning viewers that riding a motorbike without a crash helmet was dangerous. Virgin also allowed Anne to compile a scrapbook of pictures and memories under the title *The Sid Vicious Family Album*, which she did with the help of friends such as Eileen Polk.

By the summer of 1979 the record company was faced with another problem. In the months since Nancy's death in October, the Sex Pistols' popularity had risen considerably, and a whole new set of school-leavers had been turned on to a group that effectively no longer existed. What was needed was another new album. 'We knew what we were up against. We knew there was nothing new to release, but it was still a conversation that haunted every boardroom meeting,' remembers John Denton. 'Then it was mentioned that John Varnom had been compiling master tapes of all their interviews since day one. Along with this we had paid for radio ads to promote almost everything we'd ever done with them, but the bulk of these were still brand new to the kids, because they had been banned on production.' It was decided that the next move would be to compile a number of interviews and some banned radio adverts and thus *Some Product: Carri On Sex Pistols* was born. The album was housed in a sleeve that featured items from the mock cinema foyer from the film, along with a picture of the plaque outside the Chelsea Hotel in New York, although Sid's name had now been added to the list of famous writers who had stayed there. *Some Product* was released in August and made an impressive No. 6 in the UK charts.

As 1979 drew to a close Virgin were on the look-out for any other ways to exploit the Sid Vicious legend. John Tiberi informed Virgin that he had tapes from some of the Max's Kansas City shows played by Sid in September 1978. Tracks from these shows were compiled with a few numbers Sid had performed solo at the Christmas Day 1977 Sex Pistols gig in Huddersfield and a rough demo mix of 'My Way', and issued them as an album called *Sid Sings* in time for Christmas. The December 1979 release of the album was housed in a cover featuring shots of Sid in Paris taken by Tiberi on the 'My Way' video set. The collection reached No. 30 in the UK charts. 'Initially we decided that once *Sid Sings* was released, that was that – we'd done everything we could for the Sex Pistols,' recalls John Denton. 'Of course there was still no actual film, despite the soundtrack album and then Anne Beverley informed us that Punks would be travelling into London, from right across the country on 2 February 1980 to march around the capital in Sid's honour.'

Although she had been invited by numerous fanzine writers, Anne Beverley failed to attend the London march because of bad health. Rumours were rife that she was back on heroin, and despite the fact that her son had been dead for some twelve months, he was still a perfect target for the tabloid newspapers. Virgin had taken note of the planned march on the capital. 'I had been away on holiday. I was only freelancing for the label by now anyway, and on my return I thought someone was having a laugh – there was a memo on my desk regarding a Sex Pistols' greatest hits album,' remembers a grinning John Denton. 'But it wasn't a joke, it was deadly serious. Jamie Reid had been commissioned to produce what turned out to be his last piece of artwork for us – he originally turned up with both the first two album sleeves with the words "flogging a dead horse" written through both roughly in red. He was sent packing, which in hindsight was a mistake. It was a joke and a good one, but then he came back with the "Beach Boys" sleeve and another joke which fans wouldn't get until they had seen the non-existent film [the rear cover was a gold disc for *Never Mind The Bollocks* – one viewing of *Swindle* would explain everything] but we were in a rush by then, so we went with it.'

Flogging A Dead Horse was issued in February 1980. It is without doubt one of the most shameless record releases ever, but that didn't stop it making No. 21 in the charts amid a sea of dyed black spiky hair, motorbike leathers and even the odd white tuxedo.

The first 'annual' (although there would never be another) Sid Vicious memorial march around London went well, and footage of the event even shows the Punks and their police escort having a laugh together. It was a far cry from the television pictures of only three years earlier, although in those three short years plenty had changed. Punk had now evolved into the more radio-friendly 'new wave' of groups such as The Police, Blondie, Elvis Costello & The Attractions and the Ramones.

On 15 May 1980 *The Great Rock 'n' Roll Swindle* was finally let loose. It premiered in Piccadilly Circus at the Pavilion Cinema, which had been the home of all The Beatles' film debuts. Despite being a comedy version of events, padded out by old news footage, the group playing live and excellent cartoon footage care of Glitterbest management's next door neighbours Animation City, the film was well received by fans and several critics. Its premiere, however, was far from being a star-studded affair. Steve Jones and Paul Cook were now fronting The Professionals, although Steve was trapped by his own heroin addiction. John Lydon, meanwhile, had PiL to fill his days. As well as Sid, another person in the film was no longer around to see it. Mary Millington – the young porn star who had appeared opposite Steve in the closing scenes of the film – had committed suicide in the early hours of 19 August 1979. Despite their previous plans to halt further Sex Pistols releases, Virgin also issued a single-disc soundtrack album, featuring mainly the singles. Initial copies came with a free film poster. It was issued in June 1980 along with a final single 'Stepping Stone', which reinstated Rotten as the Sex Pistols' front-man. Issued on 5 June 1980 without a promo video, it limped to No. 21.

Finally, in December 1980, Virgin issued the Christmas release 'Sex Pack', a collection of six double A-side singles, featuring 'Black Leather' and 'Here We Go Again', which – while billed as 'new' Sex Pistols tracks – were effectively Steve and Paul going through the motions of what was The Professionals in all but name. The songs had already appeared in Japan on an album named *The Very Best of the Sex Pistols: And We Don't Care*, which had originally been released that summer by Nippon Columbia. Of the six singles included in the pack, both 'Holidays' and 'Swindle' were given new sleeves to replace the original banned artwork.

❀ ❀ ❀

In 1983 rumours began circulating in the music industry that film director Alex Cox and his writing partner Abbe Wool were putting together a treatment about the Sex Pistols. Cox had actually started work on a script as early as 1980. 'I tried to write a screenplay titled *Too Kool To Die*,' says Cox. 'It was about an English rock 'n' roll band in America. About halfway through writing it I realised that the most interesting thing in the story wasn't the singer or the guitarist or the drummer. It was the bass player and his girl. What became of them was ten times more interesting than what happened to the band. The pair of them were this uncontrollable unit, very bad in many ways, but more than just two isolated, paranoid, lonely individuals. They were Sid and Nancy.' But it was Cox himself who would soon grow bored with the idea. He had thought that the group was hugely different, but research had shown him that for the most part it was just another rock 'n' roll band – the same guitars, the same riffs, the same arguments and the same booze, drugs and rock 'n' roll. But if you took the tale of the group's second bass player, then you had a truly fascinating tale. His was a dark story of needles, razors, heroin, sex and murder. Cox and Wool began a re-write under the title *Love Kills*, based on the story of Sid and Nancy only. 'I came to London and I started meeting people who had known them,' recalls Cox. 'Wherever I went, it seemed like I'd meet someone who had gone to the launderette with Sid and Nancy, or reported them to the police, or been their friend. These people turned me onto other people. I made lots of notes. We started writing the outline in New York in late December 1984. We stayed at the Chelsea Hotel. The first night I was there somebody called me up at 2 a.m. saying "Sid? Sid? Sid?". Behind the mirror on the bedroom wall was written, "Sid Vicious was innocent, Nancy RIP".'

Cox's lead actor came in the form of Royal Shakespeare Company graduate Gary Oldman. At twenty-seven he was already six years older than Sid at the time of his death, but this mattered little to anyone involved. Having been impressed by Oldman when he played a skinhead opposite Tim Roth in *Made in Britain*, Cox was convinced he'd found his man. Finding his girl proved much harder. Adverts seeking actors for both roles were placed in both the UK and US music press. For the role of Sid, many lookalikes offered their services, but once Oldman was in place there was no need to keep looking. The US casting team were over-run by potential Nancys, some of whom, after three hours in make-up, would still barely resemble Nancy Spungen. Then came an unknown named Courtney Love. Apart from looking the part, Courtney was very much Nancy material, and seemed obsessed by the role – turning up for auditions even on non-audition days. Eventually Chloe Webb was chosen for the role and Courtney was offered a bit part. At the time, no one knew that Cox had set his sights much higher than two unknowns – at the start of the project he'd pencilled in Rupert Everett to play Sid and Madonna to play Nancy, but both turned him down.

Gary Oldman was determined to make this his breakthrough role. He went on a strict and impressively dedicated weight-loss programme before playing Sid. Anne Beverley was called in to act as consultant. She provided information regarding the lives of Sid and Nancy, and Oldman soaked it up like a sponge. Anne also provided the actor with Sid's original padlock and chain, plus some of her son's jewellery. The film Sex Pistols fans may always be divided upon, was shot on location in London, Paris and New York in eleven weeks. The finished rough cut lasted three hours and fifty minutes, although the finished film hit the screen at less than two hours. While it's easy to see why Hollywood started taking Gary Oldman more seriously after its release, the film frustrated some viewers who complained that it was riddled with factual errors.

'What the actors did with the end of *Sid & Nancy* differs completely from what we scripted,' says Alex Cox. 'I think it's only to the good [of the film] because they lived closer to the characters of Sid and Nancy than Abbe and I did. By the time we shot the final scenes, Chloe was really Nancy and Gary was really Sid. Their ending is better than anything we could have written. I had this revelation sitting on the set one night, alone. What Gary and Chloe had just shown me wasn't simply good acting, it was really true.'

Cox brought Glen Matlock on board to re-record Pistols songs for Gary to sing, while ex-Clash front-man Joe Strummer provided the theme tune, which sneaked through under the title 'Love Kills'. Gary also made a guest appearance in the promo video for Strummer's single. Anne Beverley's favourite scene in the film was the recreation of 'My Way'. She thought Gary brought her beloved Simon to life, and for that he was placed upon a pedestal for the rest of Anne's life. 'Sid is a real character. A lot of people still revere him. He's a British institution, like the Beefeater or the Queen Mother or John Bull,' Alex Cox said in the introduction to the film's tie-in book. 'Sid's like Arthur Askey or Eric Sykes or Hattie Jacques. It's about time Nancy was put in the same mythic pantheon as Sid. Sid wouldn't be shit without Nancy. He'd probably be around today playing in some awful band.'

❋   ❋   ❋

Sid Vicious will never grow old like the rest of us. He is frozen in time at the age of twenty-one. Through the 1980s Sid became the poster boy for the entire Punk movement. Even in countries as far away as Japan he was the Punk most likely to appear on a T-shirt or a poster bearing the Sex Pistols' name. Anne Beverley hadn't failed to notice this, and was already selling the odd item from her vast collection through various rock auctions. As already proved by Elvis Presley, Jim Morrison, Jimi Hendrix and Brian Jones, there is always money to be made from a dead rock star. 'I was first approached to do a book about Simon in early 1981, but I'd never heard of the guy in question,' Anne said. 'So I threw the letter away, didn't even respond to it. Everything felt like the timing was all wrong.' By the end of the decade though she was happier to put Sid's life into words and worked with me on a title for Omnibus Press. At the turn of the decade the Not Why Not design company in Kensal Rise, London, were producing T-shirts for major metal bands and stadium fillers, but by far their biggest turn over was in a product that featured the image of John Simon Beverley.

By the middle of the 1990s the remaining Sex Pistols reached the same conclusion as so many other bands – the need for a reunion tour. Although some fans could not forgive the band for 'selling out' and becoming part of the 'oldie' circuit, credit should perhaps be given for the band's honesty about the reasons for the shows. The dates were branded the 'Filthy Lucre' tour and John Lydon told everyone who would listen that the Sex Pistols were simply collecting their dues. Lydon, Glen Matlock, Paul Cook and Steve Jones took part in the concerts, but bad feeling was created when Sid Vicious was given a verbal beating at the March 1996 press conference to announce the reunion. Talk of Sid being 'useless' and 'little more than a coat-hanger on stage' may have brought howls of laughter from the jostling throng of journalists, but when these soundbites appeared on the news later that same evening, they brought tears to the eyes of one woman who had expected that day of all days to pass with her dead son's memory intact. Anne had at least expected Sid to be treated with a modicum of respect. The next day she was distraught. 'Did you see that yesterday?' she asked. 'What on earth was all that about? You don't talk about your mates like that, do you?' In response she put out a press statement saying that 'Sid would be turning in his grave', but no one seemed to be listening.

❀   ❀   ❀

Anne Beverley returned from holiday in the early part of September 1996 with a back problem, which, if anything, was only getting worse. She had visited specialists whose only advice was to fuse her spine, but despite asking everyone she came across she couldn't find anyone with first-hand experience of the operation and its possible outcome. The situation was bad – since arriving home she was finding both walking and eating a problem, because of the pain both actions put her through. In the afternoon of Thursday, 5 September 1996 she wrote three letters and a note. The first letter was to her nephew David and contained a cheque for £10,000, in order to sort out a funeral and take care of all other expenses. The second letter was to Steven Haywood, explaining her decision and pointing out that the police would need to be informed so that they could break into her home. The third letter was to this book's author, to finish what had been started – to prove her son's innocence. That evening Anne also wrote a note in which she informed family and friends that she was not of unsound mind, but that she couldn't cope, was unwell and in considerable pain. She then cut all her credit cards in half and labelled piles of items as gifts for various friends and family members, before sitting down one last time in her chair. It was there that she consumed large amounts of codeine, Diazepam and alcohol.

Anne Beverley was found dead, slumped in the chair, on Friday, 6 September 1996, after police were informed by Steven

Haywood. She was sixty-four. Coroner Roger Patten returned a verdict of suicide by acute poisoning. In keeping with Sid's own final wishes, Anne's ashes were later scattered on the grave of the only other man she had ever truly loved – Chris Beverley. This final act was carried out by Sid's cousin, David Ross, following a quiet family funeral.

After Anne's death the Sid Vicious market reached ever-higher turnovers. At the Sex Pistols' 2002 Crystal Palace reunion show, the crowd was dominated by a sea of Sid T-shirts. Across the globe Vicious is as likely to be found smiling back from official Sex Pistols products as the Queen (with a safety pin through her lip) or the words 'Never Mind the Bollocks'.

Ever since his death, Sid has proved to be an inspiration to young musicians everywhere – the fact that he could barely play encourages anyone to pick up an instrument and have a go for themselves. Many bands that he was associated with also had a similar effect. His influence was also marked when The Exploited wrote 'Sid Vicious Was Innocent' in 1982.

Sid's death in New York meant that he had a foothold in influencing Punks in the USA, and in the twenty-first century bands such as Green Day, Rancid and the Offspring have a great debt to pay to him. Kurt Cobain and Courtney Love used to sign into hotels as Simon John Ritchie and Nancy Laura Spungen, while Good Charlotte's leader Benji Madden has been known to use the alias 'Kid Vicious' on occasion. Even Avril Lavigne claimed she was the 'Sid Vicious for a new generation'.

John Lydon usually has a lot to say on most subjects, but he has had surprisingly little to offer regarding Sid, and even less sympathy for his old friend. 'His mother didn't help him none too much with [the drugs]' he said, in one of his few statements about Vicious. 'He didn't really stand much of a chance and he didn't help himself none in the end either.'

AUTHOR'S NOTES

The Man I Never Met

'It seems like years, when told I cried
The night I heard Sid Vicious died
Born in nineteen fifty seven, fun and young a Punk in heaven
The years that stopped at twenty-one
Were full and loud, a crazy song of
Drugs and sex and frenzied shows with
Laughter, tears, the highs and lows
Spiked and black, wild forest hair, you walked
They stopped and turned to stare.
Gentle giant the friend of we who
Copy those we'll never be.
His face becomes a misty haze,
Controlled; and deep like life, a maze
Eyes of youth that stare you cold
From photos yellow, torn and old.
That look, that smile, he stole my life,
And married death a greedy wife
She robbed your soul denied our dream
She haunts me now I wake and scream
Body drenched by cold sweat,
I miss the man I never met.'

© Neil Thompson, 2 May 1980

In the late afternoon of 6 January 2005 a passenger plan touches down at Tokyo airport, among the passengers departing that flight are myself and Mick O'Shea. We've been in the air for twelve hours, we'd love some food and we'd love some sleep. There is one thing which separates us from our fellow passengers – some are families or businessmen returning home, others are travelling salesmen here to cut deals or just plain tourists, but we are simply two friends and I'm here to promote an exhibition about the Sex Pistols. What makes us different is that, and I'm sure I can say this without fear of contradiction, our tickets and our hotel room were effectively paid for by a rock star who had been dead for nearly twenty-six years.

At the time of writing, if you enter the name Sid Vicious into a Google search, you will find 2,510,000 results. If you then do a search within these results and enter my name, you will find links to 105,000 websites, which isn't a bad achievement for two people who never met. How I came to be chosen by Anne Beverley, mother of the late Simon John, to write a book about her son, I don't know. I've been asked a hundred times and the answer is still that I haven't the first idea. All I know is that somewhere in the mid-1980s, on the exact same day that I first met Dee Dee and Johnny Ramone, I was contacted by a company called Not Why Not Design, who produced T-shirts and posters for the estate of Simon Beverley. Within half an hour of the call I had Anne Beverley's home phone number scribbled on the back of a Guinness mat. The following morning I made the call. A very clear female voice answered and we were on the phone for the best part of two hours.

Swadlincote is situated over the River Trent and linked by bridge to Burton-on-Trent. It is known by locals as 'Swad', and in its prime – if the hills and valleys surrounding are anything to go by – its main income was coal. It is also home to the largest grass ski slope in the UK. So what brings the mother of the world's most notorious Punk Rocker to Swadlincote? On 16 January 1986, fate finally favoured Anne Beverley. It was on this day that Malcolm McLaren turned his back on proceedings at the High Court (Court 35) in London, over a case regarding frozen royalties and the earnings of the Sex Pistols. The actual case title, written on the file for the world's media to see, was Lydon vs. Glitterbest, but in reality it meant that Lydon, along with Steve Jones, Paul Cook and the late Simon John Beverley – represented on that day by his estate (Anne Beverley) – had just won a case that was first kick-started on 29 March 1978. On 10 November of the same year the case finally made it to the High Court, and finally, some eight years later, justice was served. Lydon, who had countless witness statements, didn't care how long it took. Bored to the core with what looked like days of reading statements, and having been tipped off previously by his own lawyer that the group would probably win anyway, McLaren walked away.

After drawing as much money as he could carry from the company accounts, McLaren made his way to Paris. 'At Heathrow, I looked for the first flight to Paris. I bought a ticket, and then realised in a panic that I was going to have to go through a metal detector,' he told me over coffee in Paris. 'British notes have a silver metallic strip in them, and with so many plastered about me, they were certain to set off the metal detector like an alarm bell. And then an improbable stroke of luck, a security guard spotted me. "Oh," he said, "It's Malcolm McLaren!" I told him that I was late for my flight, and he said, "Oh, come on then," and I jumped the queue and avoided the machine, as I had no bags. I got on the plane to Paris with forty thousand pounds all over my body. "A fascist regime," I sang quietly to myself. "God save the Queen."'

At 3.15 p.m. that afternoon, the group won the rights to their name and their catalogue, plus a sum of money. The actual figure was £880,000, but given that the rights to their film were also included, newspapers the following day reported the fee as being 'a million'. Anne Beverley's cut was £250,000. She also won the rights to sell products bearing her son's name in any way she chose. T-shirt and poster deals were in place within weeks, but the real win for Anne was that now she could finally leave London – a place she had grown to despise.

Anne's decision regarding just where to live was made in her own unique fashion. When I first asked, she informed me that she didn't have the first clue where to go, but wanted to be 'anywhere that wasn't London. I'd had enough, love.' She simply took out a dart and threw it at a map. Other versions of this story see her sticking a pin into an atlas at the house of her sister Veronica Ross (sometimes referred to in books by her nickname Rene), but I always remember a dart being referred too, so we'll stick with that. It landed in Swadlincote – a place she hadn't even visited, but which was situated, ironically if you're a Sex Pistols fan, just over the bridge from Burton-on-Trent. This is the home of perhaps the most bootlegged Sex Pistols live show in existence – the gig took place at the now-defunct 76 Club on 24 September 1976. A visit to Swadlincote was planned with her sister, and it was during this trip that Anne saw and fell in love with a small cottage near the high street. Within three months she was resident. David Ross, Veronica's son (and Anne's nephew) says, 'I remember saying to my mum, "Did you look at any other houses?", and she just said, "No, that was the one."' Anne Beverley moved in with two greyhounds and a cat, placed a 'no hawkers and no traders' sign on the door, decorated the stairs up to the bedrooms with silver, gold and platinum discs, framed a few old art school paintings of her son's, along with some Sex Pistols promo pictures, and set up shop as the estate of Sid Vicious.

By all accounts Anne had been considering a book when Alex Cox got hold of her unlisted number and told her he was making a film. The very idea horrified her. How would it end? What would be said about the Chelsea Hotel? How much detail would be paid to her own heroin addiction? And top of the list, just who was good enough to play her beloved Simon? Sid was a boy she still had conversations with in the afternoons, while she took the dogs for a walk on the field at the bottom of the street. Cox held court with her, then made the film he wanted to make in the first place anyway. Anne loved Gary Oldman, starring in his breakthrough film role, and thought he was incredible. She even lent him some of Sid's things, but she would not watch the film beyond the first private screening. She owned the film on VHS, but never actually played it.

Anne was a huge believer in life after death and believed with all her heart that her Simon had been reunited with Nancy on the 'other side', where nothing could ever hurt either of them again. It was upon hearing this that *Sid & Nancy* director Alex Cox went away and rewrote the film's dream-sequence ending. Gary Oldman's taxi ride to heaven was OK for a film ending, but the harsh reality of the tragic saga remained – Sid was dead, aged just twenty-one.

Anne's eventual decision to be involved with a book about Sid came about after she heard Glen Matlock was writing one of his own. Although Matlock had arguably been the most gifted musician in the Sex Pistols, it was he too, who after many internal arguments, finally left the band, thus making way for Punk's true icon. Omnibus Press, who had already signed up Glen for a book, were also thinking along the lines of Sid Vicious, but they only wanted to publish an official book with his mother involved. At this point their editor received a phone call from me asking about the possibility of doing a book on Vicious. Yes, it was possible, but only if I could involve Sid's mother. Bingo! I had his mother on the team already.

The first book *Sid's Way* (we had intended calling it *My Way*, but there were legal complications) was issued in September 1991. It had originally been the result of some sixteen hours of taped interviews with Anne Beverley, yet it is largely a picture book, because when it came to be assembled, Anne decided she didn't want us using the interviews. The book was subsequently re-issued after the success of *Satellite: Sex Pistols*, with a new cover in 1999. It was, I'm told, the fastest-selling Punk book in Japan ever!

Anne Beverley and myself remained friends over the next few years. More than a few Sid Vicious live albums, posters and T-shirts have been issued because I went up to Swadlincote and sorted out the paperwork. We'd eat Chinese food, drink lager and put the world to rights. One drunken evening I told her I was going to have a go on the famous grass ski slope, which you could see clearly from the spare bedroom window at Anne's place. She laughed: 'Yeah, and I'm going to walk on the moon.' I don't know how she got on with the moon, but to date I have never even climbed the hill that leads up to the ski slope. Apart from helping out Anne, Sid Vicious pretty much dried up in my life. I'd done my bit and moved on. I still visited and we still talked on the phone, but business was over.

On 7 September 1996 a letter arrived from Anne. It wasn't very positive, and she was clearly feeling down. She was suffering from severe back pain and a constant recurring upset, which had haunted her for months. Earlier that year, on 18 March at the 100 Club on London's Oxford Street – during a lunchtime press conference to announce the first Sex Pistols gigs in eighteen years – Johnny Rotten had told the world that Sid Vicious, his old friend, was nothing more than a useless 'coat-hanger', simply filling in a space where Glen Matlock used to stand. In his defence, Rotten was right next to Matlock when he made the comment, which brought the expected chuckles from the gathered press, but in Swadlincote (witnessed on tele-vision), it brought nothing but tears. The letter also said that I should finish what we'd started, and complete a genuine book about Sid to let the world know the truth. Everything she'd ever said on tape was at my disposal. When I finished reading the letter (sat in the front room at my parents place in Lancashire), I decided I'd give her a call. It all sounded a bit too distressed, a bit too final. The last I'd heard was that she was going on holiday and would phone when she got back. A minute later my father appeared at the door. 'Telephone for you,' he said. 'It sounds urgent!' The voice at the other end of the line was that of ex-*Sounds* journalist and subsequent Matlock biographer Pete Silverton. 'Have you heard? I mean I'd like your help on a piece I'm doing? It's a sad business.' I felt cold. I half knew, deep inside I guess, but I asked anyway what the problem was. 'Anne Beverley is dead, suicide, booze and pills.' A planned out affair too by the look of things – notes left for family members, credit cards cut right through the middle. I looked at the postmark on the letter – 5 September. From the point of me doing anything to help Anne, it had arrived one day late. I told Pete to ring back in an hour – I'd get my head together, have a coffee. I nipped out to the local corner shop and bought a sympathy card. I addressed it to her sister and posted it straight away. The following morning Anne's death made all the national newspapers.

What with the Sex Pistols' world tour and Anne's subsequent suicide, I was offered three deals on a Sid Vicious book before Christmas 1996, but the timing was all wrong. None of it felt right. In 1999 I collaborated with Paul Burgess on the book *Satellite*. We did address the Sid and Anne situation in a special part of the book, and for the first time the world saw the tattoo of Sid that Anne had helped me choose and pay for. So that did feel right – the book was met with high praise indeed, and we never saw a bad review. The launch party was star-studded, and the book finished up gaining the group's blessing. It was reprinted in Japan with the same title as the film (trivia buffs should note that *The Filth & The Fury* is called *No Future* in Japan), as its official companion.

Everything went quiet again until the summer of 2003 (I had been offered another chance to do a Sid book when the Sex Pistols regrouped again to play Crystal Palace in 2002, but I turned down that one flat), when – during a meeting with Steve Woof at EMI Records – we started discussing ideas for the following year. I mentioned that Sid Vicious would have been dead for twenty-five years in 2004, and – with this in mind – we started to compile an album based on everything we could possibly find. In the next few hours I bumped into a publisher friend of mine in a pub on London's Leather Lane. I mentioned the anniversary and the album, and he was that keen to sign up a book on Sid to tie in with them he even offered to write out a personal agreement on a bar mat!

The next book was *Vicious: Too Fast To Live*, which I completed for Creation Books. It was published on 2 February 2004, along with the EMI album of the same name. The launch party was held at Bar Low Life, just off London's Baker Street, although I like to call it the launch sauna. So successful was the campaign arranged by Scruffy Bird PR that we were packed into the place. I gave a speech, but I don't remember a word of it. My friends were too busy telling me that they'd just spotted another TV or pop star. Hell, there were A-list celebrities being turned away!

The book lifted my career to a new level, and I was being made offers I could never have dreamed of. Within six months of its publication there was already another Sid Vicious book on the shelves – an excellent account of Sid's life, titled *The Art of Dying Young*, written by my friend Mark Paytress. This led, ultimately, to my agent bringing up the subject: 'What about Sid? One last time – a full written account. You're the only one who's truly been close to a lot of the central characters.' He had a point. I was given enough time between my last Sid book and now to take months off to research the entire story again, to take on board what people had said since last time, and to dig deeper. I had no idea of knowing at the time that two guardian angels were already on my case – Malcolm McLaren was sufficiently impressed with my previous work to agree to see me, and our talks led to his offer of a foreword. Then there was Eileen Polk, whom I'd heard so much about from Anne Beverley. Now we were talking via telephone and email. Her photos were amazing, and personal, and we made a pact to get it right.

On 3 December 2005 with Orion Publishing already committed to the project, myself and my researcher Mick O'Shea took a flight to a very cold New York City, only this time we wouldn't just be visiting the outside of 63 Bank Street, where Sid died. Due to Malcolm's help, Mick O'Shea and I were also lucky enough to be invited inside by its current owner/occupier. When we were kindly left alone in the bedroom where Sid died we found ourselves talking in whispers as though we were inside a church. The bedroom, which is now occupied by our new friend's absent sister, is barely large enough to incorporate the double bed, let alone any other furniture, and a touching moment came when the owner informed us that his sister had named the bear-shaped throw-over, which was lying upon the bed, Sid – in memory of the room's former occupant. I got the goose bumps, and from the look on his face so did Mick. We took a couple of pictures, enjoyed the grand tour of the rest of the place and walked into Greenwich Village for Mexican food – both trying to fight off the ghosts.

We also revisited the Chelsea Hotel. I know that you, dear reader, will undoubtedly have your own theory on what happened in room 100 in the early hours of Friday, 12 October 1978. I can honestly say, through my discussions with Anne Beverley, Malcolm McLaren, Nils Stevenson, Glen, Steve, Paul, Roadent, Alan Jones and many other of Sid's contemporaries, that I thought I'd uncovered every stone for *Too Fast Too Live.* But I was wrong. Some doors remained closed – they needed other people's help to open them. On another research trip to New York, Mick O'Shea and I paid a visit to the Chelsea Hotel on the pretence of buying T-shirts. They have started selling T-shirts bearing the logo: 'Hotel Chelsea, NYC: A rest stop for rare individuals'. We also wanted to reacquaint ourselves with the manager Stanley Bard and his colourful brother Michael ('Ya buy two T-shirts, you get one bag! What da fuck, bags don't grow on trees!'). Mick and I had often joked that our respective first visits to the hotel had not gone according to plan for we had both been given extremely short shrift by a tall black man. He was obviously an employee in one capacity or another and didn't take kindly to inquiries about one of the hotel's more ignominious former residents. Our joint second visit to 222 West 23rd Street in August 2004, however, had proved far from intimidating and we ended up sat in Stanley's private office, adjoining the reception desk, drinking coffee while discussing Sid and Nancy.

This happy turnaround came about because we were able to gain a valid entrée due to the T-shirts the hotel had recently started selling. We were paying customers, and our being English led to Michael Bard engaging us in conversation, as well as berating us for not staying at the hotel. 'Whadya stayin' der for?' he said upon hearing that we were staying at the Thirty/Thirty. 'I cudda give ya a great deal. And we have great Cwoffee!' It was while we were waiting for Michael to bag our T-shirts that Stanley came out of the lift opposite the desk and stopped dead in his tracks upon spotting my Sid tattoo. 'I know who that is,' he said coming over and introducing himself. It turned out that Stanley had been managing the Chelsea since the late 1960s and, unsurprisingly, had not forgotten the notorious residents of room 100. Although, Nancy's death might have made good copy for the *New York Post*, it wasn't going to do the Chelsea Hotel any favours – business had been bad enough without having the hotel's name splashed across the front pages in connection with a grisly 'Punk Rock murder'.

In mid-August 2006 I travelled to Leicester to meet with David Ross, Sid's cousin and now the person who oversees the Vicious estate. David was friendly and hugely helpful with documentation, a percentage of which is enclosed here. When I arrived back in London I was shattered. Forget the tube, I thought. I'll grab a cab and order some food in, have a lazy one. I hailed a taxi – once I was inside, the driver struck up a conversation. When I told him I'd been visiting Sid Vicious' cousin, his personality changed on the spot. 'They should have fuckin' horse-whipped that cunt!' I looked visibly shocked. He went on, 'He killed his fuckin' girlfriend, y'know?' I shot across a blank stare. 'Did he?' I said. 'Investigated it much beyond the report in the *Sun* did you?' When I arrived home, a pal of mine rang to see how the trip had gone. 'Great,' I said. 'Genuinely great. There's a few people who still need educating, but who knows, maybe the next book will cover that.'

Before ending, I'd like to mention Nigel Marshall, a bass guitarist, who can genuinely play the instrument, and who now makes his living in the persona of 'Kid Vicious' as part of the country's leading tribute band – The Sex Pistols Experience. Alongside Johnny Rotter (Nathan Morris), Steve Bones (Dave Donley) and founder and ideas man Paul Crook (Dave Twigg), they take to the stage – along with the hilariously named Nancy Pungent (Sophie Boyes) – on a regular basis at venues across Europe and the USA to provide a slice of Sex Pistols life, 1977-style. Let me tell you from personal experience, their attention to detail is stunning.

Finally, a funny story. During the research period of this book, I decided to visit as many of the places mentioned in it as was going to be physically possible. One afternoon on the way to my agent's office in Covent Garden, I walked down Drury Lane to check out No. 178 – an old flat once occupied by Sid and his mother. When I left I continued down Drury Lane as though heading towards the Strand. If you take this route you might notice something else – the first turning on the left after the flat in question, a street the pair would no doubt have passed a thousand times, is called Parker Street. Personally, I still can't believe it . . .

Alan Parker

(42 years adrift in an open-neck shirt)

Thanks and Acknowledgements

'Life is short, break the rules, forgive quickly, kiss slowly, love truly, laugh uncontrollably and never regret anything that made you smile!'

(New Year's Day text message 2007)

Professional thanks to:

Robert Kirby, Katie Bayer & Catherine Cameron @ Peters, Fraser, Dunlop (for everything)

Ian Marshall & Ian Preece @ Orion Publishing (keep the faith)

Malcolm McLaren & Young Kim (God bless the pair of you)

Mick O'Shea (thanks would never be enough: you lived it with me)

Anne Beverley RIP (too much too soon . . . I won't forget you)

Don Letts (as always, just The Don, thanks mate)

Nils Stevenson (RIP), Alan Jones, Eileen Polk, Glen Matlock, Steve 'Roadent' Connolly, Steve Jones, John 'Boogie' Tiberi, Rob

Jovanovic (for everything), Dee Dee Ramone (RIP), James Merberg, Ray Stevenson, Dr Michael Baden, Sgt Richard Houseman, Steve English, Kenneth 'Stinker' Gordon (and all in the 'Pure Hell' camp), John Holmstrom, Bertie 'Berlin' Marshall, Bob Gruen, Derek Green, Dennis Morris, Peter 'Kodick' Gravelle, Rusty Egan, Marky Ramone, Howie Pyro, Captain Sensible, Jah Wobble, Mick Jones, Rat Scabies, Edward Tudor Pole, Fred Vermorel, Marco Pironi, Jimmy Zero, Alex Cox, Tony James, Dave Philp, Julien Temple, Steve Dior, Simone Stenfors, Lemmy Kilmister, Steve New, Roberta Bayley, Hilly Krystal @ CBGB, Steve Woof @ EMI Records, Steve Hammonds @ Sanctuary Records, everyone at the Chelsea Hotel (thanks Stanley) and all at 63 Bank Street, NYC. Thanks to Zoe Street, for transcribing interview tapes, in some cases at about three hours' notice.

Personal thanks to:

Mum (for everything)

David Parker

Jake Burns, Steve Grantley, Ian McCallum & Ali McMordie (Everybody should have their own rock 'n' roll band, thank you)

Steve Diggle

Jakki O'Shea, Tara Rez, Allison Dore & Pete Kalhan @ Fremantle Media, Jerry White, Naomi @ Redferns Pictures, Rock 'n' Roll Ray Morrissey, Paul King & Lou Maloney @ VH1, Simon Leppington, Uncle George X (uncrowned King of the Punks), Paul Roberts, Robert Ross (it's a Sid thing!), Terry Rawlings, Keith Badman, Chris Remington, Kevin Crace, Jon Richards, David Ross @ The Vicious Files (thank you), Andre Jacquemin @ Redwood Studios, Bill Jones & Ben Timlett (hey guys!), Rav Singh, Craig Orrick (Anoraky in the UK), Mark Fletcher, Phil Singleton @ God Save The Sex Pistols, Gary

THANKS AND ACKNOWLEDGEMENTS

Carverhill, Mark Paytress, Louise Fowler, 'Foxy' Roxy Gregory, Brian '6th Pistol' Jackson, 'Jolly' Jim McDonald, Phil, Wag & Pat @ *Mojo* magazine (a bible in four-week shifts), all @ *Distorted* magazine (the killer rocks on!), everybody @ *Record Collector*, everyone at The Big Cheese, all the staff at The 'legendary' Spice of Life and The Sex Pistols Experience (especially Nigel & Sophie, without whom . . .).

www.sex-pistols.net

www.sexpistolsexperience.co.uk

www.theviciousfiles.co.uk

www.myspace.com/aparker01

www.seditionaries.com

APPENDIX

Discography, books and DVDs

Sid Vicious vocals indicated in **bold**.

VINYL RELEASES

'No One Is Innocent'/'**My Way**' (Virgin Records VS 220) Highest chart position: 7

'The Biggest Blow'/'**My Way**'/Interview (Virgin Records 12" Single VS 220) Highest chart position: 7

'**Something Else**'/'Friggin' in the Riggin'' (Virgin Records VS 240) Highest chart position: 3

From Beyond the Grave: 'Something Else'/'C'mon Everybody'/'My Way' (Barclay Records 12" Single 640 159)

'**C'mon Everybody**'/'God Save the Queen (Symph)'/'Watcha Gonna Do About It' (Virgin Records VS 272) Highest chart position: 3

Sid Sings (Virgin Records V2144) Highest chart position: 30
Recorded live and made available at budget price, packaged
with one of two possible posters and picture inner-sleeve.

Side 1: 'Born to Lose'/'I Wanna Be Your Dog'/'Take A Chance
On Me'/ 'Stepping Stone'/'My Way'

Side 2: 'Belsen Was a Gas'/'Something
Else'/'Chatterbox'/'Search and Destroy'/'Chinese Rocks'/'I
Killed the Cat'

CD RELEASES

Sid Sings (Virgin Records CDV 2144)
'Born to Lose'/'I Wanna Be Your Dog'/'Take a Chance on
Me'/'Stepping Stone'/'My Way'/'Belsen Was a Gas'/'Something
Else'/'Chatterbox'/'Search and Destroy'/'Chinese Rocks'/'I
Killed the Cat'

Sid Dead Live (Anagram Records CD Punk 86)
'Search and Destroy'/'Chatterbox'/'Something Else'/'I Wanna
Be Your Dog'/'Belsen Was a Gas'/'Stepping Stone'/'Take a
Chance on Me'/'No Lip'/'Chinese Rocks'/'My Way'/'Search
and Destroy'/'Chatterbox'/'I Wanna Be Your Dog'/'Something
Else'/'Stepping Stone'/'No Lip'/'Belsen Was a Gas'/Interview

**Sid Vicious at the Electric Ballroom (Delta Records CD
47201)**
'Something Else'/'C'mon Everybody'/'Stepping Stone'/'No
Lip'/'I Wanna Be Your Dog'/'Belsen Was a
Gas'/'Chatterbox'/'Tight Pants'/'My Way'/'Search and
Destroy'/'My Way (ALT version)'

Sid Vicious in Vicious White Kids (Castle Records CMRCD372)
'C'mon Everybody'/'Stepping Stone'/'No Lip'/'I Wanna Be Your Dog'/'Belsen Was a Gas'/'Chatterbox'/'Tight Pants'/'Something Else'/'My Way'/Interview: Rat Scabies & Glen Matlock

Vive La Rock (Alchemy Entertainment Pilot152)
(Disc 1) 'C'mon Everybody'/'Stepping Stone'/'No Lip'/'I Wanna Be Your Dog'/'Belsen Was a Gas'/'Chatterbox'/'Tight Pants'/'My Way'/'My Way (rare unreleased studio version)'

(Disc 2) 'Search and Destroy'/'I Wanna Be Your Dog'/'No Lip'/'Something Else'/'Belsen Was a Gas'/'Stepping Stone'/'Chinese Rocks'/'My Way'/'Take a Chance on Me'/'Search and Destroy'/'Chatterbox'/'Something Else'/'Belsen Was a Gas'/'Stepping Stone'/'I Wanna Be Your Dog'/'No Lip'/'Take a Chance on Me'/'Chinese Rocks'/'My Way'

Better to Provoke a Reaction Than to React to Provocation (Yeaah! Records Yeaah6)
'Search and Destroy'/'Chatterbox'/'Something Else'/'I Wanna Be Your Dog'/'Belsen Was a Gas'/'Stepping Stone'/'Take a Chance on Me'/'No Lip'/'Chinese Rocks'/'My Way'/'Search and Destroy'/'Chatterbox'/'I Wanna Be Your Dog'/'Something Else'/'Stepping Stone'/'No Lip'/'Belsen Was a Gas'

Vicious: Too Fast to Live (EMI/Virgin Records 7243 5 97857 2 1)
'Something Else'/'C'mon Everybody'/'My Way'/'Born to Lose'/'I Wanna Be Your Dog'/'Take a Chance on Me'/'Stepping Stone'/'My Way'/'Belsen Was a Gas'/'Something Else'/'Chatterbox'/'Search and Destroy'/'Chinese Rocks'/'I Killed the Cat'/'My Way (take 3)'/'From Beyond The Grave' (an interview)/'Something Else (1st Mix)'

DVD RELEASES

Sid & Nancy **(Momentum Pictures MP033D)**
Alex Cox's film in full 108-minute cut, includes an interview
with Alex Cox

The Great Rock 'n' Roll Swindle **(Sony/BMG 2028859)**
Julien Temple's film in full 104-minute cut, includes an
interview with Julien by Chris Salewicz

Never Mind the Bollocks, Here's the Sex Pistols **(Eagle Vision
EREDV282)**
Includes the 'Classic Albums' documentary and bonus footage

Live At Longhorn **(Castle Music CMP 1004)**
Features nine songs from the show, although the beginning is
missing, plus two promo clips

DOA – A Right of Passage **(King Records KIBF 146)**
Lech Kowalski's film in full 93-minute cut. Bonus material
includes: theatrical trailer, gallery and 'Sad Vacation', a song
written about Sid, performed by Johnny Thunders

The Filth & The Fury **(Film Four VCD0067)**
Julien Temple's film in full 103-minute cut. Special features
include: theatrical trailer and director's commentary. The
Japanese version of this DVD contains a bonus interview with
Johnny Rotten. It's titled *No Future* **(Klock Worx KWDV-10)**

PREVIOUS BOOKS ABOUT SID VICIOUS

Sid's Way – The Life & Death of Sid Vicious (Omnibus Press)
Alan Parker & Keith Bateson (with Anne Beverley)

Sid Vicious Family Album (Virgin Books)
Anne Beverley

Sid Vicious: Rock 'n' Roll Star (Plexus)
Malcolm Butt

Sid & Nancy (Faber & Faber)
Alex Cox & Abbe Wool

Vicious: Too Fast to Live (Creation Books)
Alan Parker

Vicious: The Art of Dying Young (Omnibus Press)
Mark Paytress

And I Don't Want to Live This Life (Fawcett Books)
Deborah Spungen

Permission to reproduce lyrics, quotes and slogans is gratefully acknowledged:

Lyrics from *Tattoos and Alibis* written by Ricky Warwick © 2002 Sanctuary Records Group

Slogan taken from a poster, released by the estate of Simon Beverley © Worldwide David Ross 2007

Lyrics from 'Card cheat' by The Clash, published by Mineden Ltd/Universal Music Publishing

Lyrics from 'Wait and See' by Stiff Little Fingers, written by John Burns/Gordon Ogilvie © Complete Music Ltd (p) 1980 Sedgenote Ltd

Woody Allen quote from *Match Point*, written & directed by Woody Allen © Jada Productions 2005

Lyrics from 'Golden Boy' by The Stranglers, written by The Stranglers and published by Complete Music Ltd

Lyrics from 'Bed of Roses Number 9' by Ian Dury, written by Dury/Jankle and published by Blackhill Music Ltd

Lyrics from 'Too Much Junkie Business' by Johnny Thunders and Walter Lure © Jungle Music/MCS Music/Virgin EMI Music

What the press said about
Vicious: Too Fast to Live

'Potentially the best rock 'n' roll book of 2004. You just won't put it down'   (Liverpool Echo)

'During the 'Vox & Roll' evening at The Garage, Alan Parker captured an audience for two hours, fifteen minutes. Rarely does an author know their subject this well'   (London Evening Standard)

'Parker took his subject matter and laid waste to every word written on Vicious to this day, but, I suspect there is more to be told . . . '
(Guitar Magazine)

'Nick Hornby, you suspect, wouldn't approve. But fuck him, as Sid might have said'   (Q Magazine)

'A touching and personal insight into a shy and reluctant star'
(Record Collector)

'Parker gains a good insight into what Sid was really like'
(Kerrang!)

'At the end of his speech in Borders book shop, Parker promised one final volume on Vicious. Well, my friend, you've got my order now – talk about knowing your subject'   (Daily Star)

'Alan Parker dramatically explodes the myths that surrounded the last months of the Sex Pistols'   (The Times)

Index

Nancy

You were my little baby girl
And I knew all your fears.
Such joy to hold you in my arms
... away your tears.
... me. there's only